HAMLYN ALL COLOUR
VEGETARIAN COOKBOOK

HAMLYN ALL COLOUR
VEGETARIAN
COOKBOOK

TED SMART

Front jacket shows, clockwise from top right, *Derby and Lentil Loaf* (37), *Potato and Cashew Curry* (65), *Tomato Roulade* (217), *Wholemeal Pasta Salad* (137)

Title page shows, clockwise from top right, *Fruit Tartlets* (265), *Cheese and Semolina Bake* (289), *Carrot Aigrettes* (169), *Iced Orange Cups* (237)

Back jacket shows, clockwise from top right, *Caerphilly Bean Salad* (105), *Melon and Grapefruit Cocktail* (13), *Leek and Chick Pea Chowder* (1), *Smokie Wheat Salad* (285)

The publishers would like to thank the following for supplying photographs: Batchelors 1, 228; Edward Billington (Sugar) Ltd 241, 258, 271, 274; Birds Eye Wall's Limited 20, 78, 115, 156, 287, 296; British Cheese 18, 37, 105, 106, 107, 108, 160, 221; Butter Information Council 86, 154, 210; California Raisin Advisory Board 242, 252, 253, 272; Concentrated Butter 173, 174, 218, 255, 261, 262; Danish Dairy Board 10, 24, 28, 35, 36, 71, 81, 83, 87, 113, 155, 171, 175, 182, 184, 223, 225, 227, 245, 248, 249, 259, 267, 268, 277, 279, 290, 292, 299; Egg Marketing 246, 265; Fresh Fruit and Vegetable Information Bureau 72, 101, 116, 124, 217, 240, 264; The Kellogg Company of Great Britain Ltd 2, 7, 118, 216, 263, 266, 270, 280; Mushroom Growers' Association 11, 12, 19, 21, 23, 25, 73, 74, 76, 102, 114, 119, 121, 122, 172, 181, 295; Pasta Information Centre 157; Potato Marketing Board 6, 67, 68, 69, 70, 104, 289; St Ivel 8, 17, 27, 42, 57, 66, 75, 82, 90, 109, 151, 153, 177, 203, 214, 222, 247, 254, 275, 276, 281, 283, 293; Seafish Kitchen 285, 301; Sun Pat Peanut Butter 111; Tabasco 39, 195, 197, 286; Twining's Information Service 273; U.S. Rice Council 47, 140, 141, 143; U.S.A. Peanuts Information Service 40, 89, 117, 133, 142, 185, 243, 269; John West Foods 15, 110, 239, 260, 278, 288, 297, 300

This edition published in 1992
by Reed Consumer Books
part of Reed International Books Limited
for The Book People
Guardian House, Borough Road,
Godalming, Surrey GU7 2AE

A catalogue record for this book is available from the British Library.

ISBN 1 85613 130 0

Produced by Mandarin Offset
Printed and bound in Hong Kong

Contents

Soups	1–12
Starters	13–36
Beans and Pulses	37–64
Vegetable Dishes	65–104
Salads	105–136
Rice and Pasta	137–168
Pastry Specialities	169–188
Suppers and Snacks	189–216
Cooking for Special Occasions	217–236
Desserts	237–264
Baking	265–284
Not Quite Vegetarian	285–304

Useful Facts and Figures

Notes on metrication

In this book quantities are given in metric and Imperial measures. Exact conversion from Imperial to metric measures does not usually give very convenient working quantities and so the metric measures have been rounded off into units of 25 grams. The table below shows the recommended equivalents.

Ounces	Approx g to nearest whole figure	Recommended conversion to nearest unit of 25	Ounces	Approx g to nearest whole figure	Recommended conversion to nearest unit of 25
1	28	25	9	255	250
2	57	50	10	283	275
3	85	75	11	312	300
4	113	100	12	340	350
5	142	150	13	368	375
6	170	175	14	396	400
7	198	200	15	425	425
8	227	225	16 (1 lb)	454	450

Note: When converting quantities over 16 oz first add the appropriate figures in the centre column, then adjust to the nearest unit of 25. As a general guide, 1 kg (1000 g) equals 2.2 lb or about 2 lb 3 oz. This method of conversion gives good results in nearly all cases, although in certain pastry and cake recipes a more accurate conversion is necessary to produce a balanced recipe.

Liquid measures

The millilitre has been used in this book and the following table gives a few examples.

Imperial	Approx ml to nearest whole figure	Recommended ml	Imperial	Approx ml to nearest whole figure	Recommended ml
$\frac{1}{4}$	142	150 ml	1 pint	567	600 ml
$\frac{1}{2}$	283	300 ml	1$\frac{1}{2}$ pints	851	900 ml
$\frac{3}{4}$	425	450 ml	1$\frac{3}{4}$ pints	992	1000 ml (1 litre)

Spoon measures All spoon measures given in this book are level unless otherwise stated.

Can sizes At present, cans are marked with the exact (usually to the nearest whole number) metric equivalent of the Imperial weight of the contents, so we have followed this practice when giving can sizes.

Oven temperatures

The table below gives recommended equivalents.

	°C	°F	Gas Mark		°C	°F	Gas Mark
Very cool	110	225	$\frac{1}{4}$	Moderately hot	190	375	5
	120	250	$\frac{1}{2}$		200	400	6
Cool	140	275	1	Hot	220	425	7
	150	300	2		230	450	8
Moderate	160	325	3	Very Hot	240	475	9
	180	350	4				

Notes for American and Australian users

In America the 8-fl oz measuring cup is used. In Australia metric measures are now used in conjunction with the standard 250-ml measuring cup. The Imperial pint, used in Britain and Australia, is 20 fl oz, while the American pint is 16 fl oz. It is important to remember that the Australian tablespoon differs from both the British and American tablespoons; the table below gives a comparison. The British standard tablespoon, which has been used throughout this book, holds 17.7 ml, the American 14.2 ml, and the Australian 20 ml. A teaspoon holds approximately 5 ml in all three countries.

British	American	Australian
1 teaspoon	1 teaspoon	1 teaspoon
1 tablespoon	1 tablespoon	1 tablespoon
2 tablespoons	3 tablespoons	2 tablespoons
3$\frac{1}{2}$ tablespoons	4 tablespoons	3 tablespoons
4 tablespoons	5 tablespoons	3$\frac{1}{2}$ tablespoons

An Imperial/American guide to solid and liquid measures

Imperial	American	Imperial	American
Solid measures		**Liquid measures**	
1 lb butter or margarine	2 cups	$\frac{1}{4}$ pint liquid	$\frac{2}{3}$ cup liquid
1 lb flour	4 cups	$\frac{1}{2}$ pint	1$\frac{1}{4}$ cups
1 lb granulated or caster sugar	2 cups	$\frac{3}{4}$ pint	2 cups
		1 pint	2$\frac{1}{2}$ cups
1 lb icing sugar	3 cups	1$\frac{1}{2}$ pints	3$\frac{3}{4}$ cups
8 oz rice	1 cup	2 pints	5 cups (2$\frac{1}{2}$ pints)

Note: When making any of the recipes in this book, only follow one set of measures as they are not interchangeable.

Introduction

Hamlyn's All Colour Vegetarian Cookbook provides an invaluable collection of recipes for aspiring vegetarian cooks as well as for cooks looking for fresh ideas to enlarge their repertoire of vegetarian dishes. The wonderful variety of recipes in this book offers convincing proof that following a vegetarian diet need not limit your choice of ingredients to eggs, cheese and lentils.

A colour photograph illustrates each recipe, so that you can see the result you are aiming for. Those important finishing touches are highlighted in the photographs as well. In addition, much useful dietary and food preparation information is provided in the Cook's tips which appear below each recipe, many of them illustrated with a line drawing to give further clarification of a particular technique, ingredient, or decoration. Every recipe is calorie counted to assist in health and weight-conscious meal planning.

Preparation and cooking times are clearly given before the recipe method, so that you can see at a glance whether you have time to cook a particular dish. And of course, when planning a special meal in advance, it is simple to leaf through selecting a starter, main course and dessert, calculating the best combination to achieve infallible timing.

So that you can turn quickly to the recipe you want, each one is numbered and attractive colour coding makes it easy to identify the chapter you are looking for as you flick through the book.

The chapter sequence is helpful for menu planning, opening with soups and starters, following with pulse-based dishes, vegetable dishes and salads. Rice and pasta and pastry specialities offer further main course options, while recipes for suppers and snacks and for special occasions give a great variety of ideas, for both speedy and more elaborate dishes. Irresistible desserts feature next, then to conclude the book, a chapter of not-quite-vegetarian dishes is provided for those who follow a vegetarian diet most of the time, but occasionally prepare fish dishes to take advantage of the highly nutritious food content of fish.

Choose from over 300 appetising recipes to find the right one for every occasion.

Soups

Choose a soup to complement the courses which follow, in both texture and flavour, and even colour if possible. Light, tangy, Mulligatawny Soup or delicately flavoured Tomato and Carrot Soup make good appetisers for a substantial main course. If the course to follow is light, consider serving a protein and fibre-rich pulse-based soup, such as Bean and Pasta soup. But don't confine soup to a permanent position of first course – extend its status to that of a nourishing snack or lunch.

1 | Leek and Chick Pea Chowder

(Illustrated on back jacket)

Preparation time
10 minutes

Cooking time
25 minutes

Serves 4

Calories
235 per portion

You will need
100 g/4 oz leeks, sliced
1 small onion, chopped
2 tablespoons oil
1 teaspoon ground cumin
1 teaspoon ground coriander
350 g/12 oz potatoes, diced
1 (415-g/14.6-oz) can chick peas
750 ml/1¼ pints vegetable stock
  or water
salt and freshly ground pepper

Sauté the leeks and onion in the oil until soft. Sprinkle over the cumin and coriander and cook for a further minute. Add the potatoes and turn them thoroughly in the mixture. Stir in the drained chick peas with 450 ml/¾ pint stock or water. Bring to the boil, cover and cook gently until the potatoes are soft, about 15 minutes. Add the remaining stock or water with seasoning to taste. Serve hot as a chowder or liquidise to make a smooth thick soup. Accompany with crusty bread.

2 | Bean and Pasta Soup

Preparation time
5 minutes

Cooking time
25 minutes

Serves 4–6

Calories
215–145 per portion

You will need
1 large onion, sliced
1.15 litres/2 pints vegetable stock
75 g/3 oz pasta shapes
2 tablespoons tomato purée
salt and pepper
50 g/2 oz All-Bran cereal
1 (275-g/10-oz) can red kidney
  beans
100 g/4 oz canned broad beans
1 tablespoon chopped parsley
  (optional)

Simmer the onion in the stock in a large covered saucepan for 10 minutes. Add the pasta and tomato purée and cook for 10 minutes. Add the salt and pepper, cereal, kidney and broad beans and cook gently for a further 5 minutes. Pour into soup bowls and sprinkle with parsley, if you like.

Cook's Tip

Buy ready-ground spices and store them in an airtight jar ready for use. Alternatively, coriander seeds grind easily in a small pestle and mortar to give the most fragrant results.

Cook's Tip

All-Bran cereal is a versatile store-cupboard item – use it to add texture and valuable fibre to plain cake, pastry or bread mixtures. Combine it with unsweetened crumble mixture and grated cheese to make a tasty savoury topping for vegetables and pulses. Combine it in nut loaves, vegetable burgers and terrines for added flavour.

3 | *Mulligatawny Soup*

Preparation time
5 minutes

Cooking time
1 hour

Serves 6

Calories
95 per portion

You will need
1 apple, chopped
1 large carrot, chopped
2 tablespoons oil
25 g/1 oz plain flour
1 tablespoon curry powder
1.15 litres/2 pints vegetable stock
1 tablespoon mango chutney
25 g/1 oz sultanas
pinch of sugar
salt and pepper
2 teaspoons lemon juice or wine or cider vinegar

Cook the apple and carrot in the hot oil for 2 minutes. Stir in the flour and curry powder to make a paste. Gradually stir in the stock, bring to the boil and cook until thickened. Add the chutney, sultanas, sugar, a little salt and pepper, and the lemon juice, wine or vinegar. Cook very gently for 45 minutes–1 hour or until the vegetables are very soft.

Cool slightly and either press through a sieve or blend until smooth in a liquidiser. Pour the purée into the rinsed pan. Taste and adjust seasoning, if necessary. Reheat gently before serving.

4 | *Pea Soup*

Preparation time
10 minutes, plus overnight to soak

Cooking time
$1\frac{1}{4}$–$1\frac{1}{2}$ hours

Serves 4

Calories
210 per portion

You will need
225 g/8 oz dried split peas
1.15 litres/2 pints vegetable stock
2 medium onions, chopped
1 medium carrot, chopped
1 small turnip, chopped
salt and pepper
1 sprig of mint
1 teaspoon sugar

Cover the split peas with water and soak them overnight. Drain well. Place in a large saucepan with the stock, onions, carrot, turnip, a little salt and pepper, and the mint. Bring slowly to the boil, then simmer for $1\frac{1}{4}$–$1\frac{1}{2}$ hours or until the peas are very soft. Cool slightly and either press through a sieve or blend until smooth in a liquidiser. Pour the purée back into the rinsed pan, add sugar to taste and adjust the seasoning. Reheat very gently and serve hot.

Cook's Tip

Try serving a basket of crisp cooked poppadoms with this soup. Look out for these flavoured with chilli, cumin seeds and other spices as well as the plain variety. Instead of frying them, cook them under **the grill, keeping them away from the hot element.**

Cook's Tip

Swirl a little soured cream, natural yogurt or plain fromage frais into this soup before serving – delicious!

5 | Chestnut Soup

Preparation time
35 minutes

Cooking time
35 minutes

Serves 4–6

Calories
360–240 per portion

You will need
450 g/1 lb chestnuts
1 large onion, sliced
40 g/1½ oz butter
1 medium potato, chopped
3 celery sticks, chopped
1.4 litres/2½ pints vegetable stock
salt and freshly ground black pepper
15 g/½ oz plain flour
½ teaspoon light brown sugar
pinch of dried mixed herbs
300 ml/½ pint milk
1 tablespoon dry sherry

For the garnish
croutons (optional)
1 tablespoon chopped parsley (optional)

Slit the hard shell of each chestnut. Put the chestnuts into a pan of boiling water and simmer for 20 minutes. Remove the hard shells, rub off the brown skins and roughly chop the chestnuts.

Put the onion and half of the butter into a pan and gently cook until soft. Add the potato, celery, chestnuts, stock, salt and pepper, and bring to the boil. Cover and simmer until the chestnuts are soft. Press through a sieve, or blend in a liquidiser.

Melt the remaining butter, work in the flour and cook for 2 minutes. Stir in the sugar, herbs and chestnut purée, and heat through gently. Add the milk and re-heat, but do not boil. Stir in the sherry and serve, garnished as shown, if you like.

Cook's Tip

If you have a garden, then try drying some herbs for the winter. For example, sage, thyme and tarragon can be tied in bunches and hung in a cool, dry place.

6 | Winter warmer

Preparation time
5 minutes

Cooking time
40 minutes

Serves 4

Calories
355 per portion

You will need
25 g/1 oz butter
450 g/1 lb onions, chopped
675 g/1½ lb potatoes, chopped
900 ml/1½ pints vegetable stock
1 (280-g/10-oz) can creamed sweetcorn
pinch of mace or nutmeg
2 bay leaves
¼ teaspoon celery salt
pepper
1 (170-g/6-oz) can evaporated milk or single cream
1 tablespoon chopped fennel to garnish (optional)

Heat the butter in a large saucepan, add the onions and cook over moderate heat until golden, about 8 minutes. Add the potatoes, stock, sweetcorn, mace or nutmeg, bay leaves, salt and pepper. Bring to the boil, stirring, cover and simmer for 30 minutes or until the potatoes are very soft. Remove the bay leaves. Stir in the evaporated milk or cream, check seasoning, heat through gently and serve in warmed individual bowls. Garnish with fennel, if using.

Cook's Tip

A delicious accompaniment for soup: clean potato peelings, dipped in a thin batter and deep fried until crisp and golden.

7 | Carrot Soup

Preparation time
15 minutes

Cooking time
35 minutes

Serves 4

Calories
145 per portion

You will need
450 g/1 lb carrots, diced
900 ml/1½ pints vegetable stock
25 g/1 oz All-Bran cereal
175 g/6 oz onions, chopped
100 g/4 oz potatoes, diced
1 celery stick, chopped
1 tablespoon chopped parsley
salt and freshly ground black
  pepper
½ teaspoon caraway seeds
150 ml/¼ pint single cream
  (optional)

Put all the ingredients, except the cream, into a large pan and bring gently to the boil. Cover and simmer for 30 minutes, or until the vegetables are soft. Allow the soup to cool slightly and then purée in a food processor or a liquidiser until smooth and thick. Alternatively press the soup through a sieve.

Return the soup to the pan and reheat when required, stirring in the cream just before serving. Accompany with Caraway Rolls (see recipe 280).

8 | Tomato and Carrot Soup

Preparation time
25 minutes

Cooking time
42 minutes

Serves 6

Calories
160 per portion

You will need
100 g/4 oz carrots, peeled and
  sliced
1 small onion, chopped
1 clove garlic, chopped
2 tablespoons oil
450 g/1 lb tomatoes, peeled and
  chopped
600 ml/1 pint vegetable stock
salt and pepper
a little grated nutmeg
25 g/1 oz tomato purée
300 ml/½ pint single cream
1 tablespoon chopped parsley
additional parsley to garnish

Cook the carrots, onion and garlic in the oil over gentle heat for about 10 minutes, without browning. Stir in the tomatoes and stock. Season well with the salt and pepper and nutmeg, then stir in the tomato purée. Bring to the boil, reduce the heat and simmer for 30 minutes.

Blend the soup in a liquidiser, return to the pan and stir in the cream and parsley. Heat gently, without boiling, then serve garnished with a sprinkling of fresh chopped parsley.

Cook's Tip

If you have a food processor, then simply roughly chop all the vegetables using the knife attachment. Take care not to over-process the ingredients so that they become too fine.

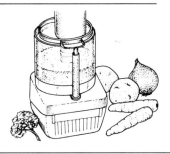

Cook's Tip

Flavour this soup with the grated rind and juice of 1 orange if you like. Add to the soup with the tomatoes and stock.

9 | *Creamy Onion soup*

Preparation time
10 minutes

Cooking time
55 minutes

Serves 4

Calories
325 per portion

You will need
*50 g/2 oz butter
3 large onions, chopped
1.15 litres/2 pints vegetable stock
450 g/1 lb potatoes, peeled and
   chopped
2–3 teaspoons soup seasoning
2 teaspoons paprika
½–1 tablespoon tomato purée
150 ml/¼ pint single cream
fried onion rings to garnish*

Melt the butter in a pan and fry the onions until soft. Add the stock, potatoes, soup seasoning, paprika and tomato purée.

Simmer for about 45 minutes. Sieve or blend the soup and reheat. Stir the cream into the hot soup and heat through very gently. Garnish with fried onion rings and serve.

Cook's Tip

Serve this soup cold as a smooth summer starter. Chill the sieved soup and add the cream just before serving. Omit the onion rings and float a spring onion curl on top of each portion instead (see Cook's Tip 227).

10 | *Leek and Potato Soup*

Preparation time
15 minutes

Cooking time
40–45 minutes

Serves 4

Calories
220 per portion

You will need
*25 g/1 oz butter
2 medium leeks, thinly sliced
350 g/12 oz potatoes, thinly sliced
750 ml/1¼ pints vegetable stock
salt and pepper
¼ teaspoon ground nutmeg
2–4 tablespoons milk or water
   (optional)
75–100 g/3–4 oz Danish Mycella
   cheese
chopped chives to garnish
   (optional)*

Melt the butter in a large pan and add the leeks. Cover and cook gently, stirring occasionally, for 8–10 minutes, until soft. Reserve a few rings for garnish. Add the potatoes to the pan with the stock, seasoning and nutmeg. Bring to the boil, cover and simmer for 25–30 minutes, until the potatoes are soft.

Cool slightly then rub the soup through a sieve, or liquidise in a blender until smooth. Return to the pan and reheat, adding a little milk or water if the soup is too thick. Just before serving, crumble in the Mycella cheese and stir until melted. Garnish with the reserved leek rings and chopped chives, if using.

Cook's Tip

To make vegetable stock, fry 2 chopped onions, 2 diced potatoes and 2 celery sticks. Stir in 1 sliced parsnip and 1 sliced turnip, add 1.2 litres/ 2 pints water. Pop in a bouquet garni, bring to the boil, lower heat and simmer for 1 hour.

11 | Cream of Mushroom Soup

Preparation time
10 minutes

Cooking time
25–30 minutes

Serves 4

Calories
135 per portion

You will need
1 tablespoon sunflower oil
1 medium onion, chopped
450 g/1 lb mushrooms, finely
    chopped
600 ml/1 pint vegetable stock
1 tablespoon chopped parsley
salt and freshly ground white
    pepper
2 teaspoons cornflour
150 ml/¼ pint single cream
croutons to garnish

Heat the oil and cook the onion gently until soft, about 5 minutes. Add the mushrooms and cook, stirring, for 3–4 minutes. Stir in the stock, parsley and seasoning; bring to the boil, cover and simmer gently for 15 minutes. Blend the cornflour with a little cold water and stir into the soup, cooking for a further 2–3 minutes until thickened. Stir in the cream and serve at once with croutons.

12 | Country Mushroom Soup

Preparation time
15 minutes

Cooking time
20 minutes

Serves 6

Calories
105 per portion

You will need
2 tablespoons oil
1 onion, finely chopped
1 clove garlic, crushed
2 teaspoons ground coriander
225 g/8 oz flat mushrooms, finely
    chopped
1.15 litres/2 pints vegetable stock
grated rind of 1 lemon
3 tablespoons chopped parsley
100 g/4 oz fresh wholewheat
    breadcrumbs
salt and pepper

For the garnish
2 tablespoons soured cream
1 tablespoon chopped parsley

Heat the oil and cook the onion gently until just soft, about 5 minutes. Stir in the garlic and coriander and cook for a minute to bring out the flavours. Add the mushrooms and cook for a further 3–4 minutes. Stir in the stock, lemon rind and parsley. Bring to the boil, cover and simmer for 10 minutes. Stir in the breadcrumbs and seasoning to taste and cook for 1 minute longer. Remove from the heat and swirl through the soured cream. Sprinkle with parsley and serve at once.

Cook's Tip

Pale button mushrooms give the best colour and a delicate flavour when making soup, but you will find that open, darker mushrooms offer a fuller flavour and are more suitable for hearty soups than creamy ones.

Cook's Tip

Make a large batch of vegetable stock (see Cook's Tip 10) leave it to cool and freeze it for future use. Fill plastic bags, supporting them in a basin, freeze, then remove the basin when hard.

Starters

Starters are designed to stimulate the taste buds, making them receptive to the courses which follow. When selecting a starter for a main meal, consider the menu as a whole and pick and choose from the recipe ideas in this chapter. A juicy, fruity starter like Melon and Grapefruit Cocktail with a fresh mint garnish will sharpen the appetite, and the unusual Crunchy Brie, served with the colourful and contrastingly flavoured cherry sauce will create enthusiastic anticipation of things to come.

13 | *Melon and Grapefruit Cocktail*

(Illustrated on back jacket)

Preparation time
10 minutes, plus 1 hour to chill

Serves 4

Calories
104 per portion

You will need
1 ripe honeydew melon, halved and deseeded
2 grapefruit, peeled
3–4 tablespoons clear honey
4 mint sprigs

Scoop out the melon flesh, using a melon baller, and place in a bowl.

Cut between the segments of the grapefruit, removing the pith and pips, and catch any juice from the fruit by working over a plate. Mix the grapefruit segments and juice with the melon, and trickle over the honey. Add the sprigs of mint to the fruit and chill thoroughly.

Serve the cocktail in glasses, carefully removing the mint to use as a garnish.

14 | *Grapefruit and Avocado Salad*

Preparation time
20 minutes

Serves 6

Calories
165 per portion

You will need
2 avocados, halved, peeled and stoned
2 grapefruit
2 oranges
$\frac{1}{2}$ teaspoon sugar
2 tablespoons olive oil
1 tablespoon chopped mint
salt and pepper
6–10 lettuce leaves, washed and torn into bite-sized pieces, or 2 heads of chicory, washed

Cut the avocado flesh into thin slices. Spread the slices out in a shallow bowl.

Holding a grapefruit over the bowl (so that the juice will go over the avocado slices), peel it with a sharp knife. Using a sawing action, cut round the fruit down to the flesh and remove all the white pith. Cut each segment of fruit away from the inner white skin. When all the segments have been removed from the grapefruit, squeeze the remaining juice from the skin over the avocado slices. Repeat this with the other grapefruit and the oranges, putting the segments on a plate.

Turn the avocado slices in the juice. Drain off any excess juice into a small bowl and add the sugar, oil, mint and salt and pepper to make a dressing.

To assemble the dish, cover individual plates with lettuce or chicory leaves, then arrange segments of grapefruit, orange and avocado on top, dividing them between the plates. Spoon a little dressing over each salad.

Cook's Tip

For special occasions, frost the tops of the glasses by dipping the rims lightly in beaten egg white, then in sugar.

Cook's Tip

Sprinkling the avocado slices with the citrus fruit juices prevents them from discolouring.

The watercress sprigs and sprinkling of herbs shown in the photograph give additional colour to the salad.

15 | Grapefruit Sorbet

Preparation time
10 minutes, plus several hours to freeze

Cooking time
7–8 minutes

Serves 6

Calories
50 per portion

You will need
25 g/1 oz honey
300 ml/½ pint water
2 (540-g/1 lb 3-oz) cans grapefruit segments in natural juice
150 ml/¼ pint lemon juice
grated rind of 2 lemons
2 egg whites
mint sprigs to decorate

Bring the honey and water gently to the boil and simmer for 5 minutes. Cool slightly. Use one can of grapefruit to make the sorbet; reserve the second can for serving. Drain the grapefruit juice from the segments in one can and add to the honey liquid with the lemon juice and rind. Cool and freeze until half frozen.

Whisk the egg whites until stiff and fold into the mixture. Freeze again until firm. Serve the sorbet on a bed of grapefruit segments, reserving a few for decoration. Top with mint sprigs.

Cook's Tip

Crystallised mint leaves make an attractive decoration for sorbets. Dip clean leaves in egg white, then in caster sugar. Dry on a wire rack.

16 | Pears with Mustard Cream Mayonnaise

Preparation time
30 minutes, plus 1 hour to chill

Serves 4

Calories
175 per portion

You will need
2 ripe eating pears
1 tablespoon lemon juice
4 tablespoons mayonnaise
1 tablespoon Dijon mustard
2 tablespoons double cream, whipped

For the garnish
flaked almonds
lettuce leaves

Peel the pears, keeping them in good shape. Using a teaspoon, scoop out the seeds and core. Brush each pear with the lemon juice to prevent from discolouring.

Whisk the mayonnaise with the mustard and whipped double cream, adding 1 teaspoon of boiling water if the consistency is too thick to coat the pears smoothly. Split the almonds and toast under the grill until golden brown. Cool.

To serve, place a few lettuce leaves on four small plates. Place a pear half, cut side down on each plate and coat with mustard mayonnaise. Sprinkle with the toasted almonds. Chill before serving.

Cook's Tip

Watch the almonds closely. It takes only a few seconds for beautifully golden nuts to become burnt offerings.

17 | Savoury Pear Mousse

Preparation time
20 minutes, plus 1–2 hours to set

Cooking time
15 minutes

Serves 8

Calories
95 per portion

You will need
2 pears, peeled and chopped
1 small onion, chopped
120 ml/4 fl oz water
pinch of chilli powder
pinch of turmeric
4 juniper berries, crushed
salt and pepper
175 g/6 oz low-fat soft cheese
4 tablespoons double cream
100 g/4 oz button mushrooms, finely chopped
2 teaspoons agar-agar or 3 teaspoons powdered gelatine
cress and capers, to garnish

To serve
Melba toast
2 hard-boiled eggs, sliced
2 tomatoes, cut into wedges

Place the pears and onion in a small pan with 2 tablespoons of the water, the chilli, turmeric, juniper berries and seasoning. Cover and cook gently for about 15 minutes, or until tender.

When the pears are soft, drain, blend in a liquidiser or press through a sieve. Add the soft cheese, cream and mushrooms and blend until smooth. Dissolve the agar-agar in the remaining cold water in a small saucepan, then bring to the boil, stirring constantly. Stir into the mousse. Pour into individual dishes and chill to set. Garnish with cress and capers, serve as shown.

Cook's Tip

To make Melba toast, toast medium-thick bread slices, cut off the crusts and slice through to give very thin pieces – work quickly before the toast cools. Lightly toast the second side.

18 | Tomato Coupé

Preparation time
10 minutes, plus 1 hour to set

Cooking time
10 minutes

Serves 6

Calories
95 per portion

You will need
1 (397-g/14-oz) can tomatoes
grated rind of ½ lemon
1 bay leaf
1 clove garlic, crushed
3 tablespoons white wine
2 teaspoons agar-agar or 3 teaspoons powdered gelatine
150 ml/¼ pint water
salt and pepper
½ teaspoon sugar
100 g/4 oz Cheddar cheese, grated
6 spring onions, thinly sliced
brown bread and butter, to serve

Pour the tomatoes and their juices into a saucepan, add the lemon rind, bay leaf and garlic. Chop the tomatoes roughly, bring to the boil, cover and simmer for 10 minutes. Press the tomato mixture through a sieve into a measuring jug and add the wine. Dissolve the agar-agar in the cold water in a small saucepan, bring to the boil, stirring constantly, then add to the tomato and wine mixture. Add more boiling water if necessary to make 600 ml/1 pint. Stir in salt, pepper and sugar to taste. Cool. Pour into 6 individual ramekins or coupé glasses and refrigerate until set.

Mix together the cheese and spring onions and top each coupé with the mixture. Serve chilled with brown bread and butter.

Cook's Tip

If you like, set the tomato mixture in one large mould, then turn it out before serving. Offer the cheese and spring onions in a separate dish.

19 | Greek Mushroom Salad

Preparation time
10 minutes, plus 1 hour to chill

Cooking time
15 minutes

Serves 6

Calories
30 per portion
180 per piece of pitta bread

You will need
2 cloves garlic, crushed
3 tablespoons tomato purée
3 tablespoons lemon juice
150 ml/¼ pint water
1 teaspoon oregano
½ teaspoon basil
225 g/8 oz button mushrooms
450 g/1 lb cauliflower florets
12 black olives, roughly chopped
salt and pepper
pitta bread to serve

Place the garlic, tomato purée, lemon juice and water in a large saucepan and mix well. Stir in the herbs, mushrooms and cauliflower. Cover and bring to the boil, then reduce the heat and simmer gently for 10 minutes, stirring frequently. Stir in the olives and seasoning to taste. Transfer to a serving bowl and leave until cold.

This is best served chilled, accompanied with warm pitta bread cut into fingers.

20 | Savoury Stuffed tomatoes

Preparation time
10 minutes

Serves 4

Calories
50 per portion

You will need
4 large firm tomatoes
75 g/3 oz cream cheese, softened
½ teaspoon finely chopped chives or onion
1 tablespoon mayonnaise
salt and pepper
100 g/4 oz frozen peas, cooked
parsley or watercress sprigs to garnish

Slice the tops off the tomatoes and scoop out the pulp with a teaspoon. Beat the cream cheese with the chives or onion and mayonnaise and season well. Stir in the peas and fill the tomatoes with the mixture, replacing the top of each. Garnish with sprigs of parsley or watercress.

Cook's Tip

If you prefer, mix tomatoes with the mushrooms in this salad instead of the cauliflower. Cook the mushrooms as above, then add 6 peeled and quartered tomatoes at the end of the cooking time.

Cook's Tip

For best results, when you have scooped out the tomatoes, leave them to drain on double-thick absorbent kitchen paper.

21 | *Mushrooms Indienne*

Preparation time
10 minutes, plus 30 minutes to chill

Serves 4

Calories
100 per portion

You will need
150 ml/¼ pint soured cream or natural yogurt
1–2 teaspoons curry paste
1 tablespoon sieved mango chutney
salt and pepper
1 dessert apple, peeled, cored and chopped
175 g/6 oz button mushrooms
Chinese leaves, shredded
4 lemon slices to garnish

Mix together the cream and curry paste according to taste. Add the chutney, seasoning, apple and mushrooms and mix well. Chill for at least 30 minutes before serving.

Pile each portion on to a bed of shredded Chinese leaves and garnish with a twist of lemon.

22 | *Peanut Dip with Crudités*

Preparation time
15–20 minutes

Cooking time
5 minutes

Serves 6

Calories
190 per portion

You will need
2 tablespoons sunflower oil
1 onion, finely chopped
2 cloves garlic, crushed
½ teaspoon chilli powder
1 teaspoon ground cumin
1 teaspoon ground coriander
6 tablespoons crunchy peanut butter
6 tablespoons water
1 teaspoon shoyu
1 teaspoon lemon juice

For the crudités
1 small cauliflower
1 bunch of radishes
1 red pepper, deseeded
6 celery sticks
6 carrots

Heat the oil in a small saucepan, add the onion and fry for a few minutes until softened. Add the garlic and spices, stir and cook for 1 minute. Mix in the peanut butter, then gradually blend in the water, stirring until thickened. Add the shoyu and lemon juice, stir well and leave to cool.

Break the cauliflower into florets and halve the radishes if large. Cut the remaining vegetables into long thin pieces.

Turn the dip into a small dish, place on a large plate and surround with the crudités.

Cook's Tip

Instead of the curry paste, you can use curry powder but halve the quantity. Cook the powder in a little butter in a small pan for 3 minutes before adding to the cream.

Cook's Tip

Wholemeal grissini – Italian breadsticks – make excellent dippers, much favoured by children. If serving the dip for a child's party, eliminate the spices.

23 | Mushroom and Avocado Starter

Preparation time
15 minutes, plus 30 minutes to chill

Serves 4

Calories
100 per portion

You will need
225 g/8 oz button mushrooms, sliced
3 tablespoons lemon juice
4 spring onions, chopped
1 tablespoon sunflower seeds, toasted
salt and pepper
1 ripe avocado

Put the mushrooms in a mixing bowl with 2 tablespoons lemon juice, the spring onions, sunflower seeds and seasoning. Mix well and chill for at least 30 minutes.

Just before serving, remove the stone and peel from the avocado, slice the flesh and sprinkle with the remaining lemon juice. Arrange the avocado slices on individual serving plates with the mushroom salad at the side.

24 | Cheese Croustades

Preparation time
15 minutes

Cooking time
24 minutes

Oven temperature
200 C, 400 F, gas 6

Makes 12

Calories
110 per croustade

You will need
25 g/1 oz butter, melted
12 slices, medium-sliced bread

For the filling
225 g/8 oz small button mushrooms
25 g/1 oz butter
125 g/4½ oz Danish Dania cheese, plain
½ teaspoon cornflour
2 tablespoons chopped parsley
salt and pepper

For the garnish
paprika
parsley sprigs

Brush a 12-hole bun tin with a little of the melted butter. Cut the crusts off the bread and flatten each slice with a rolling pin. Cut out an 8.5-cm/3½-in circle from each piece of bread, then press into the tins. Brush with the remaining melted butter and bake for 15 minutes.

To make the filling, wipe and quarter the mushrooms. Melt the butter and cook the mushrooms, covered, for 5 minutes. Remove the rind, then add the cheese to the mushrooms, stirring until melted.

Mix the cornflour to a smooth paste with a little water, stir into the mushroom mixture and bring just to boiling point to thicken, still stirring. Lower heat, add half the parsley and salt and pepper and heat for 30 seconds.

Divide the mushroom mixture between the warm croustades and sprinkle with paprika. Add a sprig of parsley to each and serve immediately.

Cook's Tip

To remove the stone easily from a halved avocado, pierce it with the point of a knife, then pull it out.

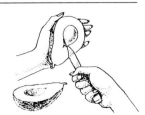

Cook's Tip

Croustades lend themselves perfectly to lots of different fillings. Try ratatouille, sautéed vegetables or leeks au gratin (Recipe 94), adding the filling of your choice just before serving to prevent the croustades becoming soggy.

25 | Mushroom Puffs with Spicy Sauce

Preparation time
15 minutes

Cooking time
20 30 minutes

Serves 4

Calories
230 per portion

You will need
225 g/8 oz mushrooms

For the sauce
1 tablespoon oil
1 small onion, finely chopped
½ clove garlic, crushed
1 teaspoon dark soft brown sugar
2 teaspoons lemon juice
1 tablespoon tomato purée
1 (227-g/8-oz) can tomatoes
1 tablespoon mushroom ketchup
salt and pepper
parsley sprigs to garnish

For the batter
50 g/2 oz plain flour
salt and pepper
4 tablespoons lukewarm water
1 egg white
oil for frying

First make the sauce: heat the oil in a pan, add the onion and garlic and cook until tender. Add the remaining ingredients and boil, season and keep warm. For the batter, place the flour and seasoning in a bowl, then beat in the water and fold in the stiffly-beaten egg white. Heat the oil for deep frying to 190 C/375 F. Dip the mushrooms in the batter, then deep fry until golden. Drain on absorbent kitchen paper, garnish with parsley sprigs and serve with the sauce.

Cook's Tip

When deep frying, make sure that the food absorbs the minimum of fat: have the oil hot before cooking, then drain the food on absorbent kitchen paper.

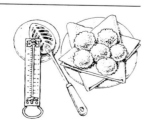

26 | Mushroom Pâté

Preparation time
15 minutes plus 1 2 hours to chill

Cooking time
20 minutes

Serves 4

Calories
190 per portion

You will need
75 g/3 oz butter
2 shallots or small onions, finely sliced
1 clove garlic, crushed (optional)
225 g/8 oz flat mushrooms, sliced
25 g/1 oz fresh wholewheat breadcrumbs
100 g/4 oz cottage cheese
pinch of grated nutmeg
pinch of ground mace
salt and pepper

For the garnish
1 tablespoon chopped parsley
lemon wedges

Melt 25 g/1 oz butter in a saucepan and cook the shallots or onions and garlic gently for 3 minutes. Add the mushrooms, cover and cook for 15 minutes. Remove the lid, turn up the heat and reduce the liquid until the mushrooms are just moist. Add a further 25 g/1 oz butter.

Cool slightly, then put the mushrooms, breadcrumbs, cheese, nutmeg, mace, salt and pepper and remaining butter in a liquidiser or food processor and blend until smooth.

Adjust the seasoning, and spoon the pâté into a small dish. Cover and chill for 1–2 hours. Just before serving sprinkle the top with parsley and garnish with lemon wedges.

Cook's Tip

A useful vegetarian spread. Tasty with chopped watercress as a sandwich filling, or served with warm granary bread and butter.

27 | *Cheese Balls*

Preparation time
30 minutes plus 1 hour
to chill

Serves 6

Calories
280 per portion

You will need
225 g/8 oz low-fat hard cheese,
    finely grated (for example Shape
    cheese)
75 g/3 oz butter
salt and pepper
1 tablespoon milk
cayenne
2 teaspoons sherry
100 g/4 oz walnuts, finely chopped

Mix all the ingredients together, except the walnuts, adding a little cayenne to taste. Take small spoonfuls of the cheese mixture and roll them into balls. Coat each with chopped walnuts. Chill for at least an hour before serving.

28 | *Crunchy Brie*

Preparation time
15 minutes, plus 30
minutes to chill

Cooking time
5–6 minutes

Serves 4

Calories
385 per portion

You will need
150 g/5 oz Blue Brie cheese
15 g/½ oz plain flour
1 egg, beaten
40 g/1½ oz fresh white
    breadcrumbs
oil for deep frying
dill sprigs to garnish (optional)

For the sauce
1 (220-g/7¾-oz) can pitted black
    cherries
1½ teaspoons arrowroot
2 teaspoons caster sugar

Cut the cheese into four equal wedges. Dip each into the flour and shake off the excess. Dip in the egg, allow excess to run off, then coat completely in the bread-crumbs. Re-coat in egg and breadcrumbs. Place on a plate, cover and refrigerate for at least 30 minutes.

Meanwhile make the sauce. Drain the juice from the cherries and reserve the fruit. In a small saucepan blend the arrowroot to a smooth paste with a little of the juice. Add the remaining juice and bring to the boil, stirring all the time, until thickened. Sweeten to taste, add the cherries and heat through gently. Pour into a sauceboat.

Heat the oil in a deep pan to 180 C/350 F, or until a day-old bread cube browns in 60 seconds. Lower the cheese portions into the hot oil, two at a time, and fry for 30–60 seconds, until the coating is golden. Remove from the pan and drain on absorbent kitchen paper. Cook the remaining cheese portions, garnish with dill if liked and serve immediately with the cherry sauce.

Cook's Tip

Serve these tasty cheese balls as a cocktail snack with drinks, instead of serving a starter. Alternatively, arrange a few balls on a little shredded lettuce on individual plates and garnish with chopped tomato for a first course.

Cook's Tip

This unusual dish can be served as a savoury at the end of a meal or even at a cheese and wine party for a change. Prepare the cheese earlier in the day ready to be cooked just before serving.

29 | *Glamorgan Sausages*

Preparation time
20 minutes

Cooking time
5–7 minutes

Serves 4

Calories
520 per portion

You will need
1 medium onion, finely chopped
175 g/6 oz Cheddar cheese, grated
275 g/10 oz fresh breadcrumbs
pinch of dried sage
pinch of mustard powder
2 eggs, separated
salt and pepper
fresh breadcrumbs for coating
oil for frying

Mix together the onion, cheese, breadcrumbs, sage, mustard, egg yolks, and salt and pepper. Divide the mixture into 12 pieces and roll each portion into a small sausage shape.

Lightly beat the egg whites in a shallow bowl. Place the breadcrumbs on a large plate. Coat each sausage shape with egg white and then press on a coating of crumbs.

Heat about 2.5 cm/1 in of oil in a large saucepan. Fry the 'sausages' for 5–7 minutes or until golden, turning once. Drain on absorbent kitchen paper. Serve hot.

Cook's Tip

Try using other types of cheese in these delicious savouries: Edam or Cheddar with chives, Sage Derby, or blue Stilton for a rich flavour.

30 | *Avocado and Cheese Mousse*

Preparation time
15 minutes, plus 2 hours to chill

Serves 4

Calories
180 per portion

You will need
1 large ripe avocado
75 g/3 oz cream cheese
1 clove garlic, crushed
juice of 1 lemon
salt and pepper
2 tablespoons single cream
watercress sprigs to garnish

Halve the avocado, remove the stone and scoop out the flesh into a bowl. Mash and mix with the cream cheese, garlic and lemon juice. Season well and stir in the cream.

Spoon the mixture into individual glasses and chill for up to 2 hours. Serve garnished with watercress and accompany with Melba toast (see Cook's Tip 17).

Cook's Tip

Do not prepare this mousse more than about 2 hours in advance as it tends to discolour.

31 | Garnished Artichoke Hearts

Preparation time
10 minutes, plus 20 minutes to chill

Serves 4

Calories
245 per portion

You will need
2 (90-g/3½-oz) packets soft cream cheese
1 clove garlic, crushed
1 egg yolk
6 tablespoons double cream, lightly whipped
pinch of paprika
2 tablespoons chopped herbs (e.g. sage, parsley, thyme)
salt and pepper
1 (400-g/14-oz) can artichoke hearts in brine, drained

For the garnish
shredded lettuce
red pepper slices

Beat the cream cheese with the crushed garlic, egg yolk, cream, paprika, herbs and salt and pepper to taste. Spoon into a piping bag fitted with a star-shaped nozzle and pipe swirls of the mixture on to the artichoke hearts.

Chill the artichoke hearts lightly before placing on a bed of lettuce on a serving plate. Garnish with red pepper slices.

32 | Vegetable Pâté

Preparation time
15 minutes

Cooking time
1 hour 25 minutes

Oven temperature
160 C, 325 F, gas 3

Serves 6

Calories
210 per portion

You will need
2 tablespoons olive oil
1 onion, thinly sliced
350 g/12 oz courgettes, sliced
1 (225-g/8-oz) carton curd cheese
50 g/2 oz fresh white breadcrumbs
2 teaspoons chopped fresh basil or 1 teaspoon dried basil
2 teaspoons chopped fresh marjoram or 1 teaspoon dried marjoram (optional)
salt and pepper
1 egg, beaten
2 tablespoons melted butter
350 g/12 oz spinach, cooked and chopped
½ teaspoon freshly grated nutmeg
blanched courgette slices to garnish

Heat the oil in a frying pan and cook the onion and courgettes until softened. Drain and purée, then dry out in a saucepan over low heat (2–3 minutes). Beat in the curd cheese, breadcrumbs, basil, marjoram, if using, seasoning and egg.

Spoon half the courgette mixture into a lined and well-buttered, 450-g/1-lb loaf tin. Season the spinach, add the nutmeg and spread in an even layer over the courgettes. Cover with the remaining courgette mixture and press down firmly. Cover with buttered foil, place in a bain-marie and cook in a moderate oven for 1¼ hours. Cool and chill overnight. Turn out and serve garnished with courgette slices.

Cook's Tip

Garnished Artichoke Hearts make a delicious party snack, or hors d'oeuvre. Serve with garlic bread and a light dry red wine.

Cook's Tip

A bain-marie is a roasting tin (or other suitable vessel) filled with hot water. Containers of food that need gentle cooking are placed in the water to ensure that the outside does not overheat during cooking.

33 | Classic Greek Salad

Preparation time
15 minutes, plus 30–60 minutes to stand

Serves 4

Calories
125 per portion

You will need
1 medium onion, sliced and
  separated into rings
1 tablespoon olive oil
1 tablespoon wine vinegar
salt and pepper
4 tomatoes, thinly sliced
$\frac{1}{2}$ cucumber, peeled and diced
10–12 black olives (optional)
100 g/4 oz feta cheese or other
  white, crumbly cheese, diced

Put the onion into a bowl with the oil, vinegar and a little salt and pepper. Mix well, then leave to stand for 30–60 minutes to allow the onion to soften slightly. Stir occasionally.

Add the tomatoes, cucumber, olives and cheese, mixing gently to distribute all the ingredients. Serve at once.

34 | Smoked Cheese and Nut Salad

Preparation time
15 minutes

Serves 6

Calories
270 per portion

You will need
50 g/2 oz hazelnuts, coarsely
  chopped
6 tablespoons vegetable oil
2 tablespoons wine vinegar
salt and pepper
pinch of cayenne
$\frac{1}{2}$ teaspoon prepared English
  mustard
$\frac{1}{2}$ teaspoon sugar
1 crisp lettuce, shredded
1 head radicchio, separated into
  leaves
2 dessert apples
1 tablespoon lemon juice
150 g/5 oz German smoked
  cheese, cut into 1-cm/$\frac{1}{2}$-inch
  cubes
watercress to garnish

To make the dressing, toast the chopped hazelnuts under a medium grill until evenly browned. Cool. Put oil, vinegar, salt and pepper, cayenne, mustard and sugar into a screwtop jar, add the hazelnuts and shake for 1 minute until well mixed.

Arrange the lettuce and radicchio on 6 individual plates. Cut the apples into 1-cm/$\frac{1}{2}$-in cubes, toss in the lemon juice and arrange with the cubes of cheese on top of the salad. Spoon the dressing over the cheese and apple just before serving and garnish with sprigs of watercress.

Cook's Tip

Feta cheese has a salty, distinct flavour which perfectly complements the other ingredients in this salad. Alternatively, you can use another mild, crumbly cheese such as Cheshire. For a creamy texture, try mozzarella.

Cook's Tip

An unusual colourful starter using radicchio. The same quantities will serve 2–3 as a main meal salad.

35 | *Speedy Party Dip*

Preparation time
5 minutes, plus 1 hour
to chill

Serves 4—6

Total calories
1075 (270 180 per
portion)

You will need
225 g/8 oz full-fat soft cheese with
   garlic
150 ml/¼ pint natural yogurt
½ small green pepper, deseeded
   and finely shredded

Beat the cheese to soften, add the yogurt and beat until
smooth. Stir in the pepper and mix well. Turn into a
serving dish and chill.
   Serve with a selection of small pieces of raw carrot,
courgette, celery, pepper, broccoli and cauliflower, and
crisp savoury biscuits.

36 | *Blue Cheese Dip*

Preparation time
10 minutes, plus 30
minutes to chill

Serves 4—6

Total calories
1100 (275 185 per
portion)

You will need
100 g/4 oz Danish Blue cheese
2 tablespoons mayonnaise
150 ml/¼ pint whipping cream
freshly ground black pepper

For the garnish
cucumber slices
parsley sprigs

Mash the blue cheese with a fork or electric mixer. Beat
in the mayonnaise until smooth. Lightly whip the cream
and fold into the cheese mixture. Add pepper to taste
and turn into a serving bowl to chill. Garnish with
cucumber and parsley before serving.
   Offer cucumber sticks, olives, breadsticks, tomato
wedges and other savoury snacks as dippers.

Cook's Tip

**This dip also makes a delicious
topping for baked potatoes.**

Cook's Tip

**Blue cheese is easier to mash
when at room temperature.
For a variation to the dip, try
adding half a green pepper,
deseeded and finely chopped,
or 25–50 g / 1–2 oz finely
chopped walnuts.**

Beans and Pulses

In a vegetarian diet versatile dried peas and beans provide valuable sources of protein and fibre. Many people will be familiar with the delicious dhals – made from lentils, chick peas and mung beans, among others – that are an integral part of an Indian meal, but may not have experimented at home to make the most of the huge variety of pulses available. The recipes in this chapter offer lots of good ideas.

37 | Derby and Lentil Loaf

(Illustrated on front jacket)

Preparation time
20 minutes

Cooking time
1½ hours

Oven temperature
180 C, 350 F, gas 4

Serves 4–6

Calories
360–240 per portion

You will need
225 g/8 oz red lentils, soaked overnight
1 vegetable stock cube
1 onion, chopped
100 g/4 oz Derby or Sage Derby cheese, grated
150 ml/¼ pint tomato juice
2 eggs, beaten
2 slices wholemeal bread, made into crumbs
2 teaspoons mixed herbs
pinch of salt
cucumber slices to garnish

Drain water from soaked lentils and put them in a saucepan with fresh water to cover. Add the vegetable stock cube; bring slowly to the boil. Cover and simmer for 20–30 minutes or until the lentils are tender. Drain away any surplus water.

Add the chopped onion and grated cheese to the lentils. Mix well. Add the tomato juice, beaten eggs, breadcrumbs, herbs and salt and stir the mixture thoroughly. Spoon the mixture into a greased 450-g/1-lb loaf tin and bake for 1 hour. Turn out the cooked loaf and serve hot or cold, garnished with cucumber.

38 | Lentil Moussaka

Preparation time
10 minutes

Cooking time
40–45 minutes

Oven temperature
200 C, 400 F, gas 6

Serves 4

Calories
205 per portion

You will need
100 g/4 oz red lentils
1 (397-g/14-oz) can tomatoes
1 clove garlic, crushed
½ teaspoon dried oregano
pinch of ground nutmeg
1 vegetable stock cube
150 ml/¼ pint boiling water
1 tablespoon oil
225 g/8 oz aubergine, sliced
1 onion, chopped

For the cheese topping
1 egg
150 g/5 oz low-fat soft cheese
pepper and nutmeg

Put the lentils in a large saucepan with the tomatoes, garlic, oregano and a generous pinch of nutmeg. Crumble in the stock cube and then pour in the boiling water. Simmer for 20 minutes.

Heat the oil and lightly cook the aubergine slices with the onion. Layer them with the lentil mixture in an ovenproof dish. Beat the egg and cheese, seasoning and nutmeg. Pour over the moussaka and cook in a moderately hot oven for about 20–25 minutes.

Cook's Tip

Although the lentils are soaked in this recipe, it is not always essential to do so. For a quick supper, just simmer them for about 30 minutes. Serve with soured cream and chopped herbs.

Cook's Tip

Low-fat soft cheese is an excellent ingredient to use in cooking since it gives a rich flavour without being too runny. For example try Shape brand and look out for varieties flavoured with herbs **and garlic to create an interesting flavour.**

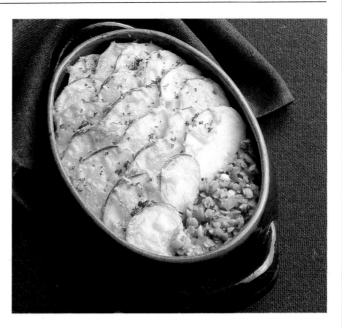

39 | Lentil and Vegetable Bake

Preparation time
10 minutes

Cooking time
40 minutes

Serves 4

Calories
405 per portion

You will need
2 tablespoons oil
1 large onion, chopped
2 medium carrots, chopped
2 celery sticks, chopped
175 g/6 oz red lentils
1 teaspoon mixed herbs
a few drops of Tabasco sauce
600 ml/1 pint vegetable stock
2 tablespoon tomato purée
salt and pepper
100 g/4 oz mushrooms, sliced
2 small courgettes, diced
1 tablespoon sunflower seeds
25 g/1 oz chopped nuts
50 g/2 oz fresh wholewheat
    breadcrumbs
50 g/2 oz Cheddar cheese, grated

Heat the oil in a large saucepan, add the onion and cook for 5 minutes until softened. Add the carrots and celery and cook for 2 minutes. Stir in the lentils, herbs, Tabasco, stock, tomato purée and salt and pepper and bring to the boil. Cover and simmer for 20 minutes or until the lentils are soft. Stir in the mushrooms and courgettes and cook for a further 10 minutes. Pour the mixture into a shallow ovenproof dish. Mix the seeds, nuts, breadcrumbs and cheese and sprinkle evenly over the top. Cook under a hot grill until golden and crisp. Serve hot.

Cook's Tip

It is a good idea to make a large batch of breadcrumbs and freeze them for future use. Reduce a whole loaf to crumbs in a liquidiser or food processor, then pack them loosely in large freezer bags.

40 | Lentil and Peanut Layer

Preparation time
20 minutes

Cooking time
45 55 minutes

Serves 4

Calories
570 per portion

You will need
2 tablespoons groundnut oil
1 onion, chopped
2 carrots, diced
2 celery sticks, chopped
175 g/6 oz red lentils
1 teaspoon dried mixed herbs
1 tablespoon soy sauce
300 ml/½ pint vegetable stock
1 (397-g/14-oz) can tomatoes
100 g/4 oz salted peanuts, roughly
    chopped
salt and pepper
675 g/1½ lb potatoes
50 g/2 oz Cheddar cheese, grated
chopped parsley to garnish

Heat the oil in a large saucepan, add the onion and fry for 5 minutes until softened. Add the carrots and celery and cook for 2 minutes more. Add the lentils, herbs and soy sauce and mix well. Stir in the stock and tomatoes and bring to the boil. Cover and simmer gently for 20–30 minutes, adding more stock if necessary, until the lentils are cooked and the mixture thickened. Stir in the peanuts and seasoning. Simmer for 5 minutes more.

Meanwhile, boil the potatoes in their jackets, drain, skin and slice thinly. Place the lentil mixture in an ovenproof dish and cover with the sliced potato. Sprinkle with the cheese and place under a hot grill for 6–8 minutes, until the cheese has melted and the potatoes are golden brown. Sprinkle with parsley and serve.

Cook's Tip

When red lentils are used in a recipe, you can substitute green ones for a change. They need longer cooking – about 40–45 minutes – and you may have to add extra liquid.

41 | Walnut and Lentil Loaf

Preparation time
10 minutes

Cooking time
1 hour 25 minutes

Oven temperature
190C, 375F, gas 5

Serves 6

Calories
245 per portion

You will need
1 tablespoon oil
1 onion, chopped
1 clove garlic, crushed
2 celery sticks, sliced
175 g/6 oz green lentils
450 ml/¾ pint water
100 g/4 oz walnuts, ground
50 g/2 oz wholewheat
    breadcrumbs
2 tablespoons chopped parsley
1 tablespoon shoyu
1 egg, beaten
salt and pepper
thyme sprigs to garnish

Heat the oil in a saucepan, add the onion and fry for a few minutes until softened. Add the garlic, celery, lentils and water and bring to the boil. Cover and simmer for 30–40 minutes, until the lentils are tender, stirring occasionally and removing the lid for the last 10 minutes to allow the moisture to evaporate.

Stir in the walnuts, breadcrumbs, parsley, shoyu, egg and salt and pepper to taste, and mix thoroughly.

Line a 450-g/1-lb loaf tin with foil to cover the bottom and long sides. Brush with oil. Spoon the mixture into the tin, cover with foil and bake in a moderately hot oven for 45–50 minutes.

Leave in the tin for 2 minutes, then loosen with a knife and turn out on to a warmed serving dish. Garnish with thyme. Serve with a tomato sauce (see recipe 154) or tomato mayonnaise.

Cook's Tip

If you do not have a food processor or liquidiser, then you will find a rotary grater useful for grinding nuts.

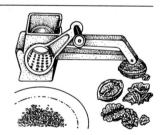

42 | Lentil Croquettes

Preparation time
15–20 minutes, plus 1 hour to chill

Cooking time
30–35 minutes

Serves 4–6

Calories
565–375 per portion

You will need
225 g/8 oz red lentils, rinsed
600 ml/1 pint water
1 tablespoon oil
175 g/6 oz low-fat hard cheese,
    grated (for example Shape
    cheese)
50 g/2 oz peanut butter
50 g/2 oz fresh wholewheat
    breadcrumbs
2 tablespoons chopped parsley
juice of 1 lemon
1–2 teaspoons yeast extract
salt and black pepper

For the coating
1 egg, beaten
50–75 g/2–3 oz wholewheat
    breadcrumbs
2–3 tablespoons oil for cooking

Place the lentils in a pan with the water and simmer, covered, for 30 minutes, until the water is absorbed and the lentils form a purée. Add the oil, cheese, peanut butter, breadcrumbs, parsley, lemon juice, yeast extract to taste and seasoning. Mix well. Cool, then chill lightly.

Shape large spoonfuls of the mixture into croquettes. Coat each with egg and breadcrumbs. Chill again. Fry the croquettes in the oil, turning once until golden all over. Drain on absorbent kitchen paper and serve with a salad.

Cook's Tip

Dry, uncooked breadcrumbs are best for coating food before frying. Make the fresh crumbs, then dry them out in a very cool oven until crisp. For a fine texture put them through the liquidiser or food processor once more. If thoroughly dried they store well in an airtight container in a cool place.

43 | Lentil Patties

Preparation time
15 minutes

Cooking time
1 hour 20 minutes

Serves 4

Calories
320 per portion

You will need
175 g/6 oz lentils, rinsed
450 ml/¾ pint cold water
1 large onion, finely chopped
4 tablespoons wholemeal flour
2 tablespoons mixed fresh herbs,
  chopped
salt and freshly ground black
  pepper
freshly grated nutmeg
oil for shallow frying

For the garnish
watercress sprigs
tomato wedges

Place the lentils and water in a saucepan and bring to the boil. Reduce the heat, cover the pan and simmer gently for 30–40 minutes until all the water has been absorbed. Remove from the heat and allow to cool.

Mix the onion into the lentils, and stir in the flour, herbs, seasoning and nutmeg. Shape the mixture into eight patties, about 10 cm/4 in. in diameter, on a floured board.

Shallow fry the patties slowly in oil until golden brown, then turn them over and brown the second side. Drain, then serve, garnished with watercress sprigs and tomato wedges.

44 | Spiced Lentil Dhal

Preparation time
5 minutes

Cooking time
35 minutes

Serves 4–6

Calories
110–70 per portion

You will need
100 g/4 oz red lentils
225 g /8 oz frozen onion slices, or 2
  small fresh onions, chopped
450 ml/¾ pint boiling vegetable
  stock
3 cloves garlic, crushed
½ teaspoon ground turmeric
1 teaspoon paprika
1 teaspoon ground coriander
1 teaspoon ground cumin

Place all the ingredients in a large saucepan, bring to the boil, then reduce heat and simmer for about 30 minutes or until cooked. The dhal should be thick and the lentils should be soft and still retain their shape. Serve the dhal as an accompaniment to an Indian main dish.

Cook's Tip

These patties are delicious served with mayonnaise or soured cream, accompanied by baked potatoes and a green salad.

Cook's Tip

Cook the dhal, pack into a rigid container, label and freeze. Use within 3 months. Reheat from frozen in a moderately hot oven (200 C, 400 F, gas 6) for about 20 minutes or cook on high in the microwave for 10–15 minutes.

45 | Crispy Pea Croquettes

Preparation time
20 minutes

Cooking time
8–10 minutes

Serves 4

Calories
320 per portion

You will need
450 g/1 lb cooked peas
100 g/4 oz cream cheese with
   herbs and garlic
100 g/4 oz fresh wholewheat
   breadcrumbs
2 eggs
1 teaspoon ground coriander
1 teaspoon chopped mixed herbs
salt and pepper
75 g/3 oz dry breadcrumbs
oil for deep-frying
dill sprig to garnish (optional)

For the garnish
1 tomato, quartered
chopped parsley
watercress sprigs

Mash the cooked peas to a purée with the cream cheese. Mix in the breadcrumbs, 1 egg, coriander, herbs and salt and pepper to taste to make a fairly stiff paste.

Shape into croquettes, about 2.5 cm/1 in in diameter and 7.5 cm/3 in long. Beat the remaining egg and dip the croquettes first into beaten egg, then into the breadcrumbs.

Heat the oil for deep-frying to 190 C, 375 F, and fry the croquettes quickly, in 2–3 batches, until crisp and golden. Serve hot or cold, garnished as shown.

Cook's Tip

For a light lunch party, serve these crisp croquettes with Creamed Lentils (Recipe 64) and ratatouille.

46 | Provencal Beans

Preparation time
15 minutes, plus
overnight to soak

Cooking time
2 hours 15 minutes

Serves 4

Calories
355 per portion

You will need
350 g/12 oz haricot beans or pinto
   beans, soaked overnight
salt and pepper
2 tablespoons olive oil
2 onions, sliced
1 red pepper, deseeded and sliced
1 green pepper, deseeded and
   sliced
2 cloves garlic, crushed
1 (397-g/14-oz) can chopped
   tomatoes
2 tablespoons tomato purée
1 teaspoon chopped marjoram
1 bouquet garni
50 g/2 oz black olives, halved and
   stoned
2 tablespoons chopped parsley

Drain the beans, place in a medium saucepan and cover with cold water. Bring to the boil, boil rapidly for 10 minutes, then cover and simmer for 1–1¼ hours, until almost tender, adding a pinch of salt towards the end of cooking. Drain, reserving 300 ml/½ pint of the liquid.

Heat the oil in a medium saucepan, add the onions and fry until softened. Add the peppers and garlic and fry gently for 10 minutes. Add the tomatoes with their juice, tomato purée, herbs, beans, reserved liquid, and salt and pepper to taste. Cover and simmer for 45 minutes, adding the olives and parsley 5 minutes before the end of the cooking time. Remove the bouquet garni and serve.

Cook's Tip

It is a good idea to make a fresh bouquet garni – tie a bay leaf, parsley sprig, thyme sprig, rosemary sprig and a few chives together. Vary the herbs according to taste and season. Make a few and freeze them for future use if you like.

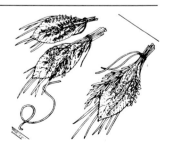

47 | Bean and Rice Casserole

Preparation time
15 minutes, plus
overnight to soak

Cooking time
2 hours

Oven temperature
180C, 350F, gas 4

Serves 4

Calories
370 per portion

You will need
175 g/6 oz haricot beans, soaked
    overnight
900 ml/1½ pints vegetable stock
salt and freshly ground black
    pepper
1 tablespoon vegetable oil
1 large onion, sliced
225 g/8 oz courgettes, sliced
1 red pepper, deseeded and sliced
1 green pepper, deseeded and
    sliced
1 aubergine, halved and sliced
150 ml/¼ pint dry cider
175 g/6 oz long-grain brown rice
salt and freshly ground black
    pepper

Drain the beans and place in a flameproof casserole with the stock and seasoning. Bring to the boil, cover and simmer for 1 hour, until the beans are tender but retain their shape.

Heat the oil and fry the onion, courgettes and peppers for 2 minutes. Add the aubergine slices a few at a time and cook for a further 5 minutes. Transfer the vegetables to the bean casserole together with the cider and rice. Cover and cook in a moderate oven for 45 minutes, or until the rice is tender and the liquid absorbed. Season to taste before serving.

48 | Sweet and Sour Butter Beans

Preparation time
10 minutes

Serves 4

Calories
140 per portion

You will need
100 g/4 oz pineapple pieces,
    canned or fresh
1 (415-g/14½-oz) can butter beans
1 medium carrot, cut into
    matchsticks
175 g/6 oz fresh beansprouts
1 tablespoon oil
1 clove garlic, crushed
1½ teaspoons cider or white wine
    vinegar
fresh marjoram to garnish

Drain the pineapple pieces, if canned. Drain the butter beans. Combine the pineapple, beans, carrot and bean sprouts in a bowl. Mix the oil, garlic and vinegar, pour over the fruit and vegetables, chill and serve. Garnish with sprigs of marjoram.

Cook's Tip

To freeze: cool quickly and transfer to foil containers. Cover, seal and freeze. To serve, defrost then reheat, covered, in a moderate oven (180C, 350F, gas 4) for 30 minutes or until heated through.

Cook's Tip

It is easy to sprout beans by placing them in a jam jar covered with a piece of muslin. If you keep the muslin in place with an elastic band, it is easy to rinse the beans every day until the sprouts are long enough.

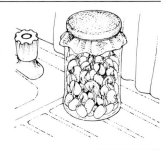

49 | Butter Beans in Sesame

Preparation time
20 minutes

Cooking time
25 30 minutes

Serves 4

Calories
575 per portion

You will need
100 ml/4 fl oz oil
1 teaspoon cumin seeds
1 large onion, chopped
100 g/4 oz sesame seeds, finely
    ground
1 tablespoon ground coriander
1 (397-g/14-oz) can chopped
    tomatoes
salt
2 teaspoons sugar
1 teaspoon chilli powder
1 teaspoon ground turmeric
2 (425-g/15-oz) cans butter beans,
    drained
1 tablespoon chopped coriander to
    garnish

Heat the oil in a pan, add the cumin seeds and fry until they begin to crackle. Add the onion and fry until soft and transparent.

Add the ground sesame seeds and fry for 3–5 minutes, then add the ground coriander and fry for a further minute. Stir in the tomatoes, salt to taste, the sugar, chilli powder and turmeric. Mix well and cook the sauce for 3–5 minutes.

Add the drained beans and stir carefully until well coated with the sauce. Simmer until the beans are thoroughly hot. Sprinkle with chopped coriander.

50 | Bean Curry

Preparation time
10 minutes, plus
overnight to soak

Cooking time
1 hour 10 minutes

Serves 4

Calories
345 per portion

You will need
350 g/12 oz red kidney beans,
    soaked overnight
2 tablespoons oil
1 clove garlic, crushed
2.5-cm/1-in piece fresh root
    ginger, grated or finely chopped
1 medium onion, chopped
2 carrots, diced
2 celery sticks, sliced
100 g/4 oz mushrooms, sliced
¼ teaspoon chilli powder
2 (397-g/14-oz) cans tomatoes
450 ml/¾ pint water
salt
2 tablespoons chopped coriander
    leaves (optional)

Drain the beans and bring them to the boil with enough water to cover them by at least 2.5 cm/ 1 in. Boil vigorously for 10 minutes, reduce heat, cover and simmer for about 1 hour or until tender. Check that the water level is maintained throughout cooking.

Meanwhile, heat the oil and cook the garlic, ginger and onion for 3 minutes. Add the carrots, celery and mushrooms and cook for 3 minutes. Stir in the chilli powder, drained cooked beans, tomatoes and their juice, water and a little salt. Cook for 15 minutes until carrots are tender and the mixture fairly thick. Check seasoning and sprinkle with coriander leaves. Serve with natural yogurt.

Cook's Tip

For textural contrast and a good protein mix, combine this curry with a nutty, crunchy salad, such as Fruit Coleslaw (Recipe 116) or Crunchy Cabbage Salad (Recipe 117).

Cook's Tip

Fresh root ginger keeps well in the salad drawer of the refrigerator. Look out for smooth, plump ginger with a fine skin that shows it is young and tender. It can also be stored in a pot of sand in a cool place.

51 | Chilli Bean Tacos

Preparation time
15 minutes

Cooking time
35 minutes

Oven temperature
200C, 400F, gas 6

Serves 2–3

Calories
505–335 per portion

You will need
100 g/4 oz frozen Mexican mix, or
an equivalent weight of fresh
vegetables including diced red
and green peppers, sweetcorn
and chopped onion
1 (415-g/14½-oz) can red kidney
beans, juice reserved
½ teaspoon Tabasco sauce
2 cloves garlic, crushed
2 tablespoons tomato purée
6 Mexican taco shells
1 small lettuce, shredded
1 small onion, chopped
50 g/2 oz Cheddar cheese, grated

Place the Mexican mix or fresh vegetables in a medium saucepan with a small amount of boiling water. Bring back to the boil, reduce heat and cook for 10 minutes. Stir the kidney beans, Tabasco, crushed garlic, and tomato purée into the vegetables, then add enough of the reserved juice to make a thick sauce. Cook for another 10 minutes. Place the tacos on a baking tray and heat in a moderately hot oven for 10 minutes until hot.

Let guests fill their own tacos. First spoon a few tablespoons of the bean and vegetable mixture into the taco shells then top with the lettuce, onion and cheese.

52 | Green Pea and Potato Curry

Preparation time
30 minutes

Cooking time
20–30 minutes

Serves 4

Calories
190 per portion

You will need
50 g/2 oz butter or margarine
225 g/8 oz fresh or frozen peas
225 g/8 oz potatoes, peeled and
diced
225 g/8 oz onions, diced
1 tablespoon garam masala
1 teaspoon ground turmeric
1 teaspoon chilli powder

Heat the butter or margarine in a pan, add all the ingredients and stir-fry for a few minutes to mix well. Cover and cook over a low heat for about 25–30 minutes or until the vegetables are tender. Stir occasionally during the cooking time to prevent sticking.

Cook's Tip

The tacos need to be eaten with the fingers so have plenty of paper napkins available.

Cook's Tip

When cooking with spices, it is a good idea to use a plastic cooking spoon instead of a wooden spoon which discolours and picks up flavours easily. Alternatively, if you prepare spicy food frequently, then set aside a special wooden spoon for the purpose.

53 | Bean and Pasta Curry

Preparation time
20 minutes

Cooking time
30 minutes

Serves 4

Calories
405 per portion

You will need
1 tablespoon vegetable oil
3 medium onions, chopped
2 cloves garlic, crushed
3 tablespoons curry powder
$\frac{1}{2}$ teaspoon ground cumin
$\frac{1}{2}$ teaspoon ground coriander
$\frac{1}{2}$ teaspoon chilli powder
2 teaspoons grated fresh root
    ginger (optional)
2 tablespoons wholemeal flour
900 ml/1$\frac{1}{2}$ pints vegetable stock
1 tablespoon lemon juice
salt (optional)
150 g/5 oz pasta shapes, such as
    quills or twists
2 (415-g/14$\frac{1}{2}$-oz) cans red kidney
    beans

To make the sauce, heat the oil in a pan with a lid and cook the onions and garlic gently for 5 minutes. Stir in the curry powder, cumin, coriander, chilli, ginger and flour. Cook for 1 minute. Pour in the stock and lemon juice, bring to the boil, cover and simmer gently for 25 minutes. Season. Cook the pasta in plenty of boiling salted water for about 10 minutes until 'al dente'. Drain and rinse. Drain the kidney beans, reserving the liquid for thinning the sauce.

Add the pasta and beans to the sauce, stirring them in gently. Thin down with the reserved bean liquor if necessary. Reheat and serve piping hot.

Cook's Tip

The curry sauce can be prepared 24 hours in advance. Cover and keep in the refrigerator.

54 | Bean Cobbler

Preparation time
20 minutes

Cooking time
50 minutes

Oven temperature
200 C, 400 F, gas 6

Serves 6

Calories
390 per portion

You will need
1 (415-g/14$\frac{1}{2}$-oz) can red kidney
    beans
1 (415-g/14$\frac{1}{2}$-oz) can butter beans
1 (415-g/14$\frac{1}{2}$-oz) can flageolet
    beans
100 g/4 oz leeks, finely sliced
225 g/8 oz courgettes, finely sliced
300 ml/$\frac{1}{2}$ pint tomato juice
150 ml/$\frac{1}{4}$ pint vegetable stock
1 teaspoon chilli powder
chopped parsley to garnish

For the scone topping
225 g/8 oz self-raising flour
$\frac{1}{4}$ teaspoon salt
2 teaspoons dried mixed herbs
2 teaspoons baking powder
50 g/2 oz margarine
6 tablespoons natural yogurt

Drain the kidney, butter and flageolet beans. Mix together with the leeks, courgettes, tomato juice, stock and chilli powder. Place in an ovenproof dish and cook in the oven for 20 minutes.

To make the scone topping, sift the flour, salt, herbs and baking powder into a bowl. Rub in the margarine until the mixture resembles fine breadcrumbs. Stir in the yogurt and mix gently. Turn on to a floured surface and knead very lightly. Roll out to about 1 cm/$\frac{1}{2}$ in thick and cut out 12 rounds using a 5-cm/2-in cutter. Place on top of the vegetables, return to the oven and cook for 30 minutes until golden and firm on top. The underside remains soft like a dumpling. Garnish with parsley.

Cook's Tip

When preparing sliced leeks for a dish, trim and slice the leeks first, then place in a colander and wash thoroughly under cold running water. Run your fingers through the slices as you wash them.

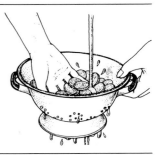

55 | West African Bean Salad

Preparation time
20 minutes, plus
overnight to soak

Cooking time
45–60 minutes

Serves 4

Calories
345 per portion

You will need
225 g/8 oz black-eyed beans,
    soaked overnight
4–5 tablespoons peanut oil
1 tablespoon lemon juice or wine
    vinegar
1 clove garlic, crushed
salt and pepper
1 medium red or white onion,
    chopped
225 g/8 oz large tomatoes, peeled
    and chopped
1 red chilli, deseeded and chopped
    (optional)

Drain the beans and cover with fresh water. Bring to the boil, lower the heat and simmer for 45–60 minutes or until tender. Drain and rinse thoroughly. Transfer to a serving dish.

Blend the oil, lemon juice and garlic and add salt and pepper to taste. Pour over the warm beans and leave to cool.

When cool, mix in the onion, tomatoes and chilli, if using. Serve at once.

Cook's Tip

The seeds of chillies are the hottest part, so always deseed chillies unless a really hot flavour is required. Never touch lips or eyes while deseeding them as a strong reaction occurs on the delicate skin.

56 | Egyptian Salad

Preparation time
15 minutes, plus 36
hours to soak

Cooking time
2 hours

Serves 4

Calories
255 per portion

You will need
175 g/6 oz ful medames, soaked
    for 36 hours or 1 (400-g/14-oz)
    can ful medames, drained and
    well rinsed
salt
coriander leaves
2–3 eggs with white or light-
    coloured shells
brown onion skins
3–4 tablespoons olive oil
1 tablespoon lemon juice
1 clove garlic, crushed
½–1 teaspoon ground cumin
2 tablespoons chopped parsley
coriander sprigs to garnish

Drain the ful medames and cover with plenty of fresh water. Bring to the boil, skim, lower the heat and simmer for 1½ hours or until tender. Add salt to taste towards the end of the cooking time.

Place a coriander leaf on each egg. Wrap an onion skin around each egg and then wrap in absorbent kitchen paper to make a parcel. Tie each with cotton and cover with cold water. Bring to the boil, cook for 10 minutes and leave to cool. When cold, unwrap the eggs and set aside in the shells. Drain and rinse the beans with fresh water, then pop each bean out of its skin, if liked. Mix the olive oil, lemon juice and garlic; pour over the beans. Taste and adjust the seasoning. Transfer the beans to a serving dish and sprinkle with cumin and parsley. Garnish with coriander sprigs and serve, accompanied by the patterned hard-boiled eggs.

Cook's Tip

Ful medames are small, light brown/beige coloured dried beans that resemble small broad beans. Available from health food shops, they must be soaked before cooking and are a common ingredient in Middle Eastern cooking.

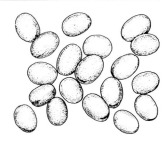

57 | Kidney Bean Coleslaw

Preparation time
30 minutes

Serves 4—6

Calories
210 140 per portion

You will need
225 g/8 oz white cabbage, shredded
175 g/6 oz carrots, grated
½ small onion, chopped
1 dessert apple, cored and grated
1 (415-g/14½-oz) can red kidney beans, drained
4 spring onions, chopped
2 tablespoons chopped parsley
salt and pepper
50 g/2 oz low-fat soft cheese (for example Shape cheese)
1 tablespoon lemon juice
2 tablespoons sunflower oil
2 tablespoons natural yogurt
watercress sprigs to garnish (optional)

Mix the cabbage, carrots, onion and apple. Add the beans, spring onions and parsley then season to taste.
   Mix the low-fat cheese with the lemon juice, oil and yogurt. Toss this dressing with the salad before serving.
   A watercress garnish may be added, if liked.

58 | Colourful Bean Salad

Preparation time
15 20 minutes

Cooking time
15 minutes

Serves 4—6

Calories
275 185 per portion

You will need
450 g/1 lb green beans, topped and tailed
salt and pepper
pinch of grated nutmeg
3 4 tomatoes, quartered
575 g/1¼ lb new potatoes, scrubbed and cooked
1 onion, chopped
1 small bunch herbs, (e.g. chives, parsley, thyme) chopped
2 tablespoons mayonnaise
6 tablespoons double or soured cream

Bring a large saucepan of water to the boil, add the beans with a little salt and the nutmeg. Bring back to the boil, then reduce heat and cook gently for 10–12 minutes until tender. Drain, rinse under cold water, drain again and place in a serving bowl. Add the tomatoes and potatoes and toss well. Scatter the onion and herbs on top.
   To make the dressing, blend the mayonnaise with the cream and salt and pepper to taste. Pour over the bean salad and toss well to mix.

Cook's Tip

Sunflower oil is a polyunsaturated fat – a good choice for the health-conscious eater. Avoid blended oils, which may contain coconut or palm oil, both high in saturated fatty acids.

Cook's Tip

Counting calories? Use low-fat yogurt in place of the double cream – you may need slightly less than the 6 tablespoons suggested above.

59 | Kidney Bean and Stilton Salad

Preparation time
10 minutes

Serves 4

Calories
192 per portion

You will need
1 (415-g/14½-oz) can red kidney beans
225 g/8 oz French beans, finely sliced or 225 g/8 oz mange tout
juice of ½ lemon
100 g/4 oz cottage cheese
75 g/3 oz blue Stilton, broken into small pieces
chopped parsley to garnish (optional)

Drain the kidney beans. Mix together with the French beans or mange tout and the lemon juice. Spoon the cottage cheese on top and sprinkle over the crumbled Stilton. Garnish with parsley, if liked. Serve with hot garlic bread.

60 | Rice and Bean Salad

Preparation time
10 minutes

Serves 4

Calories
285 per portion

You will need
1 bunch of watercress
350 g/12 oz cooked rice
1 (415-g/14½-oz) can black eyed beans, drained
6 radishes, sliced
12 olives, stoned
1 tablespoon mayonnaise
½ teaspoon salt

Reserve a sprig of watercress for the garnish. Trim and separate the rest into small sprigs.
   Mix together the rice, beans, radishes, olives, watercress, mayonnaise and salt. Serve immediately, garnished with the watercress sprig.

Cook's Tip

To make garlic bread, beat a crushed garlic clove into butter and spread on slices of French bread, leaving them attached at the base. Wrap in foil and heat through in the oven.

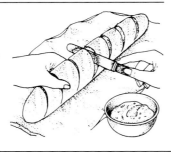

Cook's Tip

To yield 350/12 oz cooked rice, prepare 100 g/4 oz raw rice. Instead of white or brown rice you may like to try wild rice – dark, long thin grains which require a little extra cooking.

61 | Felafel in Pitta Pockets

Preparation time
20 minutes

Cooking time
20 minutes

Oven temperature
110C, 225F, gas ¼

Serves 4

Calories
520 per portion

You will need
2 (400-g/14-oz) cans chick peas
1 medium onion, grated
1 clove garlic, crushed
1 teaspoon ground cumin
1 teaspoon ground coriander
¼ teaspoon ground chilli
½ teaspoon caraway seeds
salt and pepper
3 tablespoons chopped parsley
1 egg, beaten
75 g/3 oz wholemeal flour
vegetable oil for shallow frying

To serve
4 wholewheat pitta breads
prepared salad ingredients

Drain the chick peas and reduce to a coarse paste in a liquidiser. Mix with the next eight ingredients.

Form the mixture into small balls then pat them into small flat cakes about 4 cm/1½ in across. Dip into the beaten egg, then into the flour. Shallow fry in oil in batches for about 5 minutes until crisp and brown. Drain on absorbent kitchen paper. Warm pitta breads for 5 minutes, split along one side and fill the pockets with salad and the hot felafel. Serve immediately.

62 | Bean Pâté

Preparation time
10 minutes

Cooking time
5 minutes

Serves 4

Calories
145 per portion

You will need
1 medium onion, chopped
2 cloves garlic, crushed
1 tablespoon oil
1 tablespoon peanut butter,
    smooth or crunchy, or tahini
juice of 1 lemon
2 tablespoons chopped parsley
1 (415-g/14½-oz) can butter beans
dill sprigs to garnish (optional)

Cook the onion and garlic in the oil until softened, about 5 minutes. Mix together the onion mixture, peanut butter or tahini, lemon juice and parsley. Drain the butter beans and add to the onion mixture. Mash with a fork or blend briefly in a liquidiser. Press into an oiled dish, cover and chill. Garnish with dill sprigs, if using.

Cook's Tip

For convenience, the uncooked felafel can be prepared up to 8 hours in advance and kept tightly covered with cling film to prevent the flavours permeating the other foods in the refrigerator.

Cook's Tip

This pâté looks good served in individual ramekin dishes. Place each on a saucer and garnish with wedges of lemon and parsley sprigs.

63 | Spanish Chick Peas

Preparation time
20 minutes, plus
overnight to soak

Cooking time
1½–2 hours

Serves 4

Calories
320 per portion

You will need
175 g/6 oz chick peas
900 ml/1½ pints cold water
1 tablespoon oil
1 teaspoon salt
25 g/1 oz butter
1 onion, chopped
1 clove garlic, crushed
1 green pepper, deseeded and
    chopped
1 (397-g/14-oz) can chopped
    tomatoes
1 (340-g/12-oz) can sweetcorn,
    drained
2 green chillies, deseeded and
    chopped
¼ teaspoon oregano
generous pinch of ground cumin

Soak the chick peas overnight in water to cover. Drain, discarding peas that have not absorbed any water. Place in a medium saucepan, add measured cold water, and oil and bring to the boil. Reduce the heat, cover the pan and simmer for 1–1½ hours, until the chick peas are tender, adding the salt towards the end of cooking. Drain and return the peas to the saucepan.

Melt the butter in a heavy-based frying pan and sauté the onion, garlic and green pepper until the onion is soft. Stir in the tomatoes, sweetcorn, chillies, oregano and cumin.

Add the sautéed onion mixture to the chick peas. Cover and cook gently, stirring frequently, for 20 minutes. Serve hot.

Cook's Tip

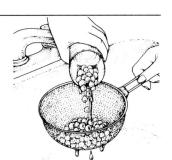

Canned chick peas can be used instead of the dried variety. They should be drained and mixed with the sautéed mixture, then cooked as above.

64 | Creamed Lentils

Preparation time
10 minutes

Cooking time
30–35 minutes

Serves 4

Calories
470 per portion

You will need
25 g/1 oz butter
1 small onion, chopped
1 clove garlic, crushed
1 leek, sliced and washed
2 medium carrots, chopped
350 g/12 oz green lentils
1 litre/1¾ pints water
2 cloves
1 bay leaf
3 white peppercorns
3 tablespoons snipped chives
300 ml/½ pint soured cream
salt and pepper

Melt the butter in a saucepan and cook the onion, garlic, leek and carrots for 3 minutes, stirring frequently. Add the lentils and cook for 1 minute, stirring. Add the water, cloves, bay leaf and peppercorns, bring to the boil, cover, and cook very gently for 25–30 minutes or until the lentils are tender but still have some bite. Check that the mixture doesn't become too dry. Remove the cloves and bay leaf. Turn into a warmed serving dish. Stir half the chives into half the soured cream and swirl through the lentils.

Swirl over the remaining soured cream and sprinkle with the remaining chives. Serve with wholewheat pasta or brown rice.

Cook's Tip

Dried flower buds of the Asian clove tree, cloves have a wonderful spicy fragrance. They are used in sweet and savoury dishes but extracted before serving to avoid the rather over powering effect of biting on them.

Vegetable Dishes

Packed with vitamins, minerals and fibre, fresh vegetables are a delight to cook with, not least because simple recipes are as successful at bringing out their natural flavours as more complicated ones, and are often more efficient in conserving nutritional content. Vegetables form a colourful accompaniment to a main course, contributing subtle or distinctive flavours. Some of the recipes in this chapter make a complete main course.

65 | Potato and Cashew Curry

Illustrated on front jacket

Preparation time
10 minutes

Cooking time
55 minutes

Serves 4

Calories
345 per portion

You will need
450 g/1 lb potatoes, scrubbed
salt
3 tablespoons oil
1 teaspoon cumin seeds
1 teaspoon mustard seeds
1 teaspoon ground coriander
½ teaspoon chilli powder
½ teaspoon ground turmeric
1 (227-g/8-oz) can tomatoes
600 ml/pint water
100 g/4 oz cashew nuts
chopped coriander to garnish

Boil the potatoes in their skins in a pan of boiling salted water for 15 minutes. Drain the potatoes, allow to cool, then peel them and cut into small cubes.

Heat the oil in a pan and add the cumin and mustard seeds. As soon as the seeds begin to pop, add the coriander, chilli, turmeric, salt to taste and the tomatoes and their juices. Cook for a few minutes, then stir in the measured water.

Bring to the boil, reduce the heat and stir in the potatoes and nuts. Simmer for 30 minutes.

Garnish with coriander and serve.

66 | Creamed Swede Duchesse

Preparation time
25 minutes

Cooking time
45 minutes

Oven temperature
200 C, 400 F, gas 6

Serves 4

Calories
245 per portion

You will need
675 g/1½ lb potatoes, peeled and cubed
350 g/12 oz swedes, peeled and cubed
salt and pepper
75 g/3 oz low-fat soft cheese (for example Shape cheese)
25 g/1 oz butter
50 g/2 oz low-fat hard cheese, grated (for example Shape cheese)
watercress sprigs to garnish

Cook the potatoes and swede in boiling salted water until tender – about 20 minutes. Mash with seasoning, the soft cheese and butter. When cool enough to handle, pipe large vegetable rosettes on to a greased baking tray. Bake for 20 minutes, until lightly browned. Sprinkle with the grated cheese and cook for a further 5–10 minutes until well browned. Serve at once, garnished with watercress.

Cook's Tip

Cover the pan when cooking the cumin and mustard seeds or they may pop right out of the pan.

Cook's Tip

For piping savoury foods such as potato you will need a large star nozzle, sometimes referred to as a potato pipe. Make sure you have a large piping bag to hold plenty of the creamed vegetables.

67 | *Mediterranean Potatoes*

Preparation time
5 minutes

Cooking time
35 minutes

Serves 4

Calories
335 per portion

You will need
675 g/1½ lb potatoes
1 tablespoon oil
50 g/2 oz butter
1 clove garlic, crushed
1 medium onion, sliced
100 g/4 oz mushrooms, sliced
1 small green pepper, deseeded
  and sliced
1 (397-g/14-oz) can tomatoes
2 teaspoons brown sugar
1 teaspoon mixed herbs
salt and pepper
50 g/2 oz fresh breadcrumbs
grated Parmesan cheese (optional)

Cut the potatoes into even-sized pieces and cook, in enough boiling water to just cover, for 10–15 minutes or until just cooked.

Meanwhile, heat the oil and half the butter in a frying pan. Add the garlic, onion, mushrooms and pepper and cook for 5 minutes or until softened. Add the tomatoes and can juices, sugar, herbs and seasoning. Break up the tomatoes and cook for 10 minutes or until the onion is tender and the sauce not too runny. Melt the remaining butter in a small pan, add the breadcrumbs and fry until brown and crisp.

Place the drained potatoes in a warm dish, pour over the sauce and sprinkle with the breadcrumbs. Serve hot with Parmesan cheese handed separately, if liked.

68 | *Almond Potatoes*

Preparation time
10 minutes

Cooking time
12 18 minutes

Serves 4

Calories
320 per portion

You will need
350 g/12 oz potatoes, cooked and
  mashed with milk and butter
plain flour seasoned with salt and
  pepper
1 egg, beaten
100 g/4 oz almonds, finely
  chopped
25 g/1 oz butter
1 tablespoon oil
parsley sprigs to garnish

Divide the mashed potato into 12 pieces. Place the seasoned flour on a plate and shape each potato piece into a medallion shape coating it with flour as you do so. Coat each medallion in the beaten egg and then the almonds.

Heat the butter and oil in a large frying pan and cook the medallions, a few at a time, for about 6 minutes, turning once, until golden. Drain on absorbent kitchen paper. Serve hot, garnished with parsley.

Cook's Tip

If you are fond of Parmesan, for example with pasta, then a cheese mill is useful. This is a cylindrical enclosed grater. The cheese is stored in it and the lid is turned to grate it straight on to the food. From cookshops only.

Cook's Tip

These crunchy cakes can be frozen. Open freeze on trays lined with cling film, then pack in bags for storage. Cook from frozen, allowing time to heat through. Also good dotted with butter and baked.

69 | *Stir-fried Potatoes*

Preparation time
15 minutes

Cooking time
20 minutes

Serves 4

Calories
225 per portion

You will need
450 g / 1 lb potatoes, grated and
  rinsed to extract starch
3 tablespoons oil
350 g / 12 oz vegetables, finely
  chopped
1 tablespoon soy sauce
1 teaspoon ground ginger
salt and pepper

Use a cloth to squeeze the excess moisture from the grated potato. Heat the oil in a large non-stick pan or wok. Fry the grated potato for 5–10 minutes or until nearly cooked, stirring frequently. Add the chosen vegetables, soy sauce, ginger and salt and pepper and fry briskly for a further 5–10 minutes to cook vegetables yet keep them crisp. Serve hot.

70 | *Potatoes Madras*

Preparation time
15 minutes

Cooking time
30 minutes

Serves 4–6

Calories
380 255 per portion

You will need
3 tablespoons oil or ghee
675 g / 1½ lb potatoes, cut into large
  dice
225 g / 8 oz cauliflower, cut into
  florets
1 large onion, sliced
2 cloves garlic, crushed (optional)
1 tablespoon curry powder
½ teaspoon ground ginger
100 g / 4 oz red lentils
1 (397-g / 14-oz) can chopped
  tomatoes
300 ml / ½ pint vegetable stock
2 tablespoons malt vinegar
1 tablespoon mango chutney
salt and pepper
chopped parsley or coriander
  leaves to garnish

Heat the oil in a large frying pan and quickly fry the potatoes, cauliflower, onion and garlic until just beginning to brown.

Stir in the curry powder and ginger. Continue to fry for a few minutes. Stir in the remaining ingredients except the parsley. Cover and simmer for about 20 minutes, stirring occasionally until the vegetables and lentils are tender. Garnish and serve.

Cook's Tip

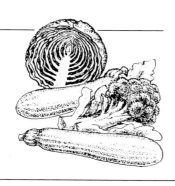

Use a combination of the following: onion, cauliflower, peppers, runner beans, sweetcorn, broccoli, celery, courgettes, mushrooms, cabbage, leeks, parsnip. Add chopped cashew nuts too if you like.

Cook's Tip

This makes a colourful main dish for a dinner party. Serve with a selection of accompaniments such as poppadoms, slices of banana, chutney, yogurt and cucumber, desiccated coconut.

71 | Potato Cake with Cheese Topping

Preparation time
15 minutes, plus 20 minutes for potatoes to cool

You will need
675 g / 1½ lb potatoes, scrubbed
75 g / 3 oz butter
1 medium onion, chopped
salt and pepper
100 g / 4 oz Danish Danbo or Havarti cheese, grated
sliced tomato to garnish

Cooking time
35 minutes

Serves 4

Calories
375 per portion

Boil the potatoes for 10 minutes. Drain and cool slightly, then peel and cool completely. Coarsely grate them into a large bowl. Melt 25 g / 1 oz of the butter in a large frying pan and gently fry the onion for 5 minutes until softened. Remove the onion with a slotted spoon and gently stir into the potato.

Melt the remaining butter in the pan, add the potato mixture, sprinkle with salt and pepper and form into a 'cake'. Cook gently for 5–7 minutes until golden on the underside. Invert a plate over the pan and turn the 'cake' on to it, slide the 'cake' back into the pan and fry for a further 7–10 minutes until golden.

Towards the end of the cooking time, heat a grill to moderate. Sprinkle the 'cake' with the cheese and grill until bubbling. Garnish with tomato slices and serve with a mixed salad.

72 | Egg Tatties

Preparation time
15 minutes

You will need
2 large potatoes
3 eggs
1 tablespoon milk
salt and freshly ground black pepper
15 g / ½ oz butter
2 tablespoons finely chopped chives
2 tablespoons thick Greek yogurt
watercress to garnish

Cooking time
1 hour 25 minutes

Oven temperature
200 C, 400 F, gas 6

Serves 2

Calories
395 per portion

Clean the skins of the potatoes and prick at regular intervals with a fork. Bake in a moderately hot oven for about 1¼ hours, until tender. Just before the potatoes are ready, beat the eggs with the milk and seasoning to taste. Melt the butter and stir in the egg mixture; scramble lightly over a gentle heat, until the egg forms soft creamy flakes. Halve each potato lengthways and scoop out the cooked centre. Mix gently with the scrambled egg, half the chives and the yogurt then spoon back into the potato shells. Cover loosely with foil and return to the oven for a further 4–5 minutes. To serve, sprinkle with the remaining chives and garnish with watercress.

Cook's Tip

If you like, then add extra topping before the cheese – sliced tomatoes, chopped walnuts and mushrooms, cooked leeks, sweetcorn and peppers or any mixed, braised vegetables can be added.

Cook's Tip

For a simple variation, why not add some diced mozzarella cheese and chopped spring onions to the egg mixture. The filled potatoes can be topped with chopped cashew nuts or walnuts and a little extra diced mozzarella.

73 | *Mushrooms Montebello*

Preparation time
10 minutes, plus
overnight to marinate

Serves 4

Calories
130 per portion

You will need
225 g/8 oz button mushrooms
4 tablespoons sunflower oil
1 clove garlic, crushed
pinch of dill
½ teaspoon oregano
2 tablespoons red wine vinegar
1 teaspoon lemon juice
salt and freshly ground pepper

Combine all the ingredients in a bowl. Cover with cling film and leave to marinate in the refrigerator overnight. Serve to accompany rice or pasta dishes, as part of a salad buffet or as a starter.

74 | *Stilton-stuffed Mushrooms*

Preparation time
10 minutes

Cooking time
6–8 minutes

Serves 4

Calories
310 per portion

You will need
50 g/2 oz butter
8 medium flat mushrooms, stalks
  removed, wiped
4 small tomatoes, thinly sliced
175 g/6 oz blue Stilton cheese,
  sliced
celery leaves to garnish (optional)

Melt the butter in a sauté pan and cook the mushrooms open side uppermost for 3–4 minutes, until tender: Place in a flameproof dish, top each one with slices of tomato and cheese, then brown under a hot grill until the cheese is melted and bubbling. Serve at once, garnished with celery leaves if liked.

Cook's Tip

These flavoursome marinated mushrooms make an excellent filling for a plain omelette. Add the well-drained mushrooms to the omelette when the egg is half set, cook until firm, then fold over and serve at once.

Cook's Tip

Serve the mushrooms with ratatouille and baked potatoes for a tasty meal. For a starter or supper dish serve them on neat rounds of wholemeal toast.

75 | Creamed Chicory and Mushrooms

Preparation time
15 minutes

Cooking time
10 minutes

Serves 4

Calories
200 per portion

You will need
50 g/2 oz onion, chopped
40 g/1½ oz butter
275 g/10 oz chicory, sliced in half
100 g/4 oz button mushrooms,
   sliced
120 ml/4 fl oz vegetable stock
120 ml/4 fl oz double cream
salt and freshly ground black
   pepper
chopped parsley to garnish

Soften the onion in the butter over a gentle heat, without browning. Add the chicory and mushrooms and cook for a few minutes. Pour in the stock and simmer, covered, for 5 minutes. Remove from the heat, add the cream, season well and reheat for a few minutes without boiling. Transfer to a warmed dish and sprinkle with chopped parsley.

76 | Mushroom Fondue

Preparation time
15 minutes

Cooking time
10–15 minutes

Serves 4

Calories
665 per portion

You will need
½ clove garlic
150 ml/¼ pint medium dry cider
1 teaspoon lemon juice
400 g/14 oz Gouda cheese, grated
1 tablespoon cornflour
1½ tablespoons gin
100 g/4 oz button mushrooms,
   chopped
freshly ground black pepper
pinch of grated nutmeg

To serve
1 stick French bread, cut into
   cubes
100 g/4 oz button mushrooms

Rub the inside of a fondue pot or flameproof casserole with the cut garlic, and place a little finely chopped garlic in the pot. Pour in the cider and lemon juice and heat slowly until nearly boiling. Gradually add the grated cheese, a little at a time, stirring continuously with a fork until all the cheese has melted. When the mixture is bubbling, blend the cornflour with the gin until smooth and add to the fondue, stirring well. Add the chopped mushrooms, pepper and nutmeg.

Serve the cheese fondue in the cooking pot at the table. There should be a fondue fork for each person, and the cubes of French bread and whole button mushrooms are speared with the fork and dipped into the fondue. This is delicious accompanied by an orange and cucumber salad.

Cook's Tip

Frozen double cream is a useful item to keep in the freezer. Packed in neat sticks, just remove the number required for the dish and defrost at room temperature.

Cook's Tip

If gin is not to your taste, substitute an equal amount of any of the following: Kirsch, whisky, brandy or dry sherry.

77 | Celery with Mushrooms

Preparation time
15 minutes

Cooking time
30 minutes

Serves 4

Calories
175 per portion

You will need
1 head celery, trimmed
salt and pepper
50 g/2 oz butter
1 medium onion, finely chopped
100 g/4 oz mushrooms, thinly
  sliced
coarsely grated rind of 1 lemon
75–100 g/3–4 oz mozzarella
  cheese, cut into thin slivers

Cut the celery diagonally into 4-cm/1½-in lengths. Blanch in a pan of boiling salted water for 5 minutes.

Melt the butter in a pan and fry the onion until soft. Add the celery and cook gently for 5–10 minutes until tender but still crisp. Add the mushrooms and fry for 5 minutes. Stir in the lemon rind and season to taste.

Transfer the mixture to a flameproof dish. Arrange the cheese slices over the vegetables and grill until golden.

Cook's Tip

Mozzarella has a delicate flavour, and is ideal for cooking as it does not become stringy when heated. Store in a bowl of water in the refrigerator, but use as soon as possible after purchase.

78 | Continental-style Pancakes

Preparation time
15 minutes

Cooking time
15 minutes

Serves 4

Calories
245 per portion

You will need
1 (283-g/10-oz) packet frozen
  Continental stir-fry vegetables
50 g/2 oz Cheddar cheese, grated
1 tablespoon finely chopped
  parsley

For the pancake batter
50 g/2 oz plain flour
pinch of salt
1 egg
150 ml/¼ pint milk
2 teaspoons melted butter
pinch of dried mixed herbs
oil for frying

First make the pancakes. Sift together the flour and salt. Beat to a smooth batter with the egg, half the milk and the melted butter. Stir in the remaining milk with a pinch of mixed herbs. Heat a little oil in a small frying pan and cook a quarter of the batter each time, to make four pancakes. Keep warm.

Cook the stir-fry vegetables according to the packet instructions. Divide between the pancakes and fold each one in half carefully. Place in a flameproof dish and sprinkle with the cheese. Place under a hot grill and cook until golden brown and bubbling. Sprinkle with chopped parsley and serve at once.

Cook's Tip

Do not worry if the batter contains a few lumps. Simply press it through a fine sieve into a clean bowl.

79 | Carrot and Mushroom Loaf

Preparation time
10 minutes

Cooking time
1 hour 5 minutes

Oven temperature
200C, 400F, gas 6

Serves 4

Calories
200 per portion

You will need
450 g/1 lb carrots, diced
40 g/1½ oz butter
2 teaspoons soft brown sugar
salt and pepper
300 ml/½ pint vegetable stock
100 g/4 oz button mushrooms, sliced
1 small onion, finely chopped
1 tablespoon chopped parsley
2 teaspoons chopped fresh or 1 teaspoon dried dill
3 eggs
25 g/1 oz Cheddar cheese, grated
parsley sprig to garnish

Cook the carrots in 25 g/1 oz of the butter until lightly browned, about 8 minutes. Sprinkle over the sugar and salt and pepper, then stir in the stock. Cook gently until the carrot is tender and the liquid has evaporated. Transfer carrot mixture to a bowl. Heat the remaining butter and cook the mushrooms and onion until softened, about 5 minutes. Stir in the parsley and dill. Beat the eggs and stir into the carrot mixture. Stir in the mushroom mixture and the cheese. Spoon into a 450-g/1-lb loaf tin. Place tin in a larger tin with enough warm water to come halfway up the sides. Cook for 30–40 minutes or until firm to the touch. Carefully turn out the loaf and garnish with parsley.

80 | Spiced Potatoes

Preparation time
30 minutes

Cooking time
30–35 minutes

Serves 4

Calories
355 per portion

You will need
1 large onion, chopped
2 cloves garlic, crushed
2 tablespoons oil
1 kg/2 lb potatoes, cubed
2 teaspoons ground coriander
½ teaspoon turmeric
2 teaspoons ground cumin
bay leaf
1 (397-g/14-oz) can chopped tomatoes
150 ml/¼ pint water
salt and pepper
100 g/4 oz frozen peas
2 dessert pears or apples, peeled cored and cubed
grated rind of ½ lemon
bay leaves to garnish (optional)

Cook the onion and garlic in the oil until soft but not browned. Add the potatoes and stir in the spices. Add the bay leaf, tomatoes and water with seasoning to taste. Bring to the boil, cover and simmer for 15 minutes. Add the remaining ingredients and re-cover. Simmer for a further 5–10 minutes or until the potatoes are tender. Serve with brown or basmati rice. Garnish with bay leaves if you like.

Cook's Tip

Try other vegetables in this loaf to replace the carrots: cauliflower broken into tiny florets, parsnips, celeriac and swede. It can also be made with a selection of different vegetables.

Cook's Tip

Keep the potato cubes fairly large – dice them and they are liable to disintegrate, which spoils the appearance of this tasty dish.

81 | Vegetable Terrine

Preparation time
25 minutes

Cooking time
1 hour

Oven temperature
180 C, 350 F, gas 4

Serves 4

Calories
305 per portion

You will need
450 g/1 lb carrots (peeled weight)
225 g/8 oz broccoli
350 g/12 oz cauliflower florets
salt and pepper
2 eggs
75 g/3 oz Danish Havarti cheese, grated
1 teaspoon mild mustard
100 g/4 oz fresh white breadcrumbs
75 g/3 oz Danish Buko soft cheese with garlic
¼ teaspoon ground coriander
sage leaves to garnish (optional)

Line and butter a 900-g/2-lb loaf tin. Cook the vegetables separately in boiling salted water until just tender. Drain, rinse in cold water and cool separately. Purée the cauliflower in a liquidiser until smooth. Add 1 egg, the Havarti cheese, mustard, seasoning and 50 g/2 oz of the breadcrumbs. Turn into the prepared tin and smooth the surface. Arrange the broccoli in small florets on top. Liquidise the carrots until smooth. Add the remaining egg, seasoning, the garlic-flavoured cheese, coriander and the remaining breadcrumbs. Mix thoroughly. Spoon carefully over the broccoli and smooth the surface. Cover with buttered greaseproof paper and aluminium foil. Bake for 45–50 minutes or until firm. Remove from the oven and stand for 10 minutes. Turn out carefully, garnish and serve with a tomato sauce (see below).

82 | Stuffed Aubergines

Preparation time
10 minutes

Cooking time
45 60 minutes

Oven temperature
200 C, 400 F, gas 6

Serves 4

Calories
305 per portion

You will need
2 tablespoons oil
2 onions, chopped
2 cloves garlic, crushed
225 g/8 oz cooked haricot beans (or use canned beans)
2 tomatoes, chopped
1 teaspoon basil
1 teaspoon thyme
2 teaspoons tomato purée
salt and pepper
2 aubergines
1 (397-g/14-oz) can chopped tomatoes
225 g/8 oz low-fat hard cheese, grated (for example Shape cheese)
watercress to garnish

Heat the oil in a saucepan. Add the onions and garlic and cook until soft but not browned. Stir in beans, tomatoes, herbs and tomato purée. Season well.

Cut the aubergines in half lengthways. Scoop out the flesh, chop this and add it to the beans; cook gently for 10 minutes. Meanwhile, parboil the aubergine shells for 5 minutes, drain well and fill with the bean mixture. Pour the tomatoes into a baking dish and arrange the aubergines on top. Sprinkle with cheese, cover with foil and bake for 20 minutes. Remove foil and cook for 15 minutes more. Garnish with watercress and serve with brown rice or potatoes.

Cook's Tip

To make a tomato sauce, place 2 (397-g/14-oz) cans tomatoes with their juices in a pan. Add 50 g/2 oz butter, 2–3 teaspoons sugar, a few drops of Tabasco and salt and pepper and mash the tomatoes as the mixture comes to the boil.

Cook for 8–10 minutes until blended and thickened. Press through a sieve to remove seeds. Reheat as required.

Cook's Tip

A quick way of scooping out and chopping aubergines: cut in half and cut the middle criss-cross with a sharp knife. Carefully cut out the flesh or scoop out with a spoon.

83 | Stuffed Marrow Rings

Preparation time
15 minutes

Cooking time
50 minutes

Oven temperature
180C, 350F, gas 4

Serves 4

Calories
325 per portion

You will need
1 medium-sized marrow
1 medium onion, chopped
1 celery stick, sliced
25 g/1 oz butter
100 g/4 oz mushrooms, sliced
1 tablespoon tomato purée
100 g/4 oz mixed nuts, chopped
½ teaspoon ground cinnamon
½ teaspoon rosemary
50 g/2 oz Danish Blue cheese, crumbled
75 g/3 oz fresh breadcrumbs
salt and pepper
1 egg, beaten
rosemary sprigs to garnish

Peel the marrow and cut it into four. Scoop out the seeds. Cook in boiling water for 4–5 minutes until just starting to soften. Drain and place the rings in a lightly buttered ovenproof dish. Gently fry the onion and celery in the butter for 5 minutes until softened. Add the mushrooms, cover and cook for a further 2 minutes. Add the purée, nuts, cinnamon, rosemary, cheese, breadcrumbs, salt and pepper and the egg and mix well.

Fill the rings with the stuffing, placing any extra in a small ovenproof dish. Cover the stuffed marrow and bake for 40 minutes or until marrow is tender. Cover the extra stuffing and bake at the same time (although it probably won't need quite as long). Garnish with sprigs of rosemary and serve with jacket potatoes.

Cook's Tip

Try using peppers: select 4 dumpy ones (about 100–150 g/ 4–5 oz); blanch in boiling water for 4 minutes. Drain and cool in water. Cut a slice from the stalk end of each pepper. Discard the core and reserve the lids. Deseed and remove white pith from peppers, taking care not to puncture the skin. Fill with the stuffing, replace the 'lids' and bake as above.

84 | Cheese Courgettes

Preparation time
10 minutes

Cooking time
40 minutes

Oven temperature
180C, 350F, gas 4

Serves 2

Calories
545 per portion

You will need
4 large courgettes
salt and pepper
100 g/4 oz butter
1 large onion, finely chopped
1 tablespoon chopped parsley
50 g/2 oz Cheddar cheese, grated

Trim the courgettes and cook whole in a saucepan of boiling salted water for 15 minutes or until just cooked. Drain. Cut the courgettes in half lengthways and carefully scoop out the flesh leaving a thin 'wall' all round. Chop the scooped-out flesh.

Heat the butter in a saucepan and fry the onion for 5 minutes until soft. Add the chopped courgette flesh and cook over high heat until pulpy. Stir in the parsley and half the cheese. Add salt and pepper to taste. Spoon mixture into courgette halves, place in an ovenproof dish, sprinkle with remaining cheese and bake for 20 minutes. Serve hot accompanied by a side salad.

Cook's Tip

A parsley chopper is useful for chopping a variety of fresh herbs. It is a small metal roller, with several round blades. Trim, wash and dry the herbs, place in a small mound on a board and roll away.

85 | Vegetable Burgers

Preparation time
25 minutes, plus 10 minutes to stand

Cooking time
20 minutes

Serves 4

Calories
355 per burger

You will need
225 g/8 oz leeks
350 g/12 oz celeriac, peeled and finely grated
225 g/8 oz carrots, finely grated
225 g/8 oz potatoes, grated
1 onion, finely chopped
2 cloves garlic, finely chopped
bunch of fresh parsley, finely chopped
2 eggs
100 g/4 oz wholewheat breadcrumbs
salt and pepper
about 6 tablespoons vegetable oil

Trim the leeks, cut a cross down through the green leaves to the white part and wash. Cut across the leeks into thin slices including about two - thirds of the green leaves. Place the leeks, celeriac, carrots and potatoes in a tea towel and squeeze well.

Place all the prepared vegetables and parsley in a bowl and mix with the eggs and breadcrumbs to make a firm, smooth and malleable mixture. Season to taste, cover and leave to stand for 10 minutes.

With moist hands, shape the mixture into flat cakes or burgers. Heat about half the oil in a frying pan. Fry the vegetable burgers, in two batches, over a high to moderate heat for about 10 minutes, turning once. Add a little more oil to the side of the pan, if necessary.

Serve hot, with a mixed salad.

Cook's Tip

Make the burgers half the usual size and use with salad as a filler for pitta pockets, instead of the traditional felafel. For instructions on preparing the pitta pockets, see Recipe 61.

86 | Vegetable Parcels

Preparation time
20 minutes

Cooking time
1 hour

Oven temperature
180 C, 350 F, gas 4

Serves 2

Calories
105 per portion

You will need
2 large cabbage leaves
1 clove garlic, crushed
1 onion, chopped
75 g/3 oz long-grain brown rice, cooked
2 walnut halves, finely chopped
50 g/2 oz yellow pepper, deseeded and finely chopped
1 stick celery, chopped
salt and pepper
300 ml/½ pint dry white wine or vegetable stock
2 tablespoons plain flour
3 tablespoons water
150 ml/¼ pint single cream

Blanch the cabbage leaves in boiling water for 1 minute, drain and pat dry. Mix together the garlic, onion, rice, walnuts, yellow pepper and celery, seasoning to taste. Divide this mixture between the cabbage leaves and roll up into parcels. Place in an ovenproof dish and pour in the white wine or stock. Season with black pepper, cover, and bake in a moderate oven for 1 hour.

Transfer the parcels to a serving dish and keep hot. Blend the flour to a smooth paste with the water, add the cooking juices from parcels and pour into a saucepan. Bring to the boil, stirring, then remove from the heat and add the cream. Heat gently without boiling, season to taste and pour over the parcels to serve.

Cook's Tip

Instead of cabbages leaves you may like to stuff vine leaves. Use packet or canned leaves, allowing about 4–6 instead of the larger cabbage leaves. They will still serve 2 as a main course or 4 as a starter.

87 | Savoury Bake

Preparation time
20 minutes

Cooking time
45–50 minutes

Oven temperature
180 C, 350 F, gas 4

Serves 4

Calories
370 per portion

You will need
1 large onion, sliced
50 g/2 oz butter
225 g/8 oz courgettes, thinly sliced
225 g/8 oz tomatoes, peeled and sliced
1 teaspoon dried mixed herbs
salt and pepper
40 g/1½ oz plain flour
450 ml/¾ pint milk
100 g/4 oz Cheddar cheese, grated
50 g/2 oz fresh breadcrumbs

For the garnish
tomato wedges
parsley sprigs

Cook the onion in 15 g/½ oz butter until just soft. Place half the courgettes in a 1.75-litre/3-pint ovenproof dish, cover with half the onion and the tomatoes. Sprinkle with the mixed herbs and seasoning, then top with the remaining onion and courgettes.

Meanwhile, make the sauce. Melt the remaining butter in a pan, stir in the flour and gradually add the milk, stirring continuously until the sauce thickens and boils. Season and add 75 g/3 oz of the cheese. Pour the sauce over the vegetables. Mix together the remaining cheese and the breadcrumbs and sprinkle over the sauce. Cook for 35–40 minutes until golden brown. Garnish with tomato wedges and parsley sprigs.

88 | Aubergine Layer

Preparation time
20 minutes

Cooking time
1 hour 12 minutes

Oven temperature
180 C, 350 F, gas 4

Serves 4

Calories
295 per portion

You will need
2 medium aubergines, trimmed and sliced
salt and pepper
4 tablespoons vegetable oil
2 onions, sliced
4 tomatoes, peeled and sliced
50 g/2 oz walnuts, chopped
300 ml/½ pint tomato juice
½ teaspoon dried basil

For the topping
15 g/½ oz margarine or butter
1 small onion, finely chopped
50 g/2 oz fresh wholewheat breadcrumbs
1 tablespoon grated Parmesan cheese
¼ teaspoon mustard powder

Place the aubergine slices in a colander set over a plate, sprinkle with salt and leave to drain for 30 minutes. Rinse and pat dry. Heat 3 tablespoons of the oil in a large frying pan, add the aubergines and fry until lightly coloured on both sides. Add the remaining oil and fry the onions until softened. Layer all the vegetables and walnuts in an ovenproof dish. Season the tomato juice, add the basil and pour over. Cover and cook in a moderate oven for 45 minutes. Melt the margarine in a saucepan, add the onion and cook for 2–3 minutes. Stir in the remaining ingredients, use to top the vegetables and cook, uncovered, for 15 minutes. Serve at once.

Cook's Tip

When selecting courgettes, look for smooth-skinned, unblemished specimens. These miniature marrows should be used as soon as possible after picking, so cook them on the day of purchase to eat them at their best.

Cook's Tip

The reason for salting aubergines before cooking is to extract bitter juices which can spoil the flavour of the finished dish. In some recipes this is not an essential process. Make sure you rinse and dry the vegetables before using them or the dish will be very salty.

89 | Aubergine Fans Georgia

Preparation time
20 minutes

Cooking time
25 30 minutes

Oven temperature
200 C, 400 F, gas 6

Serves 4

Calories
260 per portion

You will need
2 medium aubergines
175 g / 6 oz mozzarella cheese,
    thinly sliced
4 tomatoes, sliced
50 g / 2 oz salted peanuts
1 tablespoon groundnut oil
1 clove garlic, crushed
1 tablespoon chopped parsley
1 teaspoon oregano
salt and pepper

Cut the aubergines in half lengthways. Place each half cut side down on a board and make slits at 1-cm/½-in intervals from the stalk end down to the base, taking care not to cut right through. Fan out the aubergines and arrange them in a greased baking tin or individual dishes. Place cheese and tomato slices alternately in the cuts and sprinkle over the peanuts.

Mix the oil with the garlic, herbs and seasoning and brush evenly over the aubergines. Cover the tin with foil and bake in a moderately hot oven for 25–30 minutes, until the aubergines are tender. Serve hot.

90 | Macaroni and Aubergine Layer

Preparation time
10 minutes, plus 30 minutes to prepare aubergine

Cooking time
1 hour

Oven temperature
190 C, 375 F, gas 5

Serves 4

Calories
440 per portion

You will need
350 g / 12 oz aubergines, sliced
salt and pepper
175 g / 6 oz macaroni
3 tablespoons oil
1 onion, sliced
1 clove garlic, chopped
150 ml / ¼ pint natural yogurt
150 ml / ¼ pint milk
175 g / 6 oz low-fat hard cheese,
    grated (for example Shape
    cheese)
225 g / 8 oz tomatoes, sliced
parsley to garnish

Sprinkle the aubergine slices with salt and leave for 30 minutes. Cook the macaroni in boiling salted water for about 8 minutes, until tender but not soft, then drain.

Rinse and dry the aubergines. Heat the oil in a large frying pan. Quickly toss the aubergine and onion slices in the oil for 2–3 minutes. Add the garlic. Mix the yogurt, milk and two-thirds of the cheese. Layer the aubergine and onions, pasta and tomatoes in an ovenproof dish, seasoning the layers. Pour in the yogurt mixture and top with the remaining grated cheese. Bake for 45 minutes, until golden. Serve hot, garnished with parsley.

Cook's Tip

Cutting aubergines into fans is a good way of preparing them. For simplicity, sprinkle with spices, dot with butter and grill or bake. Lemon rind and Parmesan cheese make good toppings.

Cook's Tip

To make yogurt, heat milk to 50 C / 100 F, then stir in 2–3 tablespoons natural live yogurt. Pour into a vacuum flask and leave overnight, until the yogurt has formed. Remove and chill until required.

91 | Aubergines Bonne Femme

Preparation time
20 minutes

Cooking time
30 minutes

Oven temperature
200 C, 400 F, gas 6

Serves 4–6

Calories
295 200 per portion

You will need
5 tablespoons olive oil
3 medium aubergines, cut in
  quarters lengthways, then in
  2 cm/¾ in slices
1 large onion, coarsely chopped
2 cloves garlic, halved
250 g/9 oz tomatoes, roughly
  chopped
salt and pepper
1 teaspoon chopped fresh oregano
1 parsley sprig, chopped
50 g/2 oz Parmesan cheese,
  grated
1 tablespoon butter

Heat the oil in a saucepan, add the aubergines, onion and garlic and fry for 7–8 minutes. Remove and discard the garlic.

Add the tomatoes to the pan and season with salt and pepper to taste. Stir in the oregano and parsley. Cook for a few minutes then transfer the mixture to a shallow ovenproof dish. Sprinkle with the Parmesan cheese and dot with the butter. Cook in a moderately hot oven for about 20 minutes. Serve immediately.

92 | Aubergine and Onion Gratin

Preparation time
20 minutes, plus 1 hour
to prepare aubergine

Cooking time
50 minutes 1 hour

Oven temperature
200 C, 400 F, gas 6

Serves 4

Calories
350 per portion

You will need
4 medium aubergines
salt and pepper
2 3 tablespoons oil
225 g/8 oz onions, sliced
225 g/8 oz Cheddar cheese, grated
chopped parsley to garnish

Slice the aubergines and layer in a colander, sprinkling each layer with salt. Set aside for 1 hour.

Rinse the aubergine slices under cold running water, then pat dry. Heat the oil in a frying pan and fry the aubergine slices, a few at a time, for 2–3 minutes on each side. Drain on absorbent kitchen paper. Fry the onions in the pan until soft.

Arrange the aubergine and onion slices in layers in a greased ovenproof dish, seasoning each layer. Sprinkle with the cheese. Cook in a moderately hot oven for 40 minutes. Garnish with parsley and serve.

Cook's Tip

Serve this delicious dish accompanied by salad, French bread and a French red wine.

Cook's Tip

If preferred, courgettes can be used in place of the aubergines in this recipe. Courgettes do not need to be salted prior to cooking but you will need the equivalent weight of the aubergines.

93 | *Sunflower Okra with Mushrooms*

Preparation time
10 minutes

Cooking time
18 20 minutes

Serves 4

Calories
130 per portion

You will need
2 teaspoons vegetable oil
2 tablespoons sunflower seeds
350 g/12 oz okra, topped and tailed
25 g/1 oz butter
100 g/4 oz button mushrooms, halved
salt and pepper

Heat the oil in a small pan and cook the sunflower seeds for 1–2 minutes until brown. Drain on absorbent kitchen paper and set aside.

It is best to cook the okra whole but, if any are too large, cut them in half lengthways.

Melt the butter in a frying pan or wok and stir-fry the okra quickly for 3–4 minutes. Add the mushrooms and cook for a further 3–4 minutes. Sprinkle with salt and pepper, cover the pan and leave to cook for about 10 minutes until the mushrooms are soft and the okra crisply tender.

Remove the lid and cook quickly for 1–2 minutes to reduce the liquid in the pan. Spoon into a hot dish and sprinkle with the sunflower seeds.

94 | *Leeks au Gratin*

Preparation time
10 minutes

Cooking time
45 minutes

Oven temperature
180 C, 350 F, gas 4
then
200 C, 400 F, gas 6

Serves 6

Calories
280 per portion

You will need
1 kg/2 lb leeks, trimmed and cut into 2 cm/$\frac{3}{4}$ in thick rings
15 g/$\frac{1}{2}$ oz butter
1 clove garlic, halved
300 ml/$\frac{1}{2}$ pint milk
pinch of grated nutmeg
$\frac{1}{2}$ teaspoon dried tarragon
salt and pepper
150 ml/$\frac{1}{4}$ pint double cream
100 g/4 oz Emmental cheese, grated

Rinse the leeks and drain thoroughly. Place in a large ovenproof dish.

Heat the butter in a small saucepan and fry the garlic for a few minutes until golden. Remove the pieces of garlic from the pan with a slotted spoon and discard. Pour the butter over the leeks.

Heat the milk with the nutmeg, tarragon and salt and pepper to taste, until almost boiling. Stir in the cream and pour over the leeks. Cover the dish tightly with greased foil and cook in a moderate oven for 20 minutes. Remove the foil and sprinkle with the cheese. Increase the oven temperature to moderately hot and bake for a further 15–20 minutes until the cheese is golden and bubbling. Serve immediately.

Cook's Tip

Make sure the okra you buy are fresh, with no damaged ridges or brown patches.

Cook's Tip

This dish can make a filling main course when served with jacket potatoes.

95 | *Cidered Hotpot*

Preparation time
15 minutes

Cooking time
1 hour 45 minutes
2 hours 15 minutes

Oven temperature
200 C, 400 F, gas 6

Serves 4

Calories
465 per portion

You will need
225 g/8 oz swede
225 g/8 oz turnips
75 g/3 oz butter
2 medium onions, sliced
2 leeks, sliced
225 g/8 oz carrots, sliced
40 g/1½ oz plain flour
450 ml/¾ pint dry cider
1 tablespoon tomato purée
salt and pepper
1 teaspoon yeast extract
450 g/1 lb potatoes, peeled and
*   thinly sliced*
oil for brushing
75 g/3 oz Cheddar cheese, grated

Cut the swede and turnips into 2.5-cm/1-in cubes. Melt the butter in a large frying pan, add the swede, turnip, onions, leeks and carrots and cook gently for 10 minutes until softened, (see photograph). Transfer the vegetables to a lightly oiled ovenproof dish.

Mix the flour to a paste with a little of the cider in the saucepan, gradually stir in the remaining cider and bring to the boil, whisking all the time. Add the tomato purée, salt and pepper and yeast extract. Pour over the vegetables. Arrange the sliced potatoes on top. Brush the potato slices with oil and sprinkle over the cheese. Cover.

Bake for 1½–2 hours or until the vegetables are cooked. Uncover the dish for the last 30 minutes to brown the topping. Serve hot.

Cook's Tip

This delicious hotpot makes an excellent family meal. Serve chunks of crusty granary bread as an accompaniment. You can vary the vegetables to suit the season.

96 | *Parsnip Casserole*

Preparation time
10 minutes

Cooking time
1 hour 1 hour 5
minutes

Oven temperature
160 C, 325 F, gas 3

Serves 4

Calories
290 per portion

You will need
about 675 g/1½ lb parsnip
75 g/3 oz butter
1 medium onion, chopped
50 g/2 oz Cheddar cheese, grated
salt and pepper
a few drops of Tabasco sauce
300 ml/½ pint vegetable stock
2 tomatoes, thinly sliced
50 g/2 oz fresh breadcrumbs

Peel the parsnips and cut into chunks. Heat 50 g/2 oz of the butter in a large saucepan and cook the onion until softened, about 5 minutes. Remove the pan from the heat, stir in the parsnip, cheese, salt and pepper, Tabasco and stock. Spoon into a lightly greased ovenproof dish. Arrange the sliced tomatoes on top, (see picture). Bake in the oven covered for 45–50 minutes or until the parsnip is just cooked. Melt the remaining butter and stir in the breadcrumbs. Sprinkle over the tomatoes and press down.

Return to oven, uncovered, for 10 minutes. Serve hot.

Cook's Tip

Use a matured Cheddar to give the parsnip plenty of flavour. Instead of parsnip you can use courgettes, marrow or pumpkin in this dish. Serve with baked potatoes or crunchy roast potatoes if you like.

97 | Spinach, Cauliflower and Courgette Bhaji

Preparation time
5 minutes

Cooking time
35 minutes

Serves 4

Calories
50 per portion

You will need
225 g/8 oz frozen leaf spinach
225 g/8 oz frozen cauliflower
  florets
225 g/8 oz frozen sliced
  courgettes
100 g/4 oz frozen onion slices, or 1
  small fresh onion, sliced
2 cloves garlic, crushed
½ teaspoon grated or very finely
  chopped fresh root ginger or
  ¼ teaspoon garam masala
1 2 teaspoons black mustard
  seeds
1–2 tablespoons thick set natural
  yogurt

Put all the vegetables in a large saucepan with some water, garlic and ginger. Bring to the boil, then reduce heat and cook for about 20 minutes. Add the garam masala and mustard seeds and cook for a further 10 minutes, or until the vegetables are just tender.

Just before serving, stir the yogurt into the vegetables.

Cook's Tip

Try using frozen broccoli in place of the cauliflower. You could also use frozen mixed sliced peppers instead of the courgettes.

98 | Broccoli Ring

Preparation time
15 minutes

Cooking time
25 30 minutes

Oven temperature
180 C, 350 F, gas 4

Serves 6

Calories
330 per portion

You will need
450 g/1 lb frozen chopped
  broccoli, defrosted
1 onion, finely chopped
2 cloves garlic, crushed
50 g/2 oz butter
50 g/2 oz plain flour
300 ml/½ pint milk
225 g/8 oz mature Cheddar
  cheese
4 eggs, well beaten
salt and pepper

For the garnish
tomato wedges
watercress sprigs

Grease a 1.4-litre/2½-pint ring mould with oil. Drain the broccoli, squeezing out the excess moisture, and put into a large mixing bowl. Add the onion and garlic to the broccoli. Melt the butter in a saucepan, add the flour and cook together for a minute. Gradually add the milk, stirring continuously, and bring to the boil. Simmer gently for a few minutes, then remove from the heat. Grate half the quantity of cheese and add to the sauce together with the eggs. Season, beat until smooth. Add to the broccoli and mix together well. Pour into the ring mould.

Place the mould in a roasting tin filled with hot water to a depth of 2.5 cm/1 in. Bake in a moderate oven for 25–30 minutes until set. Cool in the mould for 5 minutes, before turning out the broccoli ring on to a warm serving platter. Slice the remaining cheese thinly and lay the slices over the top of the broccoli ring. Grill until golden and bubbling. Garnish as shown.

Cook's Tip

Fresh broccoli may be used instead of frozen. Trim stems, cutting into 2.5-cm/1-in pieces and florets. Steam for 3 minutes, then proceed as above.

99 | Chicory in Mustard Sauce

Preparation time	**You will need**
5 minutes	8 small heads chicory
	150 ml/¼ pint salted water
Cooking time	juice of 1 lemon
18 minutes	15 g/½ oz butter
	scant 1 tablespoon plain flour
Serves 4	150 ml/¼ pint vegetable stock
	2–3 tablespoons single cream
	scant 2 tablespoons prepared mild
Calories	mustard
85 per portion	1 teaspoon sugar
	1 tablespoon chopped dill to
	garnish

Rinse and drain the chicory and remove the thick stems. Bring the water and lemon juice to the boil. Add the chicory heads, lower the heat and cook for about 10 minutes. Drain and keep hot. Reserve cooking liquid.

Melt the butter in a small pan, stir in the flour and cook for 2–3 minutes. Gradually add the reserved cooking liquid and stock, stirring constantly.

Add the cream, mustard and sugar and bring to the boil, stirring constantly. Cook for 3 minutes, stirring. Arrange the chicory heads on a warmed serving dish, pour over the sauce. Sprinkle with the chopped dill. Serve immediately.

Cook's Tip

Look out for different mustards in delicatessens and health food shops. Try wholegrain varieties, those flavoured with herbs and continental types, such as Swedish mustard which can be slightly sweet and very mild.

100 | Spinach with Flaked Almonds

Preparation time	**You will need**
10 minutes	1 kg/2¼ lb leaf spinach
	50 g/2 oz butter
Cooking time	½ onion, finely chopped
20 minutes	salt
	grated nutmeg
Serves 4	4 tablespoons natural yogurt
	50 g/2 oz flaked almonds
Calories	
200 per portion	

Place the spinach in a sieve, rinse and drain thoroughly. Tear the leaves into manageable pieces. Melt half the butter in a large saucepan, add the onion and cook for 2–3 minutes until softened. Add the spinach, a little at a time, turning it in the butter to coat. Season with salt and nutmeg to taste. Cook over a low heat for 10–15 minutes until tender, depending upon the thickness of the spinach leaves.

Stir the natural yogurt into the spinach mixture. Remove the spinach from the heat and transfer to a warmed serving bowl. Fry the almonds in the remaining butter, stirring, until golden. Fold the almonds into the spinach and serve immediately.

Cook's Tip

Freshly grated nutmeg gives the best flavour. Keep whole nutmegs in an airtight jar, then grate them as required on a special miniature, very fine grater.

101 | Chinese-style Stir-Fry

Preparation time
15 minutes

Cooking time
5 minutes

Serves 4

Calories
155 per portion

You will need
4 tablespoons oil
175 g/6 oz Chinese leaves, shredded
175 g/6 oz Brussels sprouts, shredded
175 g/6 oz leeks, shredded
175 g/6 oz tiny cauliflower florets
salt and freshly ground black pepper
2 tablespoons soy sauce

Heat the oil in a wok or deep frying pan. Add the prepared vegetables and stir-fry for 4–5 minutes over a brisk heat. The vegetables should still be slightly crunchy. Sprinkle with salt and pepper and a generous quantity of soy sauce to taste. Serve immediately.

102 | Crispy Vegetarian Nuggets

Preparation time
25 minutes

Cooking time
15 20 minutes

Serves 4

Calories
600 per portion

You will need
1 tablespoon vegetable oil
1 onion, finely chopped
225 g/8 oz mushrooms, finely chopped
175 g/6 oz long-grain rice, cooked
1½ teaspoons chopped fresh thyme
175 g/6 oz Lancashire cheese, grated
salt and pepper
1 egg, beaten
2 tablespoons wholemeal flour

For the coating
2 tablespoons wholemeal flour
2 eggs, beaten
100 g/4 oz wholewheat breadcrumbs
2 teaspoons sesame seeds
oil for frying

Heat the tablespoon of oil in a sauté pan; fry the onion and mushrooms for 5 minutes, stirring occasionally. Mix with the remaining ingredients in a bowl and shape into 12 balls. Coat the balls in flour, then dip in beaten egg and finally roll in a mixture of breadcrumbs and sesame seeds. Heat the oil in the sauté pan and fry the balls until golden brown. Drain on absorbent kitchen paper and serve with a salad.

Cook's Tip

Stir-frying is an excellent method of cooking vegetables. They are cooked so quickly and in their own juices that very little of the nutritional content is lost. Have all the ingredients prepared before starting to cook.

Cook's Tip

Make a tasty soured cream sauce to accompany the nuggets. Mix 1 tablespoon grated onion and 2 tablespoons finely grated cucumber (with excess liquid removed) with 150 ml/¼ pint soured cream. Season to taste and chill lightly before serving.

103 | Parsnip Croquettes

Preparation time
20 minutes

Cooking time
20 25 minutes

Serves 4—6

Calories
360 240 per portion

You will need
225 g/8 oz parsnips, peeled and
   quartered
225 g/8 oz potatoes, peeled,
   halved if necessary
salt
15 g/½ oz butter
50 g/2 oz walnuts, coarsely
   chopped
2 tablespoons plain flour
1 egg, beaten
75 g/3 oz dried breadcrumbs
oil for shallow frying

Cook the parsnips and potatoes in a pan of boiling salted water for about 15 minutes, until tender. Drain well.

Chop the parsnips coarsely and mash the potatoes. Mix together with the butter and walnuts. Shape into neat round cakes, or if you prefer, into cylindrical croquettes. Coat each cake in flour, then in beaten egg and finally in breadcrumbs.

Shallow fry the croquettes in hot oil for 3 minutes on each side until golden brown. Drain on absorbent kitchen paper, sprinkle with salt and serve immediately with a simple salad of tomatoes, onions and chopped parsley.

104 | Vegetable Curry

Preparation time
20 minutes, plus 10
minutes to drain
aubergine

Cooking time
1 hour

Serves 4

Calories
380 per portion

You will need
1 aubergine, diced
salt and pepper
2 tablespoons oil
4 teaspoons mustard seeds
½ teaspoon ground turmeric
1½ teaspoons chilli powder
1 clove garlic, crushed
2.5-cm/1-in piece of fresh root
   ginger, peeled and finely
   chopped
1 small cauliflower, broken into
   florets
3 potatoes, peeled and diced
4 courgettes, thickly sliced
4 tomatoes, peeled, quartered and
   deseeded
175 g/6 oz runner beans or French
   beans, cut into 2.5-cm/1-in
   lengths
100 g/4 oz almonds, toasted

Sprinkle the aubergine with salt, allow to drain in a colander for 10 minutes. Rinse and drain thoroughly.

Heat the oil in a heavy flameproof casserole or in a large heavy frying pan with a lid. Add the mustard seeds, turmeric and chilli powder and cook, stirring constantly, until the seeds begin to pop. Stir in the garlic and ginger and fry for a few seconds. Then stir in all the vegetables and seasoning. Cover and cook very slowly for 40–50 minutes until all the vegetables are tender. Taste for seasoning and stir in the almonds.

Cook's Tip

Chill the croquettes in the refrigerator for 1–2 hours after coating in egg and breadcrumbs and they will hold their shape more satisfactorily when being fried.

Cook's Tip

To toast flaked almonds, distribute them evenly on a baking tray, then bake in a moderate oven (160 C, 325 F, gas 3), stirring frequently, until brown.

Salads

Salads offer the perfect opportunity for mingling sweet and sour flavours, for incorporating protein-rich cheese and creating piquant new dressings – not omitting classics such as French dressing. In this chapter you will find salads crunchy with celery, apple and walnuts, juicy with grapes or pineapple, made into a meal with cheese, and dressings including herbs, nuts and yogurt. Creativity can flourish in salad-making and the following recipes offer plenty of ideas.

105 | Caerphilly Bean Salad

(Illustrated on back jacket)

Preparation time
20 minutes

Cooking time
8 minutes

Serves 4

Calories
470 per portion

You will need
225 g/8 oz French beans
225 g/8 oz Caerphilly cheese
1 small red pepper

For the dressing
8 tablespoons salad oil
2 tablespoons red or white wine vinegar
salt, pepper and a little paprika
1 tablespoon single cream (optional)

Top and tail the French beans. Cook in boiling salted water until just tender. Drain, refresh with a little cold water, drain again and allow to cool.

Cut the cheese into neat pieces, either dice or thin strips. Discard the core and seeds from the red pepper and cut the flesh in thin rounds. Prepare the dressing by whisking all the ingredients together. Toss the cheese and beans in sufficient dressing to coat lightly, put in a salad bowl and scatter the rings of pepper over the top.

106 | Mushroom and Leicester Salad

Preparation time
15 minutes, plus 30 minutes to chill

Serves 4

Calories
260 per portion

You will need
225 g/8 oz very fresh cup or button mushrooms
4 6 tablespoons salad oil
salt and freshly ground black pepper
100 g/4 oz Red Leicester cheese
1 tablespoon wine vinegar
1 tablespoon chopped parsley
2 teaspoons chopped chives, (optional)

Trim and carefully wipe the mushrooms. Slice thinly and place in a wide bowl. Add enough oil to coat the mushrooms; season with salt and pepper. Cube the Leicester cheese or cut it into strips, add to the mushrooms with the vinegar and herbs. Toss together, put in a salad bowl, cover and chill briefly before serving.

Cook's Tip

To ring the changes, substitute mangetout peas for the French beans in this recipe. Like French beans, topping and tailing is the only preparation (apart from rinsing) necessary. Boil briefly in salted water so that they retain a little bite.

Cook's Tip

Red Leicester adds colour to this nutritious salad. Red Windsor, a distinctive marbled cheese flavoured with elderberry wine or annatto berries, could be used instead.

107 | Spinach Cheese Salad

Preparation time
15 minutes plus 20 30 minutes to chill

Serves 4

Calories
385 per portion

You will need
1 kg/2 lb fresh spinach, washed
4 tablespoons salad oil
salt and pepper
wine vinegar or lemon juice
  (optional)
175 g/6 oz Derby cheese
2 tablespoons mayonnaise
chopped chives to garnish
  (optional)

Blanch the spinach for 1 minute in boiling salted water. Drain and refresh with cold water. Press the spinach between two plates to remove excessive moisture. Place in a wide bowl.

Using two forks to help separate the leaves, dress the spinach with the salad oil, salt and freshly ground black pepper, adding a little wine vinegar or lemon juice if you like.

Cut the cheese into cubes, mix with the mayonnaise and extra seasoning if necessary. Spoon on top of the spinach and serve lightly chilled. Add a garnish of chopped chives, if liked.

Cook's Tip

Spinach has a very high vitamin A content and is rich in iron and vitamin C. As it is low in calories it is an excellent vegetable, especially when served raw as in this flavoursome salad.

108 | Cheshire Salad

Preparation time
10 minutes

Cooking time
5 minutes

Serves 4

Calories
115 per portion

You will need
For the dressing
4 tablespoons orange juice
1 teaspoon caster sugar
2 tablespoons oil
1 tablespoon white wine vinegar
1 tablespoon chopped parsley
1 tablespoon chopped chives

For the salad
225 g/8 oz red cabbage
100 g/4 oz cooked beetroot
2 red-skinned apples
1 tablespoon lemon juice
4 8 lettuce leaves
225 g/8 oz blue Cheshire cheese
parsley sprigs to garnish

Whisk the dressing ingredients in a bowl. Shred the cabbage and blanch in boiling water for 2 minutes. Drain and toss into the dressing. Cool, mixing occasionally. Thinly slice the beetroot. Core and chop the apples; toss in the lemon juice. Arrange lettuce leaves on individual plates, top with cabbage and apple. Cube the cheese and scatter over the salad. Garnish with parsley and serve.

Cook's Tip

Although red wine vinegar has an equally good flavour, white wine vinegar is a preferable ingredient in salad dressings as red wine vinegar can turn the dressing an odd pink colour.

109 | Light Cheese and Pineapple Salad

Preparation time
20 minutes, plus 20–30 minutes to chill

Serves 4

Calories
220 per portion

You will need
175 g/6 oz low-fat hard cheese, cubed (for example Shape cheese)
225 g/8 oz fresh pineapple, peeled and cubed
100 g/4 oz celery, chopped
100 g/4 oz apple, chopped
50 g/2 oz walnut pieces
3–4 tablespoons low-calorie mayonnaise
1 tablespoon chopped parsley
salt and freshly ground black pepper

Mix the cheese, pineapple, celery, apple and walnuts in a bowl. Coat with the mayonnaise and sprinkle with parsley. Season to taste and mix well. Chill for 25–30 minutes before serving.

110 | Blue Cheese and Mandarin Salad

Preparation time
15 minutes

Serves 6

Calories
135 per portion

You will need
1 (298-g/10½-oz) can mandarin orange segments in natural juice
75 g/3 oz blue cheese
150 ml/¼ pint soured cream or mayonnaise
salt and freshly ground black pepper
450 g/1 lb white cabbage, finely shredded
lettuce to serve

Drain the mandarins. Crumble the blue cheese into the mandarin juice then mix in the soured cream or mayonnaise. Season well before tossing with the cabbage and mandarins. Serve on a bed of lettuce.

Cook's Tip

When selecting a fresh pineapple, check for fragrance and ripeness. Discoloured, drooping leaves indicate the pineapple is not in peak condition; the fruit itself should be golden orange in colour, never green.

Cook's Tip

Blue cheese and mandarins form a highly successful combination. For an interesting starter, omit the cabbage and use the fruit and cheese mixture to fill well-drained canned pear halves.

111 | Crunchy Beansprout and Cheese Salad

Preparation time
10 minutes

Serves 4

Calories
305 per portion

You will need
4 tablespoons natural wholenut
  peanut butter
4 tablespoons lemon juice
1 red pepper, deseeded and cut
  into thin strips
175 g/6 oz beansprouts
175 g/6 oz Double Gloucester
  cheese, cubed
½ crisp lettuce, shredded

Stir the peanut butter and lemon juice together until well mixed. Combine the remaining ingredients in a salad bowl then stir in the peanut butter dressing just before serving.

112 | Two-Cheese Salad

Preparation time
20 minutes

Serves 4

Calories
485 per portion

You will need
1 green pepper, deseeded and cut
  into thin strips
1 red pepper, deseeded and cut
  into thin strips
4 tomatoes, sliced
175 g/6 oz blue cheese, cubed
175 g/6 oz Edam or Gouda cheese,
  cubed
12 stuffed green olives
2 tablespoons olive oil
1 tablespoon lemon juice
1 cos lettuce

For the sauce
300 ml/½ pint natural yogurt
salt and pepper
1 small avocado

Place the peppers, tomatoes, cheeses and olives in a bowl. Whisk the oil and lemon juice together until well blended, pour over salad and toss lightly, to coat. Wash and prepare the lettuce and arrange it on a serving platter. Pile the cheese salad in the centre.
  To make the sauce, mix yogurt with plenty of seasoning. Peel and finely chop the avocado, then fold it lightly into the yogurt. Serve separately.

Cook's Tip

If you have a grinder, making your own peanut butter is easy. Grind 100 g / 4 oz roasted peanuts finely and mash them to a paste in a bowl, adding a little vegetable oil if necessary. Hazelnuts, cashews and walnuts may also be used.

Cook's Tip

Vary the choice of cheese to suit your palate. For example try smoked cheese with Cheshire cheese or Sage Derby cheese with Edam. Strict vegetarians may prefer to make a selection from the rennet-free varieties.

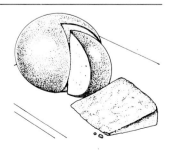

113 | Creamy Waldorf Salad

Preparation time
30 minutes, plus 1 hour to chill

Serves 6

Calories
170 per portion

You will need
2 tablespoons lemon juice
1 teaspoon caster sugar
1 tablespoon mayonnaise
3 green dessert apples
4 celery sticks
50 g/2 oz walnuts
100 g/4 oz green grapes
100 g/4 oz Danish Blue Castello cheese
6 tablespoons natural yogurt
salt and pepper
celery leaves to garnish

Whisk the lemon juice, sugar and mayonnaise together in a large bowl. Core and dice the apples and mix into the lemon mixture. Set aside and turn occasionally while preparing the other ingredients. Thinly slice the celery, chop the walnuts, halve and deseed the grapes. Add to the apple and mix to thinly coat in the lemon mixture.

Place the cheese in a bowl and beat to soften. Beat in the yogurt and seasoning to make a thick dressing. Alternatively, place the cheese, yogurt and seasoning in a liquidiser and blend until smooth. Pour over the apple mixture and turn gently with a fork until well mixed. Refrigerate for an hour then mix again. Turn into a serving bowl and garnish with celery leaves.

114 | Mushroom Slaw

Preparation time
15 minutes, plus several hours to chill

Serves 6

Calories
235 per portion

You will need
225 g/8 oz flat mushrooms, thinly sliced
225 g/8 oz white cabbage, shredded
50 g/2 oz sultanas

For the dressing
150 ml/¼ pint mayonnaise
2 tablespoons lemon juice
2 tablespoons Dijon mustard
2 tablespoons single cream
2 tablespoons chopped chives
salt and freshly ground black pepper

Mix the mushrooms with the cabbage and sultanas. In a separate bowl combine the ingredients for the dressing, seasoning to taste. Pour the dressing over the salad and mix gently together. Cover and refrigerate for several hours. Toss together well before serving.

Cook's Tip

If liked, fennel with its aniseed flavour and delicate feathery leaves may be finely chopped and substituted for the celery in this recipe.

Cook's Tip

For an unusual serving idea, make a bowl for the slaw from a Savoy cabbage; cut out the centre, wash, dry and reserve the outer leaves. Wash and shred the centre, mix with the other ingredients, dress and place in the cabbage bowl.

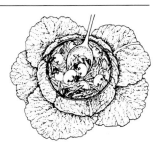

115 | Pasta Slaw

Preparation time
15 minutes, plus 30
minutes to cool

Cooking time
13–15 minutes

Serves 4

Calories
225 per portion

You will need
75 g/3 oz pasta spirals
1 (283-g/10-oz) packet frozen
   whole French beans
75 g/3 oz white cabbage, finely
   chopped
½ green pepper, deseeded and
   finely chopped
1 carrot, grated
4 spring onions, finely chopped
salt and freshly ground pepper
parsley sprigs to garnish (optional)

For the dressing
4 tablespoons mayonnaise
2 tablespoons milk or cream
1 tablespoon wine vinegar
2 teaspoons sugar
salt and freshly ground pepper

Cook the pasta in a large saucepan of boiling salted water for 10–12 minutes, until just tender. Cook the French beans in boiling salted water for 3–5 minutes. Refresh both under cold water, drain and allow to cool.

Meanwhile, mix together the remaining salad ingredients in a bowl. Combine the ingredients for the dressing and add to the salad bowl with the pasta and chopped French beans. Season to taste and garnish with sprigs of parsley to serve.

116 | Fruit Coleslaw

Preparation time
25 minutes

Serves 4

Calories
280 per portion

You will need
½ medium white cabbage, finely
   shredded
4 celery sticks, cut into matchstick
   strips
2 red dessert apples, cored and
   chopped
50 g/2 oz raisins
50 g/2 oz walnuts, chopped
100 g/4 oz grapes, halved and
   seeded
1 tablespoon chopped chives

For the dressing
4 tablespoons oil
1 tablespoon wine vinegar
pinch of mustard powder
1 teaspoon sugar
salt and pepper

To make the dressing, combine the ingredients in a screw-topped jar and shake well to blend. Place the cabbage in a large salad bowl and stir in sufficient dressing to just moisten. Add the celery, apples, raisins, walnuts, grapes and chives and toss all well together.

Cook's Tip

**For additional fibre and B
vitamins, use wholemeal pasta
in this recipe.**

Cook's Tip

**To shred cabbage finely,
choose a long-bladed, sharp
knife, secure the cabbage with
your fingers, moving them
back as you shred.**

117 | Crunchy Cabbage Salad

Preparation time
15 minutes

Serves 4

Calories
260 per portion

You will need
225 g/8 oz red cabbage, finely
    shredded
100 g/4 oz white cabbage, finely
    shredded
1 red pepper, deseeded and
    chopped
50 g/2 oz sunflower seeds
100 g/4 oz salted peanuts
50 g/2 oz raisins

For the dressing
1 tablespoon wine vinegar
1 teaspoon prepared mustard
2 tablespoons natural yogurt
2 tablespoons groundnut oil
1 tablespoon chopped parsley
salt and pepper

Place the red and white cabbage in a salad bowl with the pepper, sunflower seeds, peanuts and raisins. Mix well.

Place all the dressing ingredients in a small bowl and whisk with a fork until thickened. Pour over the salad and mix thoroughly. Serve immediately or cover and refrigerate until ready to serve.

118 | Dressed Bean and Onion Salad

Preparation time
15 minutes, plus 1 hour
to chill

Cooking time
5 minutes

Serves 4

Calories
445 per portion

You will need
50 g/2 oz butter or margarine
1 clove garlic, finely chopped
50 g/2 oz All-Bran cereal, crushed
¼ teaspoon salt
1 (227-g/8-oz) can red kidney
    beans, drained
1 (227-g/8-oz) can black-eyed
    beans or chick peas, drained
450 g/1 lb fresh or frozen green
    beans, cooked and sliced
onion rings to garnish

For the dressing
½ teaspoon salt
pinch of pepper
½ teaspoon dried basil
½ teaspoon mustard powder
3 tablespoons white wine vinegar
1 tablespoon clear honey
5 tablespoons oil

Melt the butter in a pan and sauté the garlic for 2 minutes. Stir in the cereal and salt and fry briskly for 2 minutes more. Leave to cool. Rinse the canned beans and drain well. Mix with the green beans in a salad bowl and chill. To make the dressing, combine the salt, pepper, basil, mustard, vinegar and honey in a bowl. Gradually beat in the oil. Stir the cereal mixture into the beans, garnish with the onion rings and serve.

Cook's Tip

Sunflower seeds are readily available in health food stores. As well as enhancing all kinds of salads, they provide a healthy nibble and are good toasted too.

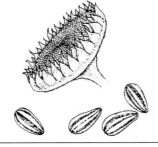

Cook's Tip

Mixing pulse protein with cereal protein in this salad makes it a well-balanced dish which supplies a good combination of amino acids.

119 | Mushroom and Mange Tout Salad

Preparation time
10 minutes, plus 20 minutes to cool

Cooking time
4–5 minutes

Serves 4

Calories
55 per portion

You will need
175 g/6 oz mange tout
225 g/8 oz small button mushrooms, sliced
6 spring onions, chopped
150 ml/¼ pint natural yogurt
salt and pepper
snipped chives to garnish

Cook the mange tout in boiling salted water for 4–5 minutes until just tender. Drain and cool. Combine the mushrooms, spring onions and yogurt with seasoning to taste.

Arrange the mange tout on a plate and top with the mushrooms. Sprinkle with chives and serve.

120 | Broad Bean Salad

Preparation time
15 minutes

Cooking time
10 minutes

Serves 4–6

Calories
420–280 per portion

You will need
350 g/12 oz fresh or frozen broad beans
salt
tarragon or parsley sprigs to garnish

For the hollandaise sauce
3 egg yolks
2 tablespoons lemon juice
175 g/6 oz unsalted butter, melted
salt and pepper

Cook the beans in boiling salted water for 5–10 minutes or until tender. Drain the beans, cool and pop the beans out of their outer skins, if liked (with young beans this will not be necessary). Put the beans into a serving bowl.

To make the hollandaise sauce, blend the egg yolks and lemon juice together in a food processor for 30 seconds. Slowly pour in the hot melted butter to make a creamy sauce. Add salt and pepper to taste. Pour over the beans immediately and garnish with the tarragon or parsley. Serve warm or cool.

Cook's Tip

The best way of preparing chives is to hold the washed bunch firmly and use a pair of scissors to snip them into a small basin.

Cook's Tip

If using fresh broad beans, do not remove from the furry lined pods until just before cooking. There is no need to shell young, tender broad beans; top, tail, cut them up, then cook and serve in the pods.

121 | Mushroom and Cucumber Side Salad

Preparation time
15 minutes

Serves 4

Calories
65 per portion

You will need
¼ Webbs lettuce, finely shredded
100 g/4 oz button mushrooms, wiped and quartered
½ cucumber, diced
4 tablespoons low-calorie mayonnaise
2 teaspoons tomato ketchup
½ teaspoon lemon juice
paprika to sprinkle

Arrange the shredded lettuce in the base of four salad bowls. Mix together the mushrooms and cucumber and place over the lettuce. Combine the mayonnaise with the tomato ketchup and lemon juice and spoon over the salad. Sprinkle with a little paprika and serve at once.

122 | Mushroom and Celeriac Salad

Preparation time
25 minutes, plus about 1 hour to chill

Serves 6

Calories
315 per portion

You will need
225 g/8 oz button mushrooms, halved if large
½ large celeriac root, coarsely grated
225 g/8 oz carrots, coarsely grated
chopped parsley to garnish

For the dressing
1 egg yolk
150 ml/¼ pint olive oil
2 tablespoons white wine vinegar
150 ml/¼ pint soured cream
salt and pepper

First make the dressing. Place the egg yolk in a small bowl and beat with 2–3 drops of the olive oil. Gradually whisk in the remaining olive oil, drop by drop, until pale and thick. Whisk in the vinegar, soured cream and seasoning to taste. Fold half the dressing into the mushrooms. Fold the rest of the dressing into the celeriac. Turn the celeriac on to a serving dish, top with the carrot and mushrooms, then sprinkle with parsley. Chill before serving.

Cook's Tip

Choose lettuces with care, avoiding any with rust spots, wilted leaves or yellowing tips. Wash the leaves carefully and quickly (do not soak), dry between sheets of absorbent kitchen paper. Store in plastic bags in the refrigerator.

Cook's Tip

For a substantial lunch or supper, serve this salad with a generous slice of quiche or flan.

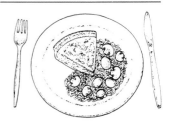

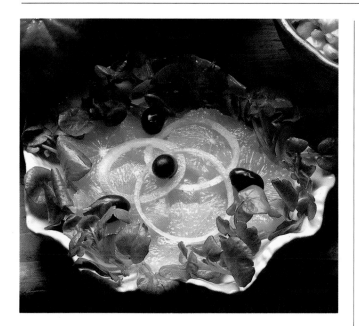

123 | *Orange and Watercress Salad*

Preparation time
15 minutes

Serves 4

Calories
185 per portion

You will need
1 large bunch watercress, trimmed
*3 oranges, peel and pith removed
and thinly sliced into rounds*
*1 onion, thinly sliced and separated
into rings*
*1 small green pepper, deseeded,
and thinly sliced into rings
(optional)*
*6 tablespoons Vinaigrette dressing
(see recipe 147)*
black olives to garnish

Put the watercress in a salad bowl. Arrange the orange slices on top with the onion and pepper rings, if using. Pour on the prepared dressing and garnish with the olives.

124 | *Brussels Sprouts and Carrot Salad*

Preparation time
*20 minutes, plus 1 hour
to chill*

Serves 4

Calories
170 per portion

You will need
450 g / 1 lb Brussels sprouts
2 medium carrots, grated
2 tablespoons sultanas
1 tablespoon finely chopped onion

For the dressing
4 tablespoons oil
1 tablespoon wine vinegar
1 teaspoon sugar
2 teaspoons Dijon mustard
salt and pepper

Wash the sprouts. Remove and discard a slice from the base of each. Slice the sprouts thinly. Mix with the carrots, sultanas and onion in a large salad bowl. Combine the ingredients for the dressing and stir sufficient into the salad to moisten. Chill for at least an hour before serving.

Cook's Tip

For an attractive and colourful garnish, shape a tomato water-lily. With a small, sharp knife, make zig-zag cuts around the middle of a tomato, through to the centre. Separate the two halves with care.

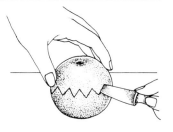

Cook's Tip

Brussels sprouts, although usually served hot, make an excellent base for a winter salad with their delicate colour and flavour. Nor are any of the valuable minerals and vitamins lost through cooking.

125 | Chicory and Sesame Salad

Preparation time
15 minutes

Serves 4—6

Calories
205 135 per portion

You will need
3 heads of chicory
2 oranges
1 bunch of watercress
25 g / 1 oz sesame seeds, roasted
4 tablespoons olive oil
1 tablespoon lemon juice
salt and pepper

Cut the chicory diagonally into 1-cm/½-in slices and place in a mixing bowl. Remove the peel and pith from the oranges and cut the flesh into segments, holding the fruit over the bowl so that any juice is retained.

Divide the watercress into sprigs and add to the bowl with the sesame seeds.

Whisk together the oil, lemon juice and salt and pepper to taste, then pour over the salad and toss thoroughly. Transfer to a salad bowl to serve.

126 | Carrot and Apple Salad

Preparation time
20 minutes

Cooking time
5 minutes

Serves 4

Calories
280 per portion

You will need
350 g / 12 oz carrots, coarsely
   grated
3 Cox's Orange Pippin apples,
   unpeeled, cored and sliced
1 tablespoon lemon juice
1 tablespoon sunflower seeds
3 tablespoons raisins
2 teaspoons vegetable oil
2 tablespoons cashew nuts
6 tablespoons French dressing
   (see recipe 135)
lettuce leaves, to serve

Put the grated carrot into a large bowl. Sprinkle the apple slices with lemon juice to prevent discoloration, then add to the bowl. Lightly mix in the sunflower seeds and raisins.

Heat the oil in a small pan and lightly brown the cashew nuts. Lift out and drain on absorbent kitchen paper, then add to the bowl.

Spoon the dressing over the salad and toss lightly. Serve on a bed of lettuce leaves.

Cook's Tip

Sesame seeds have a nutty flavour which is released more fully when they are roasted in a moderate oven (180C, 350F, gas 4) for about 15 minutes. Stir them frequently to prevent charring.

Cook's Tip

French dressing, without garlic and herbs, keeps well in a vinegar proof screw-topped jar or bottle. There is no need to refrigerate.

127 | Celery Salad Flavia

Preparation time
15 minutes, plus 30
minutes to chill

Serves 4

Calories
140 per portion

You will need
1 clove garlic, peeled and
   halved
1 head celery, cut into small strips
1 (200-g/7-oz) can artichoke hearts
   in brine, drained and halved
1 tablespoon black olives, stoned
1 tablespoon chopped parsley
3 tablespoons olive oil
1 tablespoon lemon juice
dash of Tabasco sauce
½ teaspoon prepared mustard
pinch of dried oregano
salt
few celery leaves to garnish

Using the cut side of the garlic, vigorously rub the inside
of a salad bowl, then discard. Add the celery, artichoke
hearts, olives and parsley to the bowl.

To make the dressing, beat the olive oil with the
lemon juice, Tabasco sauce, mustard, oregano and salt
to taste.

Pour the dressing over the salad and toss well. Cover
and chill for 30 minutes to allow the flavours to develop
well.

Toss the salad again before serving and garnish with
the celery leaves.

128 | Winter Radish Salad

Preparation time
5 minutes, plus 10
minutes to stand

Serves 4

Calories
90 per portion

You will need
1 large winter radish
salt
150 ml/¼ pint soured cream
1 tablespoon snipped chives to
   garnish

Scrub or thinly peel the radish. Grate or cut into very thin
slices. Place in a bowl and sprinkle generously with salt.
Leave to stand for 10–12 minutes. Rinse thoroughly and
place in a salad bowl. Spoon over the soured cream,
toss well and garnish with the chives.

Cook's Tip

To make this salad more
filling, garnish with a ring of
hard-boiled egg slices and
tomato wedges.

Cook's Tip

It is important to rinse the
radish slices thoroughly to
remove all the salt. Dry
thoroughly between sheets of
absorbent kitchen paper
before mixing with the soured
cream.

129 | Turkish Pepper Salad

Preparation time
5 minutes, plus 15
mintues to plump
raisins

Serves 4

Calories
230 per portion

You will need
2 tablespoons seedless raisins
2 medium green peppers,
 deseeded and cut into thin strips
2 spring onions, finely chopped
25 g / 1 oz pine nuts
5 tablespoons olive oil
3 tablespoons lemon juice
pinch of paprika
salt and pepper

Soak the raisins in a little warm water for about 15 minutes until plump. Drain well.

Mix together the green peppers, raisins, spring onions and pine nuts and place in a serving bowl.

Mix the oil, lemon juice, paprika and seasoning together and pour over the salad. Toss well to mix.

130 | Radish Salad

Preparation time
20 25 minutes, plus
several hours to chill

Serves 4—6

Calories
90 60 per portion

You will need
3 large bunches of radishes,
 washed, trimmed and thinly
 sliced
1 small onion, thinly sliced and
 separated into rings
2 medium tomatoes, peeled and
 chopped
1 teaspoon fresh mint, finely
 chopped
1 lettuce, washed, dried and
 shredded

For the dressing
2 tablespoons olive oil
2 tablespoons lemon juice
1½ teaspoons salt
¼ teaspoon freshly ground black
 pepper

Put the radish slices, onion rings and tomatoes in a bowl and combine with the mint.

Whisk together the oil, lemon juice, salt and pepper. Pour over the salad ingredients and toss well.

Place on a bed of shredded lettuce and chill thoroughly before serving.

Cook's Tip

Seeds of the Mediterranean
stone pine, pine nuts are pale
and oval and resemble
miniature blanched almonds.
Look for them in delicatessens
and buy in small quantities as
they do not keep indefinitely.

Cook's Tip

For an extra zesty taste, use
the large radishes that are
often found during the
summer months for this dish.

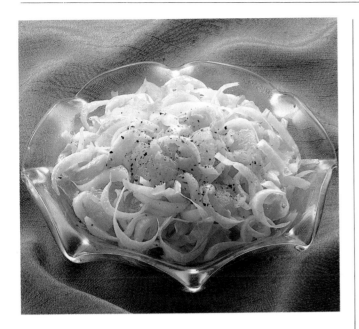

131 | *Grapefruit and Chicory Salad*

Preparation time
15 minutes, plus 30 minutes to chill

Serves 4

Calories
295 per portion

You will need
2 heads of chicory, trimmed, washed and dried
2 grapefruit

For the dressing
4 tablespoons olive oil
2 tablespoons white wine vinegar
salt and freshly ground black pepper
Tabasco sauce

Cut the chicory crossways into thin slices, and put in a salad bowl.

Squeeze and reserve the juice from half a grapefruit. Peel and remove pith from the remaining grapefruit and divide into segments. Cut each segment in half and mix with the chicory slices.

Combine the oil, vinegar and reserved grapefruit juice and season to taste with salt and pepper and a few drops of Tabasco. Pour over the salad, toss well and chill before serving.

132 | *Orange and Beetroot Salad*

Preparation time
20 minutes

Serves 4

Calories
80 per portion

You will need
2 oranges
6 small beetroot, cooked and quartered
1 small onion, thinly sliced

For the dressing
4 tablespoons natural yogurt
1 tablespoon clear honey
1 clove garlic, crushed
salt and freshly ground black pepper
freshly grated nutmeg

Grate the rind from one of the oranges and mix it with the beetroot, reserving a little for garnish, if liked. Peel both oranges and slice. Remove any obvious pips.

Combine the orange slices with the beetroot and place on a shallow serving dish or plate. Separate the onion slices into rings and sprinkle over the salad.

Place all the dressing ingredients in a bowl and blend thoroughly. Pour over the salad and serve.

Cook's Tip

This slightly sharp salad goes well with a variety of cheeses and French bread to make a tasty and quick supper.

Cook's Tip

Honey can always be substituted for sugar in salad dressings to add a pleasing flavour and to complement other ingredients with its sweetness. Use this yogurt dressing for coleslaw or Waldorf and green salads.

133 | Green Salad with Peanut Dressing

Preparation time
15 minutes

Serves 4

Calories
210 per portion

You will need
*selection of salad leaves, e.g.
  lettuce, endive, radicchio,
  watercress
½ cucumber
1 avocado (optional)*

For the dressing
*25 g/1 oz salted peanuts, finely
  chopped
1 teaspoon clear honey
1 tablespoon lemon juice
3 tablespoons groundnut oil
salt and pepper*

Wash the salad leaves and dry well. Tear into pieces and place in a salad bowl. Mix together the peanuts, honey and lemon juice. Stir in the oil until well mixed then season with salt and pepper.

Just before serving, slice the cucumber and the avocado, if using, add to the salad and toss all well together with the dressing.

134 | Tomato Ring Salad

Preparation time
*15 minutes, plus several
hours to set*

Cooking time
25 minutes

Serves 4

Calories
125 per portion

You will need
*675 g/1½ lb tomatoes, roughly
  chopped
1 onion, chopped
150 ml/¼ pint stock or water
finely grated rind and juice of
  1 orange or lemon
1 small bunch fresh herbs
1 bay leaf
1 clove garlic, crushed (optional)
salt and pepper
2 teaspoons agar-agar or 3
  teaspoons powdered gelatine
120 ml/4 fl oz water
1 teaspoon soy sauce*

Garnish
*cress
4 hard-boiled eggs*

Cook the tomatoes and onion with the stock or water, orange or lemon rind and juice, herbs, garlic, if using, and seasoning in a covered pan for 20 minutes until pulpy. Rub through a sieve to make a purée. Dissolve the agar-agar in the cold water in a small saucepan, then bring to the boil, stirring constantly. Stir into the purée, then add the soy sauce and salt and pepper to taste. Pour into a 600–900 ml/1–1½ pint ring mould, then chill until set. Unmould before serving and garnish.

Cook's Tip

In composing a greed salad, don't forget about the tiny seedling cress, bought growing in punnets and adding a welcome piquancy when sprinkled on top.

Cook's Tip

This is a perfect way to use tomatoes that are too soft for an ordinary salad.

135 | Okra Salad

Preparation time
20 minutes

Cooking time
2 minutes

Serves 4

Calories
150 per portion

You will need
450 g / 1 lb okra
1 onion, chopped
4 tablespoons sunflower oil
2 tablespoons lemon juice
1 clove garlic, crushed
1 teaspoon sugar
salt and pepper

Trim the ends off the okra and cut into short lengths. Select only the best okra for this salad – they must be in perfect condition. Drop the okra into a large pan of boiling water, bring back to the boil, then drain. Place the okra and onion in a bowl. Mix all the remaining ingredients and toss into the okra, then transfer to a dish and serve at once.

136 | Tabbouleh

Preparation time
15 minutes, plus 1 hour to soak

Serves 4

Calories
150 per portion

You will need
75 g / 3 oz bulgur wheat
40 g / 1½ oz chopped parsley
3 tablespoons chopped mint
4 spring onions, chopped
½ cucumber, finely diced
2 tablespoons olive oil
juice of 1 lemon
salt and pepper

Soak the bulgur wheat in cold water for 1 hour. Line a sieve with muslin and tip the wheat into it. Lift out the muslin and squeeze out as much moisture as possible.

Place the wheat in a salad bowl and add the remaining ingredients, seasoning with salt and pepper to taste. Add more lemon juice if preferred. Toss thoroughly, then transfer to a shallow dish to serve.

Cook's Tip

Cooked okra has a mucilaginous texture that not everyone appreciates. By merely blanching the pods, this problem is largely avoided.

Cook's Tip

Bulgur wheat is available from healthfood stores and major supermarkets.

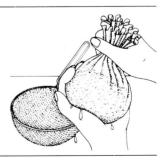

Rice and Pasta

Rice and pasta can be served with an infinite variety of sauces and ingredients and can form the main course of a meal, a tasty supper dish or lunch. The pasta recipes in this chapter are mostly based on the excellent dried packeted shapes, but do have a go at making your own pasta dough, with the added food value of eggs, then stuffing and shaping ravioli (see Recipe 161) or cutting a ribbon pasta, such as tagliatelle.

137 | Wholemeal Pasta Salad

(Illustrated on front jacket)

Preparation time
5 minutes

Cooking time
12 minutes

Serves 4

Calories
310 per portion

You will need
225 g/8 oz wholewheat pasta twists
3 tablespoons olive oil
1 tablespoon white wine vinegar
¼ teaspoon mustard powder
1 clove garlic, crushed
salt and pepper
2 spring onions, chopped
100 g/4 oz French beans, cooked
4 tomatoes, peeled, quartered and deseeded
50 g/2 oz black olives, stoned

Cook the pasta in plenty of boiling salted water for 10–12 minutes or until just tender.

Mix together the oil, vinegar, mustard, garlic and salt and pepper until thickened. Pour over the hot pasta, mix well, cover and leave until cold. Stir in the spring onions, beans and tomatoes and mix well. Turn into a large salad bowl, scatter over the olives and serve.

138 | Mung Bean and Fresh Herb Risotto

Preparation time
15 minutes, plus 6 hours to soak

Cooking time
50 minutes

Serves 4

Calories
835 per portion

You will need
350 g/12 oz mung beans, soaked for 2 hours in cold water
25 g/1 oz butter
3 tablespoons vegetable oil
1½ large onions, chopped
450 g/1 lb long-grain brown rice
1.4 litres/2½ pints vegetable stock
6 tablespoons chopped mixed fresh herbs (parsley, thyme, basil, mint)
salt and pepper
4 tablespoons pumpkin seeds

Soak the beans overnight or for 4–6 hours in cold water. Drain the beans, rinse and drain again. Using a large saucepan with a well-fitting lid, heat the butter and 1 tablespoon of the oil and fry the onion for 3 minutes, then stir in the beans and rice. Add the hot stock and bring to the boil. Cover and simmer gently for 40 minutes until beans and rice are tender and all the stock has been absorbed. Add the herbs with salt and pepper and gently fork them through the mixture. Spoon the risotto into a serving dish and keep warm. Fry the pumpkin seeds rapidly in the remaining oil for 30 seconds (take care, as they jump about in the heat) then sprinkle over the risotto. Serve hot.

Cook's Tip

If available, add some chopped fresh basil leaves to the spring onion, bean and tomato mixture.

Cook's Tip

Mung beans will probably be most familiar in their sprouted form, as beansprouts. In dried form they may be bought whole, split and skinless. These minute olive green beans are known as moong dal in Indian cooking.

139 | Risotto with Spinach and Herbs

Preparation time
15 minutes

Cooking time
35 minutes

Serves 4–6

Calories
775 520 per portion

You will need
2 tablespoons olive oil
100 g/4 oz butter
1 onion, finely chopped
100 g/4 oz mushrooms, sliced
450 g/1 lb Italian risotto rice
  (Arborio)
1.5 litres/2¾ pints hot vegetable
  stock
225 g/8 oz cooked spinach,
  chopped
1 teaspoon dried oregano
1 clove garlic, crushed
salt and pepper
75 g/3 oz grated Parmesan or
  Pecorino cheese
lemon wedges to garnish

Heat the oil and half the butter in a large saucepan. Add the onion and mushrooms and cook for a few minutes until the onions are lightly browned. Stir in the rice and cook for 5 minutes. Add the stock, spinach, oregano, garlic and salt and pepper. Stir well and cook for 20–25 minutes or until the rice is tender and has absorbed all the liquid. Stir in the remaining butter and the grated cheese. Serve the risotto garnished with lemon wedges.

140 | Rice and Mushroom Bake

Preparation time
10 minutes

Cooking time
40 45 minutes

Oven temperature
200 C, 400 F, gas 6

Serves 4

Calories
415 per portion

You will need
2 tablespoons vegetable oil
1 large onion, sliced
225 g/8 oz mushrooms, sliced
225 g/8 oz long-grain rice
1 teaspoon cumin powder
1 teaspoon mild chilli powder
1 teaspoon tomato purée
600 ml/1 pint vegetable stock
75 g/3 oz Cheddar cheese, grated
40 g/1½ oz cornflakes

Heat the oil and cook the onion and mushrooms until softened, about 5 minutes. Add the rice and fry until golden brown. Stir in the spices, tomato purée and stock. Bring to the boil and stir once. Reduce the heat, cover the pan and simmer for 15–18 minutes, until the rice is tender and the liquid absorbed. Stir in half the grated cheese and transfer to an ovenproof casserole. Mix the remaining cheese with the cornflakes, sprinkle on top of the rice and bake in a moderately hot oven for 15–20 minutes, until golden brown.

Cook's Tip

Parmesan and pecorino are both grainy, hard, grating cheeses. When young, they are eaten in chunks accompanied by white wine. Straw-coloured Parmesan is made from cows' milk and pecorino from ewes' milk. Buy fresh if possible.

Cook's Tip

Cumin, with its distinctive pungent flavour, is a spice worth investigating both as whole and ground seed. Popular in Mexico, North Africa and the East, it is sold by specialist grocers and some supermarkets. Whole seeds keep their flavour longest and may be ground very easily in an electric coffee grinder.

141 | Rice Salad Gado Gado

Preparation time
10 minutes, plus 30 minutes to cool

Cooking time
15 18 minutes

Serves 4

Calories
415 per portion

You will need
225 g/8 oz long-grain rice
50 g/2 oz mushrooms, halved
600 ml/1 pint vegetable stock
100 g/4 oz beansprouts
2 tomatoes, peeled and quartered
2 hard-boiled eggs, quartered

For the sauce
100 g/4 oz salted peanuts
4 spring onions, chopped
1 tablespoon soy sauce
1 teaspoon chilli powder

Put the rice, mushrooms and stock into a covered pan, bring to the boil and simmer gently for 15–18 minutes, until the rice is cooked and all the liquid is absorbed. Allow to cool then mix in the beansprouts, tomatoes and hard-boiled eggs.

Put the remaining ingredients in a liquidiser and blend thoroughly, adding enough water to make a smooth sauce. Pour over the rice salad and serve.

Cook's Tip

Made from fermented soya beans, soy sauce is used as extensively in Chinese cookery as salt is in the west. Most commonly dark and pungently flavoured, a more delicate – yet very salty – light soy sauce is also available.

142 | Spiced Rice and Courgette Salad

Preparation time
15 minutes, plus 1 hour to chill

Cooking time
40 45 minutes

Serves 4

Calories
530 per portion

You will need
225 g/8 oz long-grain brown rice
1 teaspoon each turmeric, curry powder, ground cumin and coriander
600 ml/1 pint water
100 g/4 oz courgettes, thinly sliced
2 tablespoons wine vinegar
5 tablespoons groundnut oil
salt
2 carrots, grated
1 onion, finely chopped
100 g/4 oz salted peanuts
1 dessert apple, unpeeled, cored and chopped

Place the rice in a saucepan with the spices and water. Bring to the boil then cover and simmer for 35–40 minutes, until the rice is tender and the liquid has been absorbed.

Meanwhile blanch the courgettes in boiling salted water for 1 minute. Drain, refresh under cold running water and drain again. Turn the rice into a large salad bowl and stir in the vinegar, oil and salt to taste. Cool slightly then add the courgettes, carrots, onion, peanuts and apple. Mix well and chill thoroughly before serving.

Cook's Tip

Flavourless peanut oil is a good choice for salad dressing, as it does not obscure the taste of other ingredients. If you want to cook with it, a pleasant flavour is imparted by first frying several slices of fresh root ginger or garlic in it.

143 | Vegetarian Gumbo

Preparation time
10 minutes

Cooking time
20–25 minutes

Serves 4

Calories
280 per portion

You will need
4 tablespoons corn oil
25 g/1 oz plain flour
1 large onion, chopped
4 celery sticks, chopped
1 small green pepper, deseeded
 and chopped
225 g/8 oz okra, sliced
1 (397-g/14-oz) can tomatoes
300 ml/½ pint vegetable stock
1 teaspoon Tabasco sauce
salt and pepper
350 g/12 oz hot cooked brown rice
 (100 g/4 oz uncooked weight)

Place half the oil in a small, heavy-based pan and heat gently. Add the flour and cook over a low heat, stirring frequently until the roux becomes a rich brown colour, but be careful not to let it burn.

In a large saucepan, heat the remaining oil and cook the onion until tender, about 5 minutes. Add the celery, green pepper and okra and sauté for 3 minutes. Stir the tomatoes, stock, Tabasco and roux into the mixture and simmer, covered, for 10 minutes. Season to taste and serve in individual bowls, topped with a portion of hot brown rice.

144 | Pasta Pesto

Preparation time
15 minutes

Cooking time
12 minutes

Serves 4

Calories
600 per portion

You will need
350 g/12 oz wholewheat caramelli
 shells, or other pasta shapes
salt and pepper
75 g/3 oz basil leaves
4 tablespoons olive oil
3 cloves garlic, crushed
50 g/2 oz pine nuts or blanched
 slivered almonds
50 g/2 oz Parmesan cheese,
 grated
25 g/1 oz butter, softened
grated Parmesan cheese to serve

Cook the pasta in plenty of boiling, salted water for about 12 minutes, or according to the directions on the packet, until just tender. Drain, refresh in hot water and drain again, tossing to ensure that no water is trapped inside the caramelli. Keep hot.

To make the sauce, blend the basil, oil, garlic and nuts in a liquidiser. Remove the mixture to a bowl, beat in the cheese and butter and season with pepper.

Spoon the sauce over the hot pasta and serve at once, with Parmesan, as an accompaniment to meat and poultry, or on its own.

Cook's Tip

Corn oil, made from the sweetcorn plant, or maize, is among the oils containing polyunsaturated fatty acids, desirable in the diet. Safflower, sunflower, and soya bean oil are others.

Cook's Tip

It is very easy to grow your own basil in a pot. Basil is also excellent sprinkled on salads, particularly tomato.

145 | Mushroom Pasta with Pine Nuts

Preparation time
25 minutes

Cooking time
40 minutes

Serves 4

Calories
480 per portion

You will need
1½ tablespoons vegetable oil
1 medium onion, sliced
450 g / 1 lb flat open mushrooms, sliced
salt
1 2 teaspoons green peppercorns
1 tablespoon soy sauce
3 tablespoons water
2 tablespoons double or whipping cream
350 g / 12 oz pasta shapes
2 tablespoons pine nuts
chopped parsley to garnish

Heat 1 tablespoon oil in a medium saucepan and cook the onion for about 5 minutes. Add the mushrooms and cook for a further few minutes. Add the salt, green peppercorns, soy sauce and water. Cover the pan and simmer gently for about 20 minutes. Remove lid and cook quickly for 1 minute to reduce liquid. Pour into a liquidiser or food processor and blend very briefly, for just a few seconds. Return to the rinsed-out pan and stir in the cream.

Bring a large pan of salted water to the boil. Add the pasta and boil briskly for 10 minutes then drain.

Meanwhile, heat the remaining oil in a small saucepan and fry the pine nuts for 2 minutes until golden brown. Drain on absorbent kitchen paper. To serve, reheat the sauce without boiling and pour over the pasta. Sprinkle with the pine nuts and parsley.

Cook's Tip

This mushroom sauce has a marvellous taste. Use the flat dark mushrooms for the best flavour. Pine nuts or kernels can be bought in health-food shops.

146 | Brown Rice and Hazelnut Salad

Preparation time
20 25 minutes

Cooking time
40 minutes

Serves 6—8

Calories
245 185 per portion

You will need
175 g / 6 oz long-grain brown rice
salt
75 g / 3 oz hazelnuts, chopped and toasted
1 red pepper, deseeded and diced
6 spring onions, finely sliced
3 celery sticks, sliced (optional)
50 g / 2 oz button mushrooms, sliced
6 tablespoons French dressing (made with 4 tablespoons oil and 2 tablespoons vinegar, 1 teaspoon French mustard, salt and pepper and a pinch of caster sugar)
3 tablespoons chopped parsley

Cook the rice in a saucepan of boiling salted water for 30–40 minutes, until tender. Rinse and drain well.

Place in a salad bowl with the remaining ingredients. Add the dressing and toss thoroughly. Serve cold.

Cook's Tip

Instead of the hazelnuts use toasted cashew nuts instead.

147 | *Brown Rice Salad*

Preparation time
10 minutes, plus 20
minutes to cool

Cooking time
35 minutes

Serves 4

Calories
395 per portion

You will need
100 g/4 oz long-grain brown rice
salt and pepper
100 g/4 oz shelled peas or sliced
  beans
100 g/4 oz sweetcorn kernels
150 ml/¼ pint Vinaigrette dressing
  (made up of 6 tablespoons oil, 2
  tablespoons vinegar, herbs and
  salt and pepper)
1 red pepper, deseeded and diced
50 g/2 oz salted peanuts
1 small onion, grated

Cook the rice in a saucepan of boiling salted water for 30 minutes or until tender. Add the peas or beans and sweetcorn and simmer for a further few minutes until just tender. Drain thoroughly.

Transfer to a medium bowl and add half of the dressing while the rice and vegetables are still hot. Toss well to mix, then leave to cool.

Add the remaining ingredients and dressing. Mix well. Taste and adjust the seasoning just before serving. Serve cold with other salad dishes.

148 | *Macaroni Special*

Preparation time
5 minutes

Cooking time
20 minutes

Serves 4

Calories
570 per portion

You will need
225 g/8 oz wholewheat macaroni
225 g/8 oz frozen mixed
  vegetables
25 g/1 oz butter
1 clove garlic, crushed
3 large tomatoes, peeled and
  chopped
225 g/8 oz mushrooms, sliced
3 tablespoons chopped parsley
  (optional)
300 ml/½ pint soured cream
50 g/2 oz mozzarella cheese,
  coarsely grated
4 tablespoons grated Parmesan
  cheese
4 slices bread, crusts removed, cut
  into triangles and toasted

Cook the macaroni in plenty of boiling water for about 5 minutes, then add the frozen mixed vegetables and cook for a further 7 minutes. Drain.

Melt the butter in a saucepan, cook the garlic for 1 minute, stir in the tomatoes and mushrooms and cook for 3 minutes. Stir in the macaroni mixture, parsley, if using, soured cream and mozzarella and heat gently until mixture is hot and the cheese just melting. Stir in the Parmesan cheese and serve immediately, garnished with the toast triangles.

Cook's Tip

**Brown rice has more protein
than polished (white) rice. It
also has traces of iron, calcium
and vitamin B. When cooked it
retains much of its bite and is
therefore an ideal basis for
salads.**

Cook's Tip

**A soured cream equivalent
may be achieved by adding a
few drops of lemon juice to
fresh double cream.**

149 | Pasta with Aubergine

Preparation time
5 minutes, plus 30 minutes to prepare aubergine

Cooking time
25 minutes

Serves 4

Calories
355 per portion

You will need
450 g / 1 lb aubergine
salt and pepper
225 g / 8 oz penne
1 medium onion, chopped
2 cloves garlic, crushed
4 tablespoons sunflower oil
1 teaspoon mustard powder
1 tablespoon tomato purée
1 (397-g / 14-oz) can tomatoes
½ teaspoon oregano
1 tablespoon chopped parsley
grated Parmesan cheese to serve

Cut the aubergine into cubes, place in a colander and sprinkle with salt. Leave for 30 minutes to extract some of the water, rinse thoroughly and pat dry. Cook the pasta in plenty of boiling salted water for 10–12 minutes or until just cooked. Drain and keep warm. Meanwhile, cook the onion and garlic gently in the oil for 5 minutes until softened. Increase the heat, add the aubergine and cook, stirring, until lightly browned. Stir in the mustard, tomato purée, tomatoes and their juices, oregano, parsley and pepper to taste and simmer the mixture gently for 10 minutes until the aubergine is cooked, stirring occasionally. Pour the sauce over the pasta and serve at once, with Parmesan cheese.

150 | Spaghetti with Walnut Sauce

Preparation time
5 minutes

Cooking time
20 minutes

Serves 4

Calories
700 per portion

You will need
450 g / 1 lb spaghetti
salt and pepper
1 medium onion, chopped
2 cloves garlic, crushed
1 tablespoon oil
50 g / 2 oz mushrooms, sliced
75 g / 3 oz walnuts, finely chopped
bunch of watercress, chopped
300 ml / ½ pint soured cream

Cook the spaghetti in plenty of boiling salted water for 10–12 minutes until just tender. Fry the onion and garlic in the oil for about 3 minutes until softened. Add the mushrooms and walnuts and cook for a further 3 minutes over moderate heat. Remove the pan from the heat, stir in the watercress, soured cream and salt and pepper to taste. Reheat very gently. Do not allow the sauce to boil.

Drain the spaghetti and place in a warm serving dish. Pour over the sauce and serve immediately.

Cook's Tip

Be adventurous in selecting pasta shapes: rigatoni and mezze maniche (short sleeves) are other short, tubular pasta shapes; the latter, as its name suggests, is served with summer sauces in Italy.

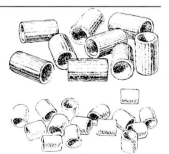

Cook's Tip

To eat pasta at its best, remember to drain it while it is al dente, which means while it still has a bit of bite to it. Test the pasta and remove it from the heat before the core has become completely soft and it will be cooked to perfection.

151 | Spinach Noodles

Preparation time
10 minutes

Cooking time
15 minutes

Serves 2–3

Calories
780 520 per portion

You will need
225 g/8 oz noodles
1 onion, chopped
50 g/2 oz butter
225 g/8 oz spinach, chopped
150 ml/¼ pint natural yogurt
100 g/4 oz low-fat soft cheese (for
  example Shape cheese)
1 teaspoon lemon juice
salt and freshly ground black
  pepper
¼ teaspoon grated nutmeg

Cook the noodles in boiling salted water for about 12 minutes until tender.

Meanwhile, cook the onion in the butter until soft, but not browned. Add the spinach and continue to cook for 2–3 minutes. Stir in the yogurt, cheese, lemon juice, seasoning and nutmeg and stir over a low heat without boiling. Drain the noodles and add to the hot spinach sauce; toss well then serve immediately.

152 | Pasta with Ratatouille Sauce

Preparation time
15 20 minutes

Cooking time
35 minutes

Serves 4–6

Calories
500 335 per portion

You will need
1 large onion, chopped
1 clove garlic, crushed
450 g/1 lb courgettes, sliced
1 large aubergine, diced
1 green pepper, deseeded and
  diced
450 g/1 lb tomatoes, peeled and
  chopped
1 tablespoon chopped oregano or
  basil
salt and pepper
450 g/1 lb pasta (spaghetti,
  noodles, etc)
1 tablespoon chopped parsley
grated Parmesan cheese to serve

Put all the ingredients, except the pasta, parsley and cheese in a large saucepan. Add enough water to cover vegetables and cook gently for 30 minutes until the vegetables are tender and the juices have thickened slightly, stirring occasionally.

Meanwhile, cook the pasta in a large saucepan in plenty of boiling salted water until just tender (about 5 minutes for freshly made pasta and 15 minutes for dried). Drain and place in a warmed serving dish.

Taste and adjust the seasoning of the sauce, then pour over the pasta. Top with the parsley and grated Parmesan cheese. Serve hot.

Cook's Tip

For special occasions, use a full-fat soft cheese such as Roulé, which is made with a blend of garlic and fine herbs.

Cook's Tip

This dish makes a filling main course. It can also be served cold as a starter, without the pasta. Served in vols-au-vent, it makes an attractive party snack (see Recipe 181 for instructions on cooking vols-au-vent).

153 | Nutty Ribbon Pasta

Preparation time
5 minutes

Cooking time
14–18 minutes

Serves 4

Calories
730 per portion

You will need
350 g/12 oz tagliarini or tagliatelli
300 ml/½ pint single cream
2 large egg yolks
freshly ground black pepper
4 sprigs fresh dill, chopped
175 g/6 oz salted peanuts, roughly chopped
chopped fresh dill, to garnish

Cook the pasta in boiling salted water for about 12–15 minutes, until tender but not soft. Meanwhile, combine the cream, egg yolks, black pepper and dill in a bowl. Stir in the peanuts. Drain the pasta and return it to the pan, then immediately add the cream mixture. Heat gently for 2–3 minutes, stirring to mix thoroughly. Serve immediately.

154 | Pasta al Pomodoro

Preparation time
10 minutes

Cooking time
25 minutes

Serves 2

Calories
430 per portion

You will need
175 g/6 oz pasta bows
salt and freshly ground black pepper
2 tablespoons grated Parmesan or other cheese

For the sauce
1 small onion, finely chopped
100 g/4 oz mushrooms, sliced
1 teaspoon sunflower oil
1 (397-g/14-oz) can tomatoes
1 tablespoon chopped fresh basil (optional)
salt and pepper

Cook the pasta bows in a large pan of boiling salted water for 10–12 minutes. Drain and keep warm. Meanwhile, sauté the onion and mushrooms in the oil for 5 minutes, stir in the tomatoes and cook gently for 15 minutes to reduce the sauce. Add the basil, if using, and simmer for a further 5 minutes. Season to taste and serve with the pasta bows, topped with Parmesan and freshly ground black pepper.

Cook's Tip

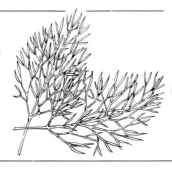

Well known for its affinity with fish, dill deserves to be more widely used. It is especially delicious with eggs, so complements the eggs in this sauce. A herb omelette is another dish in which to use fresh dill.

Cook's Tip

This simple dish is ideal for children, who will enjoy it even more if it is made with tri-coloured pasta – plain, spinach and tomato-flavoured.

155 | Pasta with Bolina Cheese Sauce

Preparation time
10 minutes

Cooking time
10 12 minutes

Serves 4

Calories
435 per portion

You will need
275 g / 10 oz tagliatelle or pasta
    shells
125 g / 4½ oz Danish Bolina cheese
25 g / 1 oz butter
4 tablespoons single cream
2 tablespoons chopped parsley
salt and pepper

Cook the pasta in a large pan of boiling salted water for 10–12 minutes until just tender.

Meanwhile, place the cheese in a bowl. Break it up with a fork, add the butter and set over a pan of boiling water. Cook, stirring occasionally, until the ingredients have melted and blended together. Add the cream and parsley. Season to taste and heat through.

Drain the cooked pasta and place on a heated serving dish. Pour the sauce over the pasta and turn gently with two forks to coat. Serve immediately with a mixed salad and crusty bread.

156 | Gratin of Pasta

Preparation time
15 minutes

Cooking time
25 minutes

Serves 4

Calories
380 per portion

You will need
100 g / 4 oz pasta shells
    salt and pepper
25 g / 1 oz butter
25 g / 1 oz plain flour
300 ml / ½ pint milk
100 g / 4 oz Cheddar cheese, grated
1 (283-g / 10-oz) packet frozen
    Country stir-fry vegetables
2 tablespoons chopped parsley
2 hard-boiled eggs, sliced

Cook the pasta shells in a large saucepan of boiling salted water for 10–12 minutes, until just tender. Melt the butter, add the flour and cook for a minute. Remove from the heat and gradually stir in the milk. Return to the heat and bring to the boil, stirring continually until the sauce bubbles and thickens. Add the cheese, season to taste and leave to cool slightly.

Cook the stir-fry vegetables according to the packet instructions. Toss the cooked pasta shells in parsley and place in a flameproof serving dish. Sprinkle with the stir-fry vegetables and arrange the egg slices on top. Pour over the cheese sauce and brown under a hot grill, if preferred. Serve immediately.

Cook's Tip

Using a big saucepan with plenty of boiling water to cook the pasta is important. The pasta swells and if it is cramped it will tend to clog together in lumps. Adding a few drops of oil to the water helps to prevent this.

Cook's Tip

Pasta shells (conchiglie) are available in a range of sizes and in both plain and wholemeal varieties. They are particularly good with chunky sauces like this one.

157 | Marrow Lasagne

Preparation time
35 minutes

Cooking time
50 minutes

Oven temperature
200 C, 400 F, gas 6

Serves 6

Calories
300 per portion

You will need
1 kg/2 lb whole marrow or squash
2 tablespoons olive oil
1 large onion, chopped
4 6 cardamom pods
2 teaspoons black peppercorns
1 teaspoon caster sugar
salt
225 g/8 oz green lasagne, cooked
225 g/8 oz small round goats'
  cheese, thinly sliced
2 tablespoons cornflour
2 tablespoons milk
450 ml/¾ pint natural yogurt
2 tablespoons grated Parmesan
  cheese

Scoop out the centre of the marrow, or squash, peel and slice the flesh. Cook in boiling water for 15 minutes, or until soft. Drain and mash coarsely.

Heat 1 tablespoon oil in a large pan and cook the onion until soft. Extract the seeds from the cardamom pods and crush with the peppercorns. Stir the ground spices, onion and sugar into the marrow and season. Brush the remaining oil over the base of a 20 × 28-cm/ 8 × 11-in ovenproof dish. Layer the lasagne, marrow and goats' cheese in the dish, ending with a last layer of lasagne.

Mix the cornflour, milk and yogurt in a saucepan. Bring gently to the boil, stirring, and cook for 2–3 minutes. Pour over the lasagne and sprinkle with Parmesan. Bake in a moderately hot oven for about 35 minutes.

Cook's Tip

Green or white cardamom pods have lots of tiny black seeds inside, which should be shiny and highly aromatic. Buy from Indian and Pakistani food stores.

158 | Vegetable Lasagne

Preparation time
10 minutes

Cooking time
1½ hours

Oven temperature
180 C, 350 F, gas 4

Serves 4

Calories
800 per portion using
cream cheese
520 per portion using
curd cheese

You will need
2 tablespoons oil
225 g/8 oz French beans, chopped
1 leek or onion, thinly sliced
salt and pepper
1 (397-g/14-oz) can tomatoes
100 g/4 oz lentils
300 ml/½ pint water
pinch of oregano
450 g/1 lb cream or curd cheese
2 eggs, beaten
100 g/4 oz lasagne, cooked
2 tablespoons chopped parsley
2 tablespoons grated Parmesan
  cheese

Heat the oil in a saucepan and fry the beans and leek or onion for 5 minutes. Season to taste. Add the tomatoes, lentils, water and oregano and bring to the boil. Simmer for about 30 minutes or until the lentils are tender.

Mix together the cream or curd cheese and the eggs. Spread half the vegetable mixture in a 1.15-litre/2-pint ovenproof dish and cover with one-third of the lasagne. Spread half the cheese mixture over, then cover with another layer of lasagne. Make a layer with the remaining vegetable mixture, cover with remaining lasagne and finally the remaining cheese mixture. Sprinkle over the Parmesan and bake for 40 minutes.

Cook's Tip

A very popular herb in Italy, oregano, like basil, perfectly complements the flavour of tomatoes. Aubergines and courgettes are also enhanced by its pronounced, aromatic flavour.

159 | Spinach Lasagne

Preparation time
20 minutes

Cooking time
45 minutes

Oven temperature
200 C, 400 F, gas 6

Serves 4

Calories
530 per portion

You will need
salt and pepper
2 (225-g/8-oz) packets frozen
    spinach, defrosted and drained
¼ teaspoon grated nutmeg
25 g/1 oz pecan nuts, chopped
40 g/1½ oz butter
40 g/1½ oz plain flour
600 ml/1 pint milk
200 g/7 oz mature Cheddar
    cheese, grated
½ teaspoon prepared English
    mustard
175 g/6 oz wholewheat lasagne,
    cooked
paprika to garnish

Season the spinach, add the nutmeg and stir in the nuts. Melt the butter in a saucepan over a low heat, then add the flour. Cook for 2 minutes, stirring. Gradually add the milk and bring the sauce to the boil, stirring constantly. Simmer gently for 2–3 minutes. Add 175 g/ 6 oz of the cheese and season with salt, pepper and mustard. Layer the spinach and lasagne in an ovenproof dish. Top with the sauce and sprinkle with the reserved cheese. Bake near the top of a moderately hot oven for 20–30 minutes until piping hot and brown on top.

Sprinkle with paprika and serve immediately.

160 | Courgette and Cauliflower Macaroni

Preparation time
30 minutes

Cooking time
20 minutes

Serves 4

Calories
605 per portion

You will need
225 g/8 oz macaroni
salt
225 g/8 oz cauliflower, broken into
    small florets
225 g/8 oz courgettes, finely
    chopped

For the sauce
450 ml/¾ pint milk
50 g/2 oz plain flour
50 g/2 oz margarine, cut up
175 g/6 oz Cheddar cheese, grated
salt and pepper
paprika to garnish (optional)

Cook the macaroni in boiling salted water for 15 minutes, then drain. Cook the cauliflower in salted boiling water for 5 minutes, adding courgettes for the final 2 minutes. Drain well and reserve 150 ml/¼ pint of the water. Place the vegetables and macaroni in an ovenproof dish.

Whisk the milk, flour and margarine with the reserved vegetable water in a pan over low heat until boiling and thickened. Stir in most of the cheese with seasoning to taste. Pour over the macaroni, sprinkle with the remaining cheese and a little paprika (if used). Brown under a moderate grill, then serve piping hot.

Cook's Tip

A roasting tin is the best container to use for cooking lasagne as it gives the pasta sheets plenty of room. When cooked, lift each sheet from the water separately with a fish slice and place in a pan or bowl of warm water. Keep the lasagne sheets in the warm water until needed but no longer than necessary, as they can absorb too much water. No-need-to-precook lasagne works very well too, provided there is plenty of sauce.

Cook's Tip

Chop a few sprigs of parsley and stir into the vegetable and macaroni mixture for additional flavour.

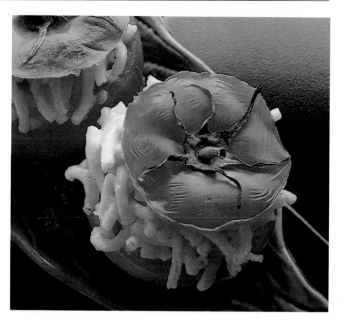

161 | Ravioli

Preparation time
40 minutes

Cooking time
5 minutes

Serves 4

Calories
720 per portion

You will need
225 g/8 oz frozen chopped
 spinach, cooked and drained
100 g/4 oz Cheddar cheese, grated
25 g/1 oz Parmesan cheese,
 grated
1 egg plus 1 yolk, beaten
¼ teaspoon grated nutmeg
salt and pepper
500 g/18 oz strong plain flour
5 eggs
½ beaten egg mixed with 1
 tablespoon water for brushing

Mix the spinach with the cheeses, whole egg and yolk, nutmeg and salt and pepper, cover and chill. Heap the flour on to a working surface and make a well in the centre. Break the 5 eggs into it and with a fork lightly beat them into the flour. Gradually work in all the flour. Use your hands to knead the soft dough for 10 minutes until it becomes satiny smooth. Rest the dough for 5 minutes, covered. Halve the dough and roll out each portion thinly to equal size. Brush one with a little of the beaten egg wash, and top with rows of teaspoons of stuffing, placing them about 2.5-cm/1-in apart. Cover with the second sheet of pasta. Press together around the stuffing. Using a pastry wheel, cut the dough into 2.5-cm/1-in squares. Sprinkle lightly with flour.

Have ready a large pan of boiling salted water, drop in the ravioli, bring back to the boil and cook for 5 minutes. Lift out with a slotted spoon and keep warm if cooked in two batches. Serve with tomato sauce (see Cook's Tip 81) and grated Parmesan cheese.

Cook's Tip

If you want to go Italian replace the Cheddar cheese in the filling with soft ricotta cheese. You will need to double the quantity to 225 g/8 oz. Made from whey, ricotta is lighter in flavour and texture than cream cheese, but not *tangy like curd cheese. Italian food stores, delicatessens, or good delicatessen counters in supermarkets stock it.*

162 | Macaroni Tomatoes

Preparation time
15 minutes

Cooking time
30 minutes

Oven temperature
180 C, 350 F, gas 4

Serves 4

Calories
255 per portion

You will need
4 beefsteak tomatoes
2 teaspoons oil
1 small onion, finely chopped
1 clove garlic, crushed
½ teaspoon mustard powder
pinch of paprika
2 drops of Tabasco sauce
salt and pepper
100 g/4 oz Cheddar cheese, grated
100 g/4 oz macaroni, cooked and
 drained

Cut a lid off the tomatoes, scoop out the centres to leave a thin wall of flesh in each. Place the pulp in a small saucepan with the oil, onion, garlic, mustard, paprika, Tabasco and seasoning. Cover and cook over a low heat for 10 minutes until pulpy, then press through a sieve and mix with the cheese and macaroni. Divide the mixture between the tomatoes and place the 'lids' on top. Bake for 15 to 20 minutes until the tomatoes are soft and the macaroni is beginning to brown. Serve at once.

Cook's Tip

If you happen to grow rosemary in your garden, then snip off a sprig, chop finely and add to the tomato pulp and the other seasonings before cooking and sieving.

163 | Corsican Cannelloni

Preparation time
15 minutes

Cooking time
55 minutes

Oven temperature
180C, 350F, gas 4

Serves 4

Calories
275 per portion

You will need
750 ml/1¼ pints boiling water
½ teaspoon vegetable oil
8 sheets 'No-need-to-precook'
   lasagne verde
225 g/8 oz frozen Ratatouille mix
100 g/4 oz frozen broad beans
2 teaspoons chopped fresh mixed
   herbs
freshly ground black pepper
1 (397-g/14-oz) can chopped
   tomatoes
100 g/4 oz mature Cheddar
   cheese, grated to serve

Pour the boiling water into a suitably shaped large shallow ovenproof dish. Add a few drops of oil. Slide the sheets of lasagne into the dish and leave for 4–5 minutes to soften. Cook the ratatouille and beans in boiling water in a medium saucepan for about 10 minutes or until cooked. Drain well. Add the herbs and freshly ground black pepper to taste.

Lift out the lasagne sheets from the water and drain. Spread out on a clean working surface or large board. Divide the vegetable filling between the lasagne then roll up the strips. Place the cannelloni in a shallow ovenproof dish and spoon over the tomatoes. Cook in a moderate oven for 30 minutes. To serve, sprinkle with grated cheese and place under a preheated hot grill until brown.

Freezer Tip

Cover the cannelloni with foil and freeze for up to 3 months. Reheat from frozen in a moderate oven (180C, 350F, gas 4) for about 30 minutes, then top with the cheese and place under a hot grill to brown.

164 | Tropical Salad

Preparation time
15 minutes

Cooking time
5 minutes

Serves 4

Calories
475 per portion

You will need
275 g/10 oz long-grain brown rice,
   cooked
50 g/2 oz dried coconut flakes
½ cucumber, unpeeled and cut into
   1-cm/½-in cubes
1 small ripe pineapple, peeled,
   cored and cut into 2.5-cm/1-in
   pieces
1 tablespoon olive oil
1 teaspoon lemon juice
salt and pepper
2 teaspoons olive oil for shallow
   frying
50 g/2 oz whole blanched almonds
pineapple leaves to garnish

Put the rice, coconut, cucumber and pineapple into a bowl. Add the oil and lemon juice and a little salt and pepper, taste and adjust the seasoning if necessary. Spoon the salad into a serving dish.

Heat the 2 teaspoons of oil in a small pan and quickly fry the almonds until golden brown. Scatter the almonds over the salad and garnish with the pineapple leaves.

Cook's Tip

To remove the centre core from a slice of pineapple, stamp out with a small plain pastry cutter.

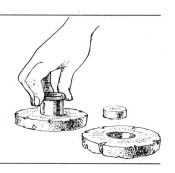

165 | *Szechuan Noodles*

Preparation time
10 minutes, plus 15 minutes to prepare cucumber

Cooking time
8 minutes

Serves 4

Calories
720 per portion

You will need
½ cucumber, cut into 1-cm/½-in dice
salt
small bunch of radishes, trimmed
1 spring onion, trimmed
450 g/1 lb fresh egg noodles or dried noodles
100 g/4 oz beansprouts
4 tablespoons peanut oil
3 4 tablespoons crunchy peanut butter
1 teaspoon sesame oil
25 g/1 oz salted peanuts, lightly crushed

Sprinkle the cucumber with salt and leave to drain for 15 minutes. Rinse and dry on absorbent kitchen paper. Slice a third of the radishes, leaving the remainder whole. Slice the spring onion diagonally. Meanwhile, cook the fresh noodles for 1 minute in boiling salted water, then drain thoroughly. Cook dried noodles as directed on the packet. Blanch the beansprouts in boiling water for 1 minute. Plunge into cold water, then drain thoroughly.

Fry the drained noodles quickly in 3 tablespoons of the peanut oil, stirring constantly. Transfer to a hot serving plate. Put the remaining oil into a pan with the peanut butter and sesame oil and heat gently. Pour over the noodles and mix lightly.

Arrange the prepared ingredients attractively on top and serve. Serve the remaining radishes in a bowl.

Cook's Tip

Peanut and sesame oil are used in this recipe as they add a distinctive flavour, favoured by the Chinese.

166 | *Rice and Beans*

Preparation time
10 minutes

Cooking time
40 minutes

Serves 4

Calories
475 per portion

You will need
225 g/8 oz long-grain brown rice
750 ml/1¼ pints boiling water
3 tablespoons sunflower oil
1 tablespoon red wine vinegar
salt and pepper
4 spring onions, chopped
1 (415-g/14½-oz) can red kidney beans
50 g/2 oz button mushrooms, sliced
225 g/8 oz tomatoes
4 tablespoons French dressing (see recipe 146)
50 g/2 oz black olives
chopped parsley to garnish

Cook the rice in the water for 40 minutes or until cooked and the water absorbed. Mix together the oil, vinegar and salt and pepper. Fluff up the rice with a fork and stir in the spring onions and oil and vinegar dressing. Cool.

Mix together the kidney beans and mushrooms. Slice the tomatoes and pour over the French dressing. Stir in the olives and salt and pepper to taste.

On a large serving plate, arrange a circle of rice salad round the edge, a circle of bean salad inside, and the tomato mixture in the middle. Scatter over the parsley to garnish.

Cook's Tip

The difference between black and green olives is that the black ones are ripe. Black olives vary from plump and succulent to small and wrinkly specimens. You can sometimes sample them before buying.

167 | Vegetable Risotto

Preparation time
15 minutes

Cooking time
55 60 minutes

Serves 4

Calories
465 per portion

You will need
4 tablespoons oil
1 onion, chopped
175 g/6 oz long-grain brown rice
3 cloves garlic, crushed
450 ml/¾ pint water
1 teaspoon salt
2 celery sticks, thinly sliced
1 red pepper, deseeded and diced
225 g/8 oz button mushrooms, sliced
1 (415-g/14½-oz) can red kidney beans
3 tablespoons chopped parsley
1 tablespoon soy sauce
50 g/2 oz cashew nuts, roasted
chopped parsley to garnish

Heat 2 tablespoons oil in a pan, add the onion and cook until softened, about 5 minutes. Add the rice and 2 cloves garlic and sautè, stirring, for 2 minutes. Pour in the water, add salt and bring to the boil. Cover and simmer gently for 35–40 minutes, until all the water has been absorbed and the rice is tender.

Heat the remaining oil in a large frying pan, add the celery and red pepper and cook for 5 minutes, until softened. Stir in the mushrooms and remaining garlic and sauté for 3 minutes. Add the cooked rice, drained kidney beans, parsley, soy sauce and nuts. Cook, stirring to mix, until the beans are heated through. Garnish with parsley, and serve with a green salad.

Cook's Tip

It is unnecessary to wash cultivated mushrooms, as well as being detrimental to their nutritional content. Simply wipe them with a clean, damp cloth before use.

168 | Creamy Curried Pasta

Preparation time
10 minutes

Cooking time
15 minutes

Serves 4

Calories
465 per portion

You will need
225 g/8 oz pasta shapes
salt and pepper
3 tablespoons olive oil
1 tablespoon white wine vinegar
1 teaspoon chopped fresh mint
1 medium onion, finely chopped
4 tablespoons dry vermouth
2 teaspoons mild concentrated curry paste
2 teaspoons apricot jam
50 g/2 oz slivered or flaked almonds, toasted
150 ml/¼ pint soured cream
½ bunch watercress, chopped

Cook the pasta in plenty of boiling salted water for 10–12 minutes or until just tender. Drain.

Meanwhile, mix together the oil, vinegar, mint and salt and pepper to make a dressing. Pour over the hot pasta and leave until cold.

Place the onion and vermouth in a pan and bring to the boil. Simmer for 3 minutes, then cool. Stir the curry paste and jam into the pasta mixture. Stir in the onion mixture. Turn the mixture into a serving dish and scatter the almonds on top. Mix together the soured cream and watercress and serve separately with the salad.

Cook's Tip

Choose small, chunky shapes, such as orecchiette, little ears, or conchiglie, shells, which provide ideal surfaces for the delicious dressing; or lumachine, little snails, which trap the sauce like containers.

Pastry Specialities

A freshly baked flan or pie is a fragrant and welcome ingredient on any menu and, when served with a salad, makes a sustaining, nutritious meal. Many of the pastry specialities in this chapter help create a sense of occasion – for example, Carrot Aigrettes or Gougère look quite festive as well as tasting delicious.

169 | Carrot Aigrettes

(Illustrated on title page)

Preparation time
15 minutes

Cooking time
30 minutes

Serves 4–6

Calories
415–315 per portion

You will need
65 g/2½ oz plain flour
salt and pepper
pinch of cayenne·
50 g/2 oz butter
150 ml/¼ pint water
2 eggs, lightly beaten
50 g/2 oz mature Cheddar cheese, grated
100 g/4 oz carrots, finely grated
50 g/2 oz hazelnuts, finely chopped
oil for deep-frying
grated Parmesan cheese to garnish

Sift the flour and seasonings on to a plate. Put the butter and water in a heavy-based saucepan and place over a low heat until the butter has melted, then increase the heat and bring to the boil.

Remove from the heat and tip in all the flour mixture. Beat with a wooden spoon until the liquid has been absorbed. Continue to beat the mixture until it leaves the sides of the pan clean. Allow to cool.

Beat in the eggs, one at a time, until the mixture becomes shiny. Beat in the cheese, carrots and nuts.

Heat the oil for deep-frying. Drop in a few teaspoonfuls of the mixture at a time so that they have room to puff up. Fry in batches for 4–6 minutes until the aigrettes are puffy and golden brown. Remove with a slotted spoon and drain on absorbent kitchen paper.

Pile the aigrettes into a warmed dish and serve sprinkled with grated Parmesan cheese.

Cook's Tip

To test whether the oil is hot enough for the aigrettes, carefully drop in a cube of day-old bread. It should turn golden in 1 minute.

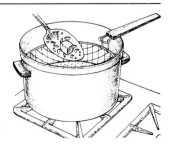

170 | Gougère

Preparation time
30 minutes

Cooking time
1 hour

Oven temperature
200 C, 400 F, gas 6

Serves 4

Calories
425 per portion

You will need
For the choux pastry
50 g/2 oz margarine
150 ml/¼ pint water
65 g/2½ oz wholemeal flour
2 eggs
50 g/2 oz Cheddar cheese, grated

For the filling
2 tablespoons oil
1 onion, chopped
225 g/8 oz mushrooms, sliced
2 cloves garlic, crushed
1 tablespoon wholemeal flour
150 ml/¼ pint vegetable stock
75 g/3 oz walnuts, chopped
2 tablespoons chopped parsley
salt and pepper

Melt the margarine in a large pan, add the water and bring to the boil. Add the flour all at once and beat until the mixture leaves the sides of the pan. Cool slightly, then add the eggs, one at a time, beating vigorously until glossy. Beat in the cheese. Spoon the pastry around the edge of a greased 1.15-litre/2-pint ovenproof dish. Heat the oil and cook the onion until softened. Add the mushrooms and garlic and fry for 2 minutes. Stir in the flour, then add the stock and bring to the boil, stirring. Cook for 3 minutes until thickened. Reserve 2 tablespoons of the walnuts and stir the remainder into the mushroom mixture, with the parsley and seasoning. Pour the filling into the centre of the dish and sprinkle with the reserved walnuts. Bake in a moderately hot oven for 40–45 minutes.

Cook's Tip

To avoid choux pastry collapsing, do not open the oven door to check the pastry until three-quarters of the cooking time is completed.

171 | Broccoli Flan

Preparation time
35 minutes, plus 30 minutes to chill

Cooking time
50 55 minutes

Oven temperature
200 C, 400 F, gas 6
then
190 C, 375 F, gas 5

Serves 4

Calories
530 per portion

You will need
1 quantity shortcrust pastry (recipe 175)

For the filling
225 g/8 oz frozen broccoli, defrosted
100 g/4 oz Danish Blue cheese
3 eggs, beaten
150 ml/¼ pint single cream
salt and pepper
¼ teaspoon ground nutmeg

Make the shortcrust pastry as instructed in recipe 175. Roll out on a lightly floured surface to line a 20-cm/8-in flan dish or tin and chill for 30 minutes. Bake blind in a moderately hot oven for 15 minutes (see Cook's Tip 173). Reduce the oven setting to the lower temperature.

Thoroughly drain the defrosted broccoli on absorbent kitchen paper and cut into 2.5-cm/1-in pieces, breaking up any large florets. Place over the base of the flan. Beat the cheese to soften slightly. Add the eggs and beat until smooth. Mix in the cream, seasoning and nutmeg and pour over the broccoli. Cook for 35–40 minutes until the filling has set.

Serve with baked jacket potatoes and a tomato salad.

Cook's Tip

Danish blue cheese (Danablu) is white with blue veins. The texture should be creamy and slightly crumbly. Avoid any cheeses that have a dull bloom or show signs of sweating.

172 | Mushroom Flan

Preparation time
35 minutes, plus 1 hour to set the glaze

Cooking time
55 60 minutes

Oven temperature
200 C, 400 F, gas 6
then
180 C, 350 F, gas 4

Serves 6

Calories
425 per portion

You will need
1 quantity shortcrust pastry (recipe 175)
1 tablespoon horseradish mustard
225 g/8 oz flat mushrooms
4 tablespoons oil
350 g/12 oz cottage cheese
2 eggs, beaten
1 tablespoon chopped parsley
salt and pepper
1½ teaspoons agar-agar or 2 teaspoons powdered gelatine
200 ml/7 fl oz very hot clear vegetable stock

Roll out the pastry to line a 23-cm/9-in flan tin. Bake blind in a moderately hot oven for 15 minutes then remove the beans and cook for 5 minutes (see Cook's Tip 173). Reduce the oven temperature. Spread the flan case with the mustard. Reserve one large mushroom; slice the remainder. Heat the oil and cook all the mushrooms in two batches until softened. Drain well on absorbent kitchen paper and scatter half over the mustard. Beat the cheese, eggs, parsley and seasoning together, then turn into the flan case. Cook in a moderate oven for 30 minutes. Place the cooked whole mushroom in the centre of the flan and surround with the reserved mushroom slices. Dissolve the agar-agar or gelatine in the hot stock, use to glaze the flan when half set.

Cook's Tip

The fully mature open or flat mushrooms are the richest in flavour. When a mushroom is small and firm it is called a button; if a little larger but still closed underneath, it is called a cup mushroom.

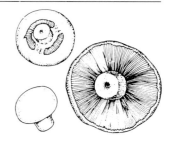

173 | Watercress and Brie Quiche

Preparation time
25 minutes

Cooking time
50 minutes

Oven temperature
200 C, 400 F, gas 6
then
180 C, 350 F, gas 4

Serves 6

Calories
445 per portion

You will need
For the pastry
100 g/4 oz plain flour
100 g/4 oz wholemeal flour
½ teaspoon salt
50 g/2 oz concentrated butter,
    softened
25 g/1 oz lard
about 3 tablespoons water

For the filling
275 g/10 oz ripe Brie cheese
300 ml/½ pint milk
100 g/4 oz watercress, trimmed
3 eggs, beaten
1 teaspoon mustard powder
freshly ground black pepper

Sift the flours and salt into a bowl or food processor, adding the bran remaining in the sieve to the bowl. Rub in the fats or process until the mixture resembles bread-crumbs. Add just enough water to mix to a firm dough. Roll out on a lightly floured surface and use to line a 23-cm/9-in loose-bottomed flan tin. Bake blind in a moderately hot oven for 10 minutes (see Cook's Tip).

Meanwhile remove the rind from the Brie. Dice the cheese, place in a saucepan with the milk and stir over a low heat until blended. Remove from the heat, stir in the watercress, beaten eggs, mustard and seasoning. Pour into the flan case and cook in a moderate oven for 35 minutes. Cool slightly before removing from the tin.

Cook's Tip

To bake blind, line the pie shell with greaseproof paper and fill with baking beans. Bake in a moderately hot oven for 10 minutes, then remove paper and beans. Proceed as in the recipe above. If, however, the pie shell is to have a cold (or *separately cooked) filling, bake for 15 minutes with the beans, and a further 5 minutes after the beans and paper have been removed.*

174 | Rainbow Quiche

Preparation time
25 minutes

Cooking time
35 40 minutes

Oven temperature
220 C, 425 F, gas 7
then
190 C, 375 F, gas 5

Serves 4

Calories
555 per portion

You will need
For the pastry
100 g/4 oz wholemeal flour
50 g/2 oz plain flour
pinch of salt
50 g/2 oz concentrated butter,
    softened
2 tablespoons poppy seeds
2 3 tablespoons water

For the filling
15 g/½ oz concentrated butter
1 red onion, sliced
175 g/6 oz red, green or yellow
    pepper, deseeded and sliced
1 courgette, sliced
1 tablespoon chopped basil
freshly ground black pepper
100 g/4 oz Cheddar cheese, grated
1 tomato, sliced
3 eggs
150 ml/¼ pint single cream
basil leaves to garnish (optional)

Mix the flours and salt in a large bowl and rub in the butter. Stir in the poppy seeds and enough water to mix to a firm dough. Roll out and use to line a 19-cm/7½-in flan tin. Melt the butter for the filling in a large pan and fry the onion, pepper and courgette until softened. Place in the flan case with the basil, black pepper, grated cheese and tomato. Beat the eggs and cream and pour over. Cook in a hot oven for 15 minutes, reducing to moderately hot for a further 15 minutes, until set. Garnish with basil if liked.

Cook's Tip

If possible, do use the red or purple onion, and red, yellow or green peppers, or even a combination, to make this quiche live up to its name.

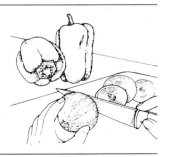

175 | Leek Flans

Preparation time
25 minutes

Cooking time
45 minutes

Oven temperature
200 C, 400 F, gas 6
then
190 C, 375 F, gas 5

Serves 4

Calories
540 per portion

You will need

For the shortcrust pastry
175 g 6 oz wholemeal or plain flour
75 g 3 oz butter
2–3 tablespoons cold water

For the filling
2 medium leeks, halved
1 celery stick
25 g 1 oz butter
125 g 4½ oz Danish Bolina cheese
2 eggs, beaten
150 ml ¼ pint milk
salt and pepper
¼ teaspoon grated nutmeg
15 g ½ oz flaked almonds (optional)

Place the flour in a bowl and rub in the butter until the mixture resembles fine breadcrumbs. Add enough water to make a stiff dough. Roll out on a lightly floured board and use to line 4 individual flan tins. Bake blind in a moderately hot oven for 10 minutes, removing the baking beans and greaseproof paper after 7 minutes (see Cook's Tip 173). Reduce oven temperature.

Slice the leeks and celery. Melt the butter and cook the vegetables, covered, for 5–7 minutes until softened. Crumble the cheese into a bowl, beat to soften, then work in the eggs, a little at a time, to make a smooth mixture. Stir in the milk, seasoning and nutmeg.

Divide the vegetables between the flan cases, pour the cheese mixture over, scatter with the almonds, if using, and bake for 20–25 minutes.

Cook's Tip

The flans make a superb summer starter; alternatively, make them a feature of a summer picnic basket – much more impressive than a pile of sandwiches!

176 | Carrot and Cumin Quiche

Preparation time
20 minutes

Cooking time
40 minutes

Oven temperature
200 C, 400 F, gas 6

Serves 4

Calories
510 per portion

You will need
175 g/6 oz plain flour
pinch of salt
75 g/3 oz margarine
2 tablespoons cold water

For the filling
175 g/6 oz cooked carrots
1 (415-g/14½-oz) can butter beans, drained
¾ teaspoon ground cumin
3 eggs
100 g/4 oz Cheddar cheese, grated

Sift the flour and salt into a bowl. Cut the margarine into small pieces and rub into the flour until the mixture resembles fine breadcrumbs. Add enough water to mix to a dough. Roll out on a lightly floured board to line a 20-cm/8-in flan dish or ring placed on a baking tray.

To make the filling, blend the carrots, beans, cumin and eggs in a liquidiser. Pour half the mixture into the flan case, sprinkle with half the cheese, cover with the remaining mixture and top with remaining cheese. Bake for 40 minutes. Serve hot or cold.

If liked, follow the attractive serving suggestion in the photograph by bordering the quiche on a serving plate with mixed salad leaves, for example, curly endive and radicchio.

Cook's Tip

When buying, look for firm bright orange carrots without splits. From the point of view of nutrition, they are best eaten raw, but if cooked whole, and scrubbed rather than peeled, you will still be rewarded with plenty of vitamin A.

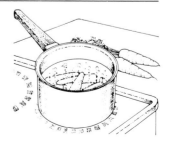

177 | Vegetable Pie

Preparation time
45 minutes

Cooking time
55 65 minutes

Oven temperature
190C, 375F, gas 5

Serves 4

Calories
650 per portion

You will need
1 turnip, diced and cooked
1 parsnip, diced and cooked
4 carrots, diced and cooked
100 g/4 oz cooked yellow split
   peas
1 leek, washed, sliced and cooked
2 courgettes, diced and cooked

For the sauce
40 g/1½ oz butter
2 tablespoons plain flour
4 tablespoons natural yogurt
250 ml/8 fl oz milk
salt and pepper
1 teaspoon mixed herbs
1 teaspoon paprika

For the cheese pastry
100 g/4 oz plain flour
100 g/4 oz wholemeal flour
100 g/4 oz margarine
100 g/4 oz low-fat hard cheese,
   grated (for example Shape)
2 3 tablespoons cold water
1 egg, beaten, to glaze

Put the vegetables in a pie dish. Whisk all the sauce ingredients in a pan over a low heat until smooth and thickened. Pour over the vegetables. Mix the flours in a bowl, then rub in the fat and stir in the cheese. Mix in enough water to bind the pastry. Roll out to a shape slightly larger than the top of the pie dish. Cover the pie, sealing the edges well. Use trimmings for decoration. Brush with beaten egg. Bake for 40–50 minutes.

Cook's Tip

Pastry trimmings bring out the artist in every cook. Shape leaves or flowers, make letters that spell out a guest's name or use pastry cutters to add decorative shapes like Christmas trees or hearts.

178 | Leek Pie

Preparation time
25 minutes

Cooking time
45 minutes

Oven temperature
200C, 400F, gas 6

Serves 4

Calories
455 per portion

You will need

For the shortcrust pastry
225 g/8 oz plain flour
pinch of salt
100 g/4 oz margarine
3 tablespoons cold water

For the filling
6 large leeks, sliced
25 g/1 oz butter
300 ml/½ pint creamy milk
2 eggs
salt and pepper
25 g/1 oz Cheddar cheese, grated

Sift the flour and salt into a bowl. Cut the margarine into small pieces and rub into the flour until the mixture resembles fine breadcrumbs. Add enough water to mix to a dough. Roll out half on a lightly floured board to line an 18-cm/7-inch sandwich cake tin.

To make the filling, cook the leeks with the butter in a large saucepan until softened, about 5 minutes. Cool and place in the pie case. Beat the milk and eggs together and season well. Pour over the leeks and sprinkle with the cheese. Roll out remaining pastry and use to cover filling. Seal the edges with water. Brush dough with a little extra milk. Bake for 40 minutes or until golden. Serve hot.

Cook's Tip

A piecrust may be decorated before it is placed on the pie. Roll out the pastry to a round 2.5 cm/1 in larger than the top of the pie, cut out a simple design, then flip the pastry over a rolling pin to transfer to the pie.

179 | Pumpkin Pie

Preparation time
30 minutes, plus 15
minutes to chill

Cooking time
1 hour

Oven temperature
220 C, 425 F, gas 7
then
190 C, 375 F, gas 5

Serves 6–8

Calories
455 340 per portion

You will need
450 g 1 lb pumpkin
salt and pepper
50 g 2 oz butter
1 large onion, sliced
225 g 8 oz potatoes
100 g 4 oz cooked peas
100 g 4 oz Cheshire cheese,
  crumbled
1 (368-g 13-oz) packet frozen puff
  pastry, defrosted
beaten egg to glaze

Peel the pumpkin and cut the flesh into cubes, discarding the seeds. Cook the cubes in simmering salted water for 15 minutes. Drain very thoroughly. Melt the butter in a pan and gently cook the onion until browned. Mix with the pumpkin. Dice and cook the potatoes; add to the pumpkin with the peas, cheese and seasoning. Roll out the pastry thinly and cut out two circles – one 25 cm / 10 in in diameter, the other 30 cm / 12 in in diameter. Place the smaller circle on a greased baking tray. Pile the filling on the pastry, leaving a 1-cm/½-in border. Brush the border with beaten egg, then top with the second pastry circle. Seal the edges and decorate with pastry trimmings. Glaze and bake in a hot oven for 15 minutes, then reduce the oven temperature to moderately hot and bake for a further 15 minutes.

Cook's Tip

Pumpkins shouldn't be reserved for Halloween lanterns. A nutritious vegetable, high in vitamin A, it is delicious roasted in the oven or boiled and mashed with a little butter and lots of black pepper and nutmeg.

180 | Family Pie

Preparation time
35 40 minutes

Cooking time
45 minutes

Oven temperature
200 C, 400 F, gas 6

Serves 6

Calories
350 per portion

You will need
175 g / 6 oz wholemeal self-raising
  flour
1 teaspoon mixed dried herbs
100 g / 4 oz margarine
3 tablespoons water
1 tablespoon vegetable oil

For the filling
100 g / 4 oz carrots, sliced
100 g / 4 oz leeks, washed and
  sliced
100 g / 4 oz celery, sliced
100 g / 4 oz cauliflower florets
300 ml / ½ pint water
about 300 ml / ½ pint milk
25 g / 1 oz butter
25 g / 1 oz plain flour
salt and pepper
2 tablespoons chopped parsley
1 (225-g/8-oz) can red kidney
  beans, drained
beaten egg, for brushing

Use the first five ingredients to make shortcrust pastry. Cook the vegetables in the water until tender. Strain and make up the cooking liquid to 600 ml / 1 pint with milk. Whisk this with the butter, flour and seasoning over a low heat until boiling and thickened. Mix the vegetables, sauce, parsley and beans in a 1.2-litre / 2-pint pie dish.

Roll out the pastry to cover the pie, sealing the edges well. Use trimmings to decorate the top and glaze with egg. Bake in a moderately hot oven for 25–30 minutes.

Cook's Tip

Two ways to make shortcrust: rub the fat into the flour, when crumbly bind with liquid; a quick way is to use chilled, hard fat, then grate it into the flour and stir in the liquid to bind.

181 | Mushroom Vols-au-Vent

Preparation time
20 minutes

Cooking time
35 minutes

Oven temperature
220C, 425F, gas 7

Makes 12

Calories
130 per vol-au-vent

You will need
12 frozen puff pastry vol-au-vent
  cases
beaten egg to glaze

For the filling
1 tablespoon oil
1 onion, finely chopped
100 g/4 oz carrot, diced
225 g/8 oz mushrooms, sliced
2 tablespoons plain flour
200 ml/7 fl oz skimmed milk
¼ teaspoon dried sage
salt and pepper
75 g/3 oz Sage Derby cheese,
  cubed
salad ingredients to garnish

Place the vol-au-vent cases on a dampened baking tray. Brush with beaten egg and bake in a hot oven for 15–20 minutes, or as directed on the packet.

Heat the oil and cook the onion and carrot slowly in a covered pan for 5 minutes. Add the mushrooms and cook for a further 3 minutes. Stir in the flour and cook for 1 minute. Gradually add the milk and bring to the boil, stirring. Add the sage, seasoning and cheese. Spoon into the cooked vol-au-vent cases and serve at once, garnished with salad ingredients.

Cook's Tip

Don't save vols-au-vent for parties and weddings. With interesting fillings they make tasty suppers or quick starters for unexpected guests. Children enjoy them too, particularly if they can choose their own fillings.

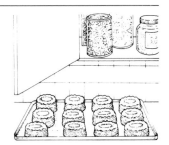

182 | Feta Parcels

Preparation time
30 minutes

Cooking time
35 minutes

Oven temperature
180C, 350F, gas 4

Makes 6

Calories
570 per parcel

You will need
150 g/5 oz butter
1 large onion, chopped
675 g/1½ lb frozen chopped
  spinach, defrosted and drained
225 g/8 oz feta cheese
2 bunches spring onions, chopped
25 g/1 oz chopped parsley
1 tablespoon dill
salt and pepper
2 eggs, beaten
10 sheets filo pastry

Melt 25 g/1 oz of the butter and cook the onion for 5 minutes until softened. Place the spinach in a bowl, crumble the cheese over it, then stir in the spring onions, parsley, dill, seasoning and eggs and mix well.

Melt the remaining butter. Unwrap the filo pastry sheets. Place one on the work surface and brush with some of the butter, cover with a second sheet and brush with butter. Continue until 5 sheets have been brushed with butter. Brush the top sheet. (Cover any pastry not being used with a cloth.) Cut the layered pastry into three, widthways. Divide half of the spinach mixture between the strips leaving a 2.5-cm/1-in border down the long edges. Fold in the long edges, brush with butter and fold up the short edges to make parcels 13 × 9 cm/5 × 3½ in. Place on a baking tray, mark the tops and brush with butter.

Repeat with the remaining filo pastry sheets and spinach mixture. Bake for 25–30 minutes until golden.

Cook's Tip

Filo pastry is available in continental delicatessens and large supermarkets. If it's not to hand, the parcels may be made with puff pastry instead. Use 1 (368-g/13-oz) packet, defrosted. Cut it in half and roll each piece to a rectangle 30 × *37.5 cm/12 × 15 in. The parcels will be slightly smaller.*

183 | Quick Pasties

Preparation time
15 minutes

Cooking time
20 25 minutes

Oven temperature
220 C. 425 F, gas 7

Serves 4

Calories
540 per portion

You will need
225 g 8 oz shortcrust pastry (see recipe 178)
4 vegeburgers
100 g 4 oz cream cheese
½ teaspoon oregano or marjoram
1 clove garlic, crushed
4 large mushrooms, stalks removed and chopped
beaten egg or milk to glaze

Roll out the pastry on a lightly floured board and cut out 8 rounds slightly larger than the vegeburgers. Place a vegeburger on four of the circles. Mix together the cream cheese, herb, garlic, and chopped mushroom stalks and spread equal amounts on each burger. Top with a mushroom. Cover each with a circle of pastry and seal the edges with water. Flute the edges and brush with beaten egg or milk. Decorate with pastry 'leaves', if liked. Bake for 20–25 minutes or until crisp and golden. Serve hot or cold.

184 | Blue Cheese Parcels

Preparation time
35 minutes

Cooking time
35 40 minutes

Oven temperature
200 C, 400 F, gas 6
then
180 C, 350 F, gas 4

Makes 4

Calories
655 per parcel

You will need
225 g/8 oz wholemeal flour
100 g/4 oz plain flour
100 g/4 oz butter
100 g/4 oz Danish Blue cheese, grated
about 4 tablespoons water

For the filling
175 g/6 oz carrots, coarsely grated
225 g/8 oz potatoes, diced
175 g/6 oz onions, finely chopped
25 g/1 oz Danish Blue cheese, grated
1½ teaspoons dried mixed herbs
3 tablespoons vegetable stock
salt and pepper

Place the flours in a bowl and rub in the butter. Stir in the grated cheese and add enough water to give a soft but not sticky dough. Knead lightly and divide the dough into four equal pieces. Roll out each on a lightly floured surface and cut to an 18-cm/7-in circle, using a tea plate as a guide.

Mix together the ingredients for the filling, seasoning to taste. Divide the mixture evenly between the pastry rounds, then lightly dampen the edges and draw together to meet in the centre, pressing well to seal. Place on a baking tray and cook in a moderately hot oven for 20 minutes, then reduce to moderate for a further 15–20 minutes. Serve hot or cold.

Cook's Tip

It's worth pointing out that home-made Vegetable Burgers (see recipe 85) are delicious when cooked in this way.

Cook's Tip

Save time by grating the butter into the flour mixture. Grate the cheese first, then the firm butter. Run the grater under hot water and it will be very easy to clean.

185 | Cheese and Onion Flans

Preparation time
30 minutes, plus 20
minutes to chill

Cooking time
30 35 minutes

**Oven
temperature**
200 C, 400 F, gas 6
then
180 C, 350 F, gas 4

Makes 4

Calories
515 per flan

You will need
175 g/6 oz self-raising wholemeal
flour
75 g/3 oz margarine
2 tablespoons crunchy peanut
butter
1 2 tablespoons water

For the filling
1 tablespoon groundnut oil
2 onions, thinly sliced
1 egg
150 ml/¼ pint milk
salt and pepper
75 g/3 oz Edam cheese, grated
25 g/1 oz salted peanuts, chopped

Place the flour in a bowl, add the margarine and rub in until the mixture resembles fine breadcrumbs. Stir in the peanut butter and sufficient water to form a firm dough. Knead lightly then chill for 20 minutes. Roll out on a floured surface to line four 10-cm/4-in flan dishes.

Heat the oil in a pan, add the onions and cook gently until very soft, about 5 minutes. Cool slightly. Beat together the egg, milk and seasoning. Divide the onion between the flan cases and pour the egg mixture over the top. Sprinkle with the cheese and peanuts. Bake in a moderately hot oven for 15 minutes, then reduce to moderate for a further 10–15 minutes until the filling is set and golden brown. Serve warm or cold.

Cook's Tip

**To make a large flan, roll out
the pastry to line a 20-cm/8-in
flan dish. Fill and bake in a
moderately hot oven for 15
minutes, as above, then
reduce to moderate for a
further 20–25 minutes.**

186 | Tomato Triangles

Preparation time
20 minutes

Cooking time
20 minutes

Oven temperature
220 C, 425 F, gas 7

Makes 4

Calories
405 per triangle

You will need
225 g/8 oz frozen wholemeal puff
pastry, defrosted
beaten egg to glaze

For the filling
250 g/9 oz ripe tomatoes
225 g/8 oz feta cheese, mashed
1 clove garlic, finely chopped
2 tablespoons chopped parsley
2 tablespoons fresh wholewheat
breadcrumbs

To make the filling, blanch the tomatoes in boiling water for 30 seconds. Rinse in cold water and peel. Dice the tomatoes, removing the core and the seeds. Mix the tomatoes with the cheese, garlic, parsley and breadcrumbs.

Roll out the pastry into a square just larger than 25 × 25 cm/10 × 10 in. Cut out four 13-cm/5-in squares. Divide the filling between the pastry squares and dampen the edges. Fold the pieces of pastry in half diagonally and press the edges with a fork to seal in the filling. Glaze with beaten egg. Bake in a hot oven for 20 minutes until puffed and golden.

Cook's Tip

**These triangles make perfect
picnic fare. When cool, pack
them in rigid plastic boxes,
using crumpled greaseproof
paper to fill up any gaps and
prevent them moving (and
possibly disintegrating) en
route.**

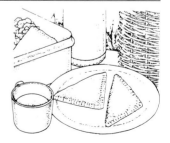

187 | Mushroom Puffs

Preparation time
20 minutes

Cooking time
3 minutes

Makes 18

Calories
55 per puff, before
frying
Total for dressing 540

You will need
225 g 8 oz frozen wholemeal puff
    pastry, defrosted
18 medium-sized button
    mushrooms
oil for deep frying

For the dressing
100 g 4 oz Stilton cheese, finely
    crumbled or grated
150 ml ¼ pint natural yogurt
2 tablespoons chopped coriander
    leaves or snipped chives

Roll out the pastry to a 30-cm/12-in square. Cut the square into six 10 × 15-cm/4 × 6-in strips. Cut each of these strips into 5-cm/2-in squares (total 36).

Clean the mushrooms, remove the stalks and use for another recipe, and place each mushroom on a square of pastry. Dampen the edges with water and place a pastry square on top. Press the edges together to seal. Heat the oil to 180 C, 360 F and deep fry the pastry squares a few at a time for 2–3 minutes or until puffed and golden. Drain on absorbent kitchen paper and keep warm while cooking the remainder.

To make the dressing, mash the Stilton with the yogurt until creamy. Stir in the coriander or chives. Serve the puffs hot or warm with the dressing.

188 | Cheese and Apple Pie

Preparation time
10 minutes

Cooking time
30 minutes

Oven temperature
200 C, 400 F, gas 6

Serves 4

Calories
700 per portion

You will need
225 g/8 oz frozen puff pastry,
    defrosted
50 g/2 oz butter
1 large onion, finely chopped
450 g/1 lb cooking apples, peeled,
    cored and sliced
75 g/3 oz walnuts, chopped
225 g/8 oz Sage Derby cheese,
    sliced
salt and pepper
a little beaten egg or milk to glaze

Roll out the pastry on a lightly floured working surface until slightly larger than the top of a 1.15-litre/2-pint pie dish. Cut a strip from the edge and use to line the dampened rim of the dish. Melt the butter in a frying pan, add the onion and apple and cook for 5 minutes until slightly softened. Layer the onion and apple mixture with the walnuts and cheese in the pie dish, seasoning each layer. Dampen the pastry strip and cover with the pastry lid. Trim and flute the edges. If liked, use the pastry trimmings to decorate. Brush with beaten egg or milk and bake for 20–25 minutes until crisp and golden.

Cook's Tip

Do not add too many pastry-coated mushrooms to the oil at a time or the temperature will drop and the pastry will fail to puff up properly.

Cook's Tip

The combination of onion, apple, walnuts and cheese would be just as good in a double crust pie and in that form would be ideal for a picnic. Serve it with a simple salad (transported separately).

Suppers and Snacks

Choose a super-speedy snack when in a hurry, a gratin or bake for a satisfying supper dish. All are highly nutritious. The recipes in this chapter make good use of a large number of store-cupboard items, as well as incorporating fresh ingredients, such as vegetables, herbs, fresh cheeses and eggs.

189 | Cheese and Semolina Bake

(Illustrated on title page)

Preparation time
10 minutes, plus 10 minutes to stand

Cooking time
35 minutes

Oven temperature
200C, 400F, gas 6
then
240C, 475F, gas 9

Serves 4

Calories
335 per portion

You will need
250 ml/8 fl oz vegetable stock
250 ml/8 fl oz milk
salt and white pepper
grated nutmeg
100 g/4 oz wholemeal semolina
2 eggs
150 g/5 oz Emmental cheese, grated
25 g/1 oz butter
2 tablespoons chopped mixed herbs

Bring the vegetable stock to the boil in a pan with the milk and a little salt, pepper and nutmeg. Remove the pan from the heat and gradually stir in the semolina. Cover the pan and leave to stand for about 10 minutes.

Beat the eggs with a fork until frothy. Stir into the semolina mixture with half the Emmental. Grease a baking dish with a little of the butter. Fill with the semolina mixture and smooth the top. Bake in a moderately hot oven for 10 minutes. Increase the temperature to very hot. Bake for 10 minutes more.

Mix the remaining Emmental with the herbs and spread over the dish. Dot with the remaining butter and bake for a further 10 minutes until the top is golden brown. Serve with a colourful mixed salad.

Cook's Tip

Semolina is a granular durum (hard) wheat flour rich in protein. It is often used with plain flour to increase the gluten content and so enable pastries to be made which hold their shape successfully.

190 | Aubergines au Gratin

Preparation time
15 minutes, plus 15 minutes to prepare aubergine

Cooking time
20 minutes

Oven temperature
220C, 425F, gas 7

Serves 4

Calories
290 per portion

You will need
2 large aubergines, cut into large cubes
salt and pepper
3 tomatoes, sliced
1 courgette, sliced
1 bunch of mixed herbs (e.g. parsley, basil, rosemary), chopped
150 ml/¼ pint double cream
2 eggs, beaten
15 g/½ oz butter
1 clove garlic, peeled and halved
2 tablespoons dry white breadcrumbs

Sprinkle the aubergines with salt and leave to drain for about 15 minutes. Rinse and wipe dry with absorbent kitchen paper. Arrange alternate layers of aubergine, tomato and courgette in a greased ovenproof dish. Sprinkle with the chopped herbs.

Mix the cream with the eggs, add salt and pepper to taste and pour over the vegetable mixture.

Melt the butter in a small saucepan, add the garlic and fry for a few minutes until golden brown. Remove and discard the garlic. Add the breadcrumbs to the garlic-flavoured butter and cook for 1–2 minutes. Sprinkle over the vegetables in the dish. Cook in a hot oven for 12–15 minutes, or until golden brown. Serve hot.

Cook's Tip

Individual cloves of garlic vary enormously in size. When a recipe calls for 1 clove garlic, choose one about the size of the top joint on your little finger.

191 | Red Pepper Macaroni Cheese

Preparation time
20 minutes

Cooking time
20 minutes

Serves 4

Calories
740 per portion

You will need
25 g / 1 oz butter
25 g / 1 oz plain flour
750 ml / 1¼ pints milk
salt and pepper
½ teaspoon prepared English
  mustard
large pinch of cayenne
¼ teaspoon grated nutmeg
1 red pepper, deseeded, cut into
  1-cm / ½-in dice and blanched
225 g / 8 oz mature Cheddar
  cheese, grated
175 g / 6 oz wholewheat macaroni,
  cooked
2 tablespoons chopped parsley
12 triangles wholewheat bread,
  fried, to garnish

Melt the butter in a large saucepan over a low heat, then add the flour. Cook for 2 minutes, stirring. Gradually add the milk and bring to the boil, stirring constantly. Simmer for 2–3 minutes. Add salt, pepper, mustard, cayenne, nutmeg, red pepper and 200 g / 7 oz of the cheese. Add the macaroni and parsley, and heat through. Transfer to a flameproof dish, top with the remaining cheese and grill to brown. Garnish and serve.

192 | Crumbly Nut Roast

Preparation time
30 minutes

Cooking time
1 hour 10 minutes

Oven temperature
220 C, 425 F, gas 7

Serves 4

Calories
535 per portion

You will need
40 g / 1½ oz butter
1 medium onion, chopped
1 celery stick, trimmed,
  scrubbed and chopped
225 g / 8 oz mixed nuts (walnuts,
  brazils and hazelnuts in equal
  quantities), coarsely chopped
3 large tomatoes, peeled and
  chopped
175 g / 6 oz fresh wholewheat
  breadcrumbs
salt and pepper
1 teaspoon mixed dried herbs
¼ teaspoon chilli powder
2 eggs, lightly beaten

Oil a 450-g / 1-lb loaf tin and line the base with oiled greaseproof paper. Melt the butter in a large saucepan and fry the onion and celery gently for 5 minutes without browning. Add the nuts, tomatoes, breadcrumbs, salt and pepper, mixed herbs and chilli. Add the eggs and mix to a fairly soft consistency, then taste and adjust seasoning if necessary.

Spoon the mixture into the prepared tin, cover with oiled foil and bake in a hot oven for 50–60 minutes, or until set.

Ease off the foil and run a knife around the sides of the tin. Turn the loaf out on to a warm dish and serve with salad and buttered pasta, if liked.

Cook's Tip

To add extra flavour, place a few tomato slices and some chopped fried onion on the base of the dish before adding the macaroni cheese.

Cook's Tip

The uncooked nut roast mixture can be prepared up to 8 hours in advance and kept covered.

193 | *Courgette Gratin*

Preparation time
20 minutes

Cooking time
45 minutes

Oven temperature
180 C, 350 F, gas 4

Serves 4

Calories
320 per portion

You will need
2 tablespoons oil
2 onions, sliced
1 clove garlic, crushed
350 g/12 oz courgettes, sliced
1 tablespoon chopped parsley
1 teaspoon chopped thyme
salt and pepper
4 large tomatoes, peeled and
sliced
25 g/1 oz margarine
25 g/1 oz wholemeal flour
300 ml/½ pint milk
100 g/4 oz Cheddar cheese, grated
1 tablespoon fresh wholewheat
breadcrumbs

Heat the oil in a pan and cook the onions until softened. Add the garlic, courgettes, herbs and salt and pepper to taste, and cook for 5 minutes, stirring occasionally. Put half in an ovenproof dish and top with tomatoes, then spread the remaining mixture on top.

Melt the margarine in a saucepan over a low heat, then add the flour. Cook for 2 minutes, stirring. Gradually add the milk and bring the sauce to the boil, stirring constantly. Simmer gently for 2–3 minutes. Add half of the cheese, and salt and pepper to taste, then pour over the courgettes. Sprinkle with the breadcrumbs, then the remaining cheese. Bake in a moderate oven for 30 minutes until golden.

194 | *Leek, Potato and Coriander Bake*

Preparation time
15 minutes

Cooking time
1¼ hours

Oven temperature
200 C, 400 F, gas 6

Serves 4

Calories
315 per portion

You will need
450 g/1 lb leeks, trimmed and
washed
1 kg/2 lb small potatoes, scrubbed
and dried
1 tablespoon oil
25 g/1 oz butter
1 teaspoon black peppercorns
2 teaspoons coriander seeds
1 teaspoon sea salt

Slice the leeks into 2-cm/¾-in rings and cut the potatoes into 1-cm/½-in slices.

Put the oil and butter in a large shallow roasting tin and place in the oven until the butter is just melted. Add the leeks and potatoes, turning them over several times to coat them with the oil and butter. Crush the peppercorns with the coriander seeds in a pestle and mortar.

Put the crushed pepper and coriander in a small bowl and add the salt. Sprinkle evenly over the potatoes and leeks and stir through.

Cover the tin tightly with foil. Bake in a moderately hot oven for 45 minutes. Remove the foil, turn the potatoes and leeks over and put back near the top of the oven for a further 30 minutes until brown. Serve hot.

Cook's Tip

To peel tomatoes, place them in a bowl and pour on freshly boiling water. Leave for 30–60 seconds, depending on ripeness, then drain and slit the skins which should slide off easily. Alternatively, hold a tomato on a fork over a gas flame until the skin splits. Turn the tomato slowly all the time.

Cook's Tip

If you do not have a pestle and mortar, put the seeds and peppercorns between 2 double sheets of absorbent kitchen paper or greaseproof paper and crush firmly with a rolling pin.

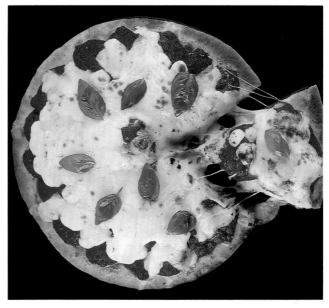

195 | *Provencal Eggs*

Preparation time
10 minutes

Cooking time
25 minutes

Oven temperature
190 C, 375 F, gas 5

Serves 4

Calories
235 per portion

You will need
2 tablespoons oil
1 large onion, thinly sliced
1 clove garlic, crushed
1 red pepper, deseeded and sliced
225 g 8 oz courgettes, sliced
1 teaspoon oregano
1 (397-g 14-oz) can tomatoes
salt and pepper
a few drops of Tabasco sauce
4 eggs
50 g 2 oz Cheddar cheese, grated

Heat the oil in a large saucepan, add the onion and garlic and cook until softened, about 5 minutes. Add the pepper and courgettes and cook for 5 minutes. Stir in the oregano, tomatoes and their juices, salt and pepper and Tabasco and heat through. Pour mixture into a shallow ovenproof dish. Make four hollows in the mixture and break an egg into each. Sprinkle cheese over eggs. Bake for 12–15 minutes or until the eggs are just set. Serve hot.

196 | *Pizza Margherita*

Preparation time
35 minutes, plus time to rise and prove

Cooking time
30 minutes

Oven temperature
220 C, 425 F, gas 7

Serves 4

Calories
360 per portion

You will need
For the dough
225 g/8 oz strong plain flour
1 teaspoon salt
7 g/¼ oz fresh yeast
150 ml/¼ pint lukewarm water

For the topping
1 tablespoon oil
1 large onion, chopped
1 clove garlic, crushed
1 (397-g/14-oz) can tomatoes, chopped if liked
salt and pepper
100 g/4 oz mozzarella, sliced
basil leaves to garnish

To make the dough, put the flour and salt in a bowl. Blend the fresh yeast with water until dissolved, add to the flour and mix to a firm dough. Knead on a lightly floured surface for 10 minutes. Put the dough in a warm, greased bowl, cover with greased polythene and leave in a warm place until doubled in size.

Heat the oil in a saucepan. Add the onion and garlic and fry until soft. Add the tomatoes and seasoning. Knead the dough for 2 minutes, roll to a 23-cm/9-in circle and place on a greased baking tray. Top with the tomato mixture and mozzarella slices. Leave to rise in a warm place for 15 minutes. Bake in a hot oven for 20–25 minutes. Garnish with basil leaves.

Cook's Tip

Tabasco sauce gets its name from the part of Mexico which produced the peppers from which it was originally made. The peppers are pulped, salted and matured for 3 years, then mixed with distilled vinegar. After being clarified, the sauce is bottled. It keeps very well. A fiery relish, a few drops are sufficient to impart a pleasing tang.

Cook's Tip

Instead of fresh yeast use 1 teaspoon dried yeast. To prepare dried yeast dissolve ¼ teaspoon sugar in the water, sprinkle in the yeast and set aside until frothy.

197 | Potato and Courgette Omelette

Preparation time
5 minutes

Cooking time
20 minutes

Serves 4

Calories
300 per portion

You will need
450 g / 1 lb potatoes, grated
2 tablespoons olive oil
225 g / 8 oz courgettes, coarsely
   grated
1 clove garlic, crushed
6 eggs, beaten
a few drops of Tabasco sauce
salt and pepper

Place the potatoes in a sieve and press out the excess moisture. Heat the oil in a large frying pan, add the potatoes and fry quickly until browned and almost cooked, about 10 minutes. Add the courgettes and garlic and cook gently for 5 minutes. Stir in the eggs, Tabasco and salt and pepper and cook gently until just set, about 5 minutes. Remove pan from heat, cut omelette into wedges and serve hot with a fresh mixed salad.

Cook's Tip

Accompany each omelette with a simple side salad of tomato and basil, served with a vinaigrette dressing enlivened by a splash of soy sauce.

198 | Cauliflower Omelettes

Preparation time
5 minutes

Cooking time
45 minutes

Serves 4

Calories
310 per portion

You will need
½ cauliflower, cut into florets
salt
2 tablespoons double cream
pinch of grated nutmeg
1 egg yolk
1 tablespoon grated Parmesan
   cheese
pinch of dried basil
6 eggs
oil for frying
75 g / 3 oz Emmental cheese,
   grated

For the garnish
tomato wedges
parsley sprigs

Place the cauliflower florets in a medium saucepan. Add boiling water to cover and a pinch of salt. Bring to the boil, then lower the heat and cook for about 20 minutes.

Drain and blend in a liquidiser or pass through a fine sieve. Add the cream, nutmeg, egg yolk, Parmesan cheese and basil, mixing well.

Beat the eggs with a little salt. Heat a little oil in a frying pan. When hot, add one quarter of the egg mixture and cook for 2–3 minutes or until set.

Spread with one quarter of the cauliflower purée, fold over to enclose and sprinkle generously with one quarter of the Emmental cheese. Place under a hot grill until the cheese melts; keep warm. Make three more omelettes in the same way. Garnish and serve.

Cook's Tip

The oil should be very hot before the omelette mixture is added to the pan. Immediately turn down the heat (eggs toughen at high temperatures) and as the omelette begins to cook, draw the sides towards the centre with a spatula.

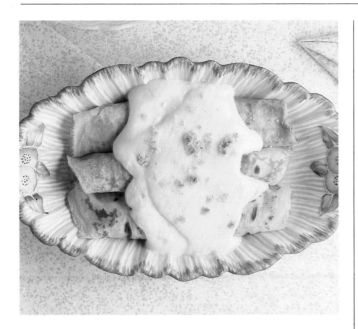

199 | Stuffed Pancakes

Preparation time
50 minutes

Cooking time
1 hour 5 minutes

Oven temperature
200 C, 400 F, gas 6

Serves 5

Calories
705 per portion

You will need
For the batter
100 g/4 oz plain flour
pinch of salt
1 egg, plus 1 yolk, beaten
300 ml/½ pint milk
1 tablespoon vegetable oil
50 g/2 oz lard or oil for frying

For the filling
10 leeks, trimmed, slit and washed

For the sauce
75 g/3 oz butter or margarine
75 g/3 oz plain flour
1 litre/1¾ pints milk
salt and pepper
125 g/5 oz Parmesan cheese,
  grated

To make the batter, place all the ingredients in a liquid-iser and blend until smooth. Use to make 10 pancakes (see Cook's Tip). Set the leeks in a steamer over a pan of boiling water. Cover and cook for 10 minutes until tender. Set aside. To make the sauce, melt the butter or margarine in a saucepan over a low heat, then add the flour. Cook for 2 minutes, stirring. Gradually add the milk and bring the sauce to the boil, stirring constantly. Simmer gently for 2–3 minutes. Season to taste. Cool a little and add 100 g/4 oz of the cheese.

Place a leek and a little sauce on each pancake. Roll up and arrange in a greased, ovenproof dish. Pour over remaining sauce and sprinkle with the 25 g/1 oz cheese. Bake in a moderately hot oven for 25–30 minutes.

Cook's Tip

For good pancakes use a frying pan that does not stick. Grease with oil, heat slowly until very hot, then pour in a little batter. Tilt pan to cover the base, cook to set, turn the pancake and brown the second side.

200 | Frittata

Preparation time
15 minutes

Cooking time
7 minutes

Serves 2

Calories
310 per portion

You will need
25 g/1 oz butter
4 eggs, beaten
275 g/10 oz spinach, cooked and
  lightly chopped, or 100 g/4 oz
  frozen spinach, cooked
3 firm tomatoes, peeled and
  coarsely chopped
100 g/4 oz cooked potatoes, diced,
  or 75 g/3 oz cooked brown rice
salt and pepper
1 teaspoon chopped sage or
  ¼ teaspoon dried sage
few drops of Tabasco sauce

Heat half the butter in a large frying pan until sizzling. Pour in the beaten eggs and stir for a few seconds. Allow the eggs to settle in the pan and then distribute the spinach, tomatoes and potatoes or rice evenly over the surface. Sprinkle with salt, pepper, sage and Tabasco sauce. Cook gently for about 4 minutes until the underside is set and golden brown. Gently lift the edge with a fish slice to check. When the underside is done, tip the omelette out on to a large plate so that the cooked side is on top.

Add the remaining butter to the pan and melt, coating the base. Slide the omelette back into the pan and cook the other side for about 3 minutes. Cut into quarters and serve hot or cold.

Cook's Tip

Butter burns more readily than oil and must be carefully watched while melting. To alleviate this problem, use a mixture of butter and oil when frying the frittata.

201 | Aubergine Galette

Preparation time
20 minutes, plus 1 hour
to prepare aubergines

Cooking time
1 hour 10 minutes

**Oven
temperature**
180C, 350F, gas 4

Serves 4

Calories
460 per portion

You will need
2 large aubergines
salt and pepper
150 ml/¼ pint olive oil
1 onion, chopped
1 clove garlic, crushed
450 g/1 lb tomatoes, peeled and
 chopped
1 egg
225 g/8 oz ricotta or curd cheese
1 tablespoon sesame seeds,
 toasted
crusty wholewheat bread, to serve

Slice the aubergines, sprinkle with salt and leave in a colander for 1 hour. Rinse well and dry on absorbent kitchen paper. Heat 2 tablespoons of the oil in a pan and cook the onion until softened. Add the garlic and tomatoes and simmer, uncovered, for 5–7 minutes.

Mix the egg with the cheese, adding salt and pepper to taste. Heat the remaining oil in a frying pan and cook the aubergine slices on both sides until golden. Drain on absorbent kitchen paper.

Arrange a layer of overlapping aubergine slices on the base and sides of an 18-cm/7-in springform cake tin. Cover with half the tomato mixture, then top with half the cheese mixture. Repeat the layers, finishing with aubergine. Cover with foil and bake in a moderate oven for 40–50 minutes. Turn out on to a hot serving dish and sprinkle with the sesame seeds.

Cook's Tip

Toast sesame seeds under the grill or in a dry frying pan for 3–4 minutes, shaking the pan continuously. Alternatively, roast the seeds in the oven (see Cook's Tip 125).

202 | Spinach and Potato Patties

Preparation time
15 minutes

Cooking time
20 minutes

Serves 3–4

Calories
450–340 per portion

You will need
1 tablespoon oil
1 onion, chopped
1 clove garlic, crushed
225 g/8 oz frozen chopped
 spinach, defrosted and drained
450 g/1 lb potatoes, boiled and
 mashed
¼ teaspoon grated nutmeg
100 g/4 oz Cheddar cheese, grated
salt and pepper
wholemeal flour for coating
oil for shallow frying
watercress sprigs to garnish

Heat the oil in a pan and cook the onion and garlic until softened. Squeeze the spinach dry and add to the pan with the potato, nutmeg, cheese, and salt and pepper to taste; mix thoroughly.

Shape the mixture into eight balls, using dampened hands, and flatten slightly. Place some flour in a plastic bag, add the patties one at a time and shake to coat completely.

Fry the patties in hot oil for 2 minutes on each side until golden brown. Garnish with watercress and serve with salad and crusty bread.

Cook's Tip

The peppery flavour of mineral-rich watercress is the perfect foil for these patties.

203 | Cheesy Banana Muffins

Preparation time
5 minutes

Serves 4

Calories
210 per portion

You will need
4 wholewheat muffins, split in half
  and toasted
butter to spread
a little yeast extract, to spread
  (optional)
75 g 3 oz low-fat hard cheese,
  grated (for example Shape
  cheese)
a little cress
1 banana, thinly sliced

Lightly spread the muffins with butter and spread four halves with yeast extract (if liked). Top the yeast-spread muffins with cheese, a sprinkling of cress and a few banana slices. Replace the muffin tops and serve at once with fresh salad ingredients.

204 | Tofu Cakes

Preparation time
15 minutes

Cooking time
10 15 minutes

Serves 4

Calories
210 per cake

You will need
350 g/12 oz tofu
6 spring onions, chopped
2 tablespoons chopped parsley
3 tablespoons finely chopped
  walnuts
100 g/4 oz fine wholewheat
  breadcrumbs
2 tablespoons grated Parmesan
  cheese
salt and pepper
oil for shallow-frying

Mix the tofu with the spring onions, parsley, nuts, breadcrumbs and Parmesan. Season to taste. Knead by hand to bind together and season to taste. Shape the mixture into eight round cakes.

  Heat the oil for shallow-frying and fry the cakes in batches until light golden brown, turning once. Drain on absorbent kitchen paper and keep hot while frying the remainder.

  Serve with a crisp salad.

Cook's Tip

For a school lunchbox treat, use bread rolls (untoasted) instead of muffins, wrapping them in foil to keep the filling in place. Add a tangerine as a thirst-quencher.

Cook's Tip

Caper cream sauce goes well with these tofu cakes. Simply stir 1 tablespoon chopped capers and 1 teaspoon tomato purée into 150 ml/¼ pint soured cream or fromage frais and serve as an accompaniment.

205 | Crunchy Tofu

Preparation time
15 minutes, plus 1 hour
to chill

Cooking time
10 15 minutes

Serves 4

Calories
280 per portion

You will need
450 g/1 lb tofu
4 tablespoons plain flour
grated nutmeg
salt and pepper
1 egg, beaten
75 100 g/3 4 oz dry white
    breadcrumbs
900 ml/1½ pints oil for deep frying

For the sauce
1 large clove garlic, crushed
2 tablespoons tomato purée
4 tablespoons chopped herbs
150 ml/¼ pint double cream,
    lightly whipped

For the garnish
watercress sprigs
lemon wedges

Cut the tofu into slices. Mix the flour, nutmeg and seasoning. Coat the tofu in the seasoned flour, beaten egg and breadcrumbs. Chill. Mix the ingredients for the sauce and chill until required. Heat the oil for deep frying to 190C/375F. Fry the tofu until crisp and golden, then drain on absorbent kitchen paper. Garnish and serve piping hot with the chilled sauce.

206 | Savoury Waffles

Preparation time
10 minutes

Cooking time
20 25 minutes

Makes 10–12

Calories
195 160 per waffle

You will need
100 g/4 oz wholemeal flour
2 teaspoons baking powder
pinch of salt
50 g/2 oz fine oat flakes
2 eggs, separated
50 g/2 oz butter or margarine
300 ml/½ pint milk

For the topping
225 g/8 oz ricotta cheese
2 tablespoons toasted sunflower
    seeds
1 tablespoon sesame seeds
4 tomatoes, chopped
4 spring onions, chopped

Mix together the flour, baking powder and salt and stir in the oats. Combine the egg yolks with the butter or margarine and the milk, blending well. Make a well in the dry ingredients, pour in the milk mixture and beat until well blended. Whisk the egg whites until stiff and fold them into the batter.

Prepare a waffle iron, following the manufacturer's instructions. Pour in just enough batter to cover the plates, close the iron and cook quickly for 2 minutes or until the waffle is golden and crisp. Use the rest of the batter in the same way.

To make the topping, lightly mix all the ingredients together. For serving, place a spoonful of savoury cheese topping on each waffle.

Cook's Tip

Tofu makes a creamy salad dressing. Simply mash 150 g/ 5 oz tofu with 2 tablespoons vegetable oil, 1 tablespoon cider vinegar, 1 teaspoon minced onion and salt and pepper to taste.

Cook's Tip

The oats in these waffles add valuable fibre and a delicious flavour. Buckwheat flakes may be used instead.

207 | Chinese-style Tofu

Preparation time
10 minutes

Cooking time
12 minutes

Serves 4

Calories
250 per portion

You will need
1 (227-g 8-oz) can bamboo shoots drained
350 g 12 oz tofu
4 tablespoons oil
1 clove garlic, peeled
175 g 6 oz mange tout, trimmed
4 tablespoons soy sauce
2 tablespoons roasted sesame seeds

Slice, then shred the bamboo shoots. Cut the tofu into 5-mm/$\frac{1}{4}$-in thick slices.

Heat the oil in a wok or large frying pan and crush the garlic into it. Add the tofu and fry the slices until crisp and golden, then remove them from the wok with a slotted spoon and drain on absorbent kitchen paper.

Add the mange tout and bamboo shoots to the wok and stir-fry for 5 minutes. Sprinkle the soy sauce and sesame seeds over them. Return the tofu to the wok and cook for a further minute before serving. A rice dish makes the ideal accompaniment.

208 | Tofu with Leeks

Preparation time
15 minutes, plus 30 minutes to marinate

Cooking time
20 minutes

Serves 4

Calories
155 per portion

You will need
300 g / 11 oz tofu, cubed
4 tablespoons soy sauce
1 tablespoon dry sherry
1½ tablespoons wholemeal flour
2 tablespoons oil
225 g / 8 oz leeks, washed and thinly sliced
1 clove garlic, finely chopped
120 ml / 4 fl oz vegetable stock
white pepper
1 red pepper, deseeded and diced
2 tablespoons chopped parsley
gomasio for sprinkling

Place the tofu in a bowl. Pour over the soy sauce and sherry and marinate for at least 30 minutes.

Drain the tofu, reserving the marinade, and coat in the flour. Heat the oil in a frying pan and fry the tofu until brown and crisp, stirring frequently. Remove and keep hot.

Add the leeks and garlic to the pan and fry over a moderate to high heat until coated in oil. Add the stock and tofu marinade. Bring to the boil, cover and simmer for 5–7 minutes.

Season to taste with pepper. Arrange the tofu on the vegetables and serve sprinkled with red pepper, parsley and gomasio.

Cook's Tip

Tofu, or bean curd, is made from ground, soaked soya beans – it is a sort of soya cheese. To eat on its own it is tasteless and has a texture which is reminiscent of a chilled custard. However, it is high in food value (protein) and can be seasoned and flavoured in any number of dishes. You can buy tofu in health food stores and Chinese supermarkets. Traditionally used in Chinese cooking, it is also used in lots of vegetarian dishes.

Cook's Tip

Salt substitute, gomasio or sesame salt, is available from health food stores. To make your own, simply grind 4–5 parts roasted sesame seeds with one part salt. Gomasio will keep in an airtight container for up to 2–3 weeks.

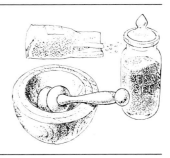

209 | Sunflower Snacks

Preparation time 20 minutes	**You will need** 100 g/4 oz sunflower seeds, ground

Cooking time
10 12 minutes
	100 g/4 oz fresh wholewheat
	   breadcrumbs
	2 tablespoons grated Parmesan
	   cheese
	salt and pepper

Serves 4	1 clove garlic, crushed 1 large egg, lightly beaten
Calories 285 per portion	about 50 g/2 oz wholemeal flour oil for deep-frying

Mix together the ground sunflower seeds, bread-crumbs, Parmesan, a little salt and a pinch of pepper in a bowl. Stir in the garlic, then add the beaten egg and mix well to bind the ingredients together.

Using floured hands, roll the mixture into small balls. Season the flour with salt and pepper and dip each ball into the flour to coat thoroughly.

Heat the oil for deep-frying and fry the balls, in batches, until crisp and golden. Drain on absorbent kitchen paper.

210 | Nutty Fruit Salad

Preparation time 5 10 minutes	**You will need** 2 medium dessert apples, cored and chopped
Serves 2	2 celery sticks, chopped 2 tablespoons sultanas 8 walnut halves, chopped

Calories
210 per portion
	50 g/2 oz drained canned kidney
	   beans
	4 tablespoons natural yogurt
	shredded crisp lettuce leaves
	2 kiwi fruit, peeled and sliced, to
	   decorate

Mix the apples, celery, sultanas, walnuts and kidney beans, then coat with the yogurt.

Serve on a bed of shredded lettuce and kiwi fruit slices. This salad is ideal for a packed lunch.

Cook's Tip

Serve these irresistible morsels as a cocktail party snack. Supply plenty of cocktail sticks with which to spear them.

Cook's Tip

Kiwi fruit came originally from China and are now largely grown in New Zealand, hence the name. They are rich in vitamin C. Peel before cutting in slices or wedges to reveal the pretty interior.

211 | Walnut Dip

Preparation time
15 minutes, plus 1
hour to chill

Serves 6

Calories
350 per portion

You will need
350 g/12 oz Lancashire cheese,
  grated
150 ml/¼ pint single cream
3 tablespoons milk
4 spring onions, chopped
salt and pepper
100 g/4 oz walnuts, finely chopped

Pound the cheese with the cream until well mixed, then beat in the milk, onions, reserving a few rings for garnish if liked, and seasoning until creamy. Add the walnuts, spoon into a dish and chill for 1 hour before serving. Plain biscuits or toast, celery and crisp apples make good accompaniments.

212 | Hummous

Preparation time
5 minutes, plus
overnight to soak

Cooking time
2¼ hours

Serves 8–10

Calories
210 170 per portion

You will need
250 g/8 oz chick peas, soaked
  overnight
150 ml/¼ pint tahini
3 cloves garlic, roughly chopped
juice of 1 2 lemons
salt and pepper

For the garnish
1 tablespoon olive oil blended with
  1 teaspoon paprika
1 teaspoon chopped parsley

Drain the chick peas, place in a saucepan and cover with cold water. Bring to the boil, cover and boil rapidly for 10 minutes, then simmer gently for 1½–2 hours, until soft; the time will vary depending on the age and quality of the peas. Drain, reserving 300 ml/½ pint of the liquid.

Place the chick peas in a liquidiser or food processor, add the remaining ingredients and season with salt and pepper to taste. Add some of the reserved cooking liquid and blend to a soft creamy paste.

Turn into a shallow serving dish, drizzle over the blended oil and sprinkle with the parsley. Serve with pitta bread.

Cook's Tip

A white cheese with a crumbly texture, Lancashire has a mild flavour which develops as it matures. It is regarded as the perfect cheese for toasting.

Cook's Tip

This is a tasty starter which is easy to make. It will keep for up to a week, covered, in the refrigerator.

213 | Tofu and Avocado Spread

Preparation time
10 minutes

Serves 2

Calories
320 per portion

You will need
225 g/8 oz silken tofu
1 ripe avocado
2 tablespoons mayonnaise
½ teaspoon salt
1 teaspoon lemon juice
2 teaspoons finely chopped onion
4 drops of Tabasco sauce
a little cayenne

Break up the tofu with a fork. Halve the avocado, remove the stone and scoop out all the flesh. Mash it and add to the tofu together with the mayonnaise, salt, lemon juice, onion, Tabasco and cayenne to taste. Mix well and chill for about an hour. Serve with toast or wholewheat bread or rolls.

214 | Breakfast Special

Preparation time
10 minutes

Serves 8

Calories
250 per portion

You will need
225 g/8 oz rolled oats
50 g/2 oz wheatgerm
100 g/4 oz small dried apricots, chopped
175 g/6 oz sultanas
50 g/2 oz walnuts, roughly chopped
½ pear (per portion), peeled, cored and grated
brown sugar or honey, optional
milk or natural yogurt to serve

Mix the cereals, dried fruit and nuts together. Store in an airtight container. To serve, add grated pear to each portion, sprinkle with sugar or honey and serve with milk or yogurt.

Cook's Tip

What a combination! Protein-rich tofu and vitamin-packed avocado. With wholewheat bread providing carbohydrate, this makes a well-balanced meal.

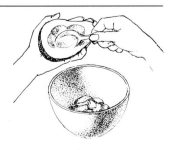

Cook's Tip

Seasonal fruits make a juicy addition: fresh peach slices, cherry halves, raspberries and strawberries are among the naturally sweet possibilities.

215 | Spiced Muesli

Preparation time
5 minutes

**Makes 575 g/
1¼ lb muesli**

Calories
360 per 100 g 4 oz

You will need
225 g 8 oz rolled oats
225 g 8 oz barley flakes or kernels,
  sesame and sunflower seeds,
  bran and wheatgerm, mixed
  according to taste
2 teaspoons cinnamon
1 teaspoon grated nutmeg
grated rind of 1 lemon
50 g 2 oz mixed nuts, chopped
50 g 2 oz seedless raisins and
  coarsely chopped dried fruit
  (apples, apricots, dates, figs),
  mixed according to taste

Put the oats in a bowl, then stir in all the remaining ingredients.

Store in a tin or another suitable airtight container and use as required. Serve with brown sugar or honey and milk, cream or yogurt. Seasonal fresh fruit may be added, if liked.

216 | Hazelnut Toasts

Preparation time
5 minutes

Cooking time
3 4 minutes

Serves 1

Calories
135 per portion

You will need
1 tablespoon nutri-grain cereal (rye
  and oats with hazelnuts)
1 tablespoon cottage cheese
½ small tomato, peeled and
  chopped
2 mushrooms, chopped
pinch of dried mixed herbs
1 slice wholewheat bread, toasted

Mix together the cereal, cottage cheese, tomato, mushrooms and mixed herbs. Spread this over the slice of toast, making sure it comes right to the edge. Heat under a moderate grill and cook until the topping is golden brown. Serve hot.

Cook's Tip

*To get a good muesli base
make with a mixture of
different grains and seeds.
Bran is dry, wheatgerm has a
strong flavour and sesame
seeds are dry so use sparingly.*

Cook's Tip

*For children cut the bread into
fancy shapes, using large
biscuit cutters.*

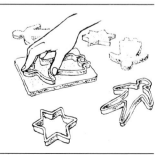

Cooking for Special Occasions

Many of the dishes in this chapter look very impressive when served to guests, although they do not necessarily involve complicated preparation processes. Without exception they are scrumptious to eat and will convert sceptical meat-eating friends!

217 | Tomato Roulade

(Illustrated on front jacket)

Preparation time
30 minutes

Cooking time
30 minutes

Oven temperature
190 C, 375 F, gas 5

Serves 4

Calories
200 per portion

You will need
15 g/½ oz butter
450 g/1 lb tomatoes, peeled and
  finely chopped
25 g/1 oz wholemeal flour
salt and pepper
3 egg yolks
4 egg whites

For the filling
50 g/2 oz Cheddar cheese, grated
2 tablespoons chutney
½ teaspoon prepared mustard
2 tablespoons chopped
  watercress
salt and pepper

Line and grease a 23 × 30-cm/9 × 12-in Swiss roll tin. Melt the butter in a pan, add the tomatoes and cook for about 4 minutes until pulpy. Stir in the flour and cook over a gentle heat for 1 minute. Remove from the heat, season and beat in the egg yolks. Whisk the egg whites until stiff and fold into the tomato mixture. Spread evenly into the prepared tin, making sure that the mixture reaches right to the edges. Cook in a moderately hot oven for about 20 minutes, until firm. Mix three-quarters of the grated cheese with the chutney, mustard, half the watercress and seasoning. Quickly turn the cooked roulade out on to a clean sheet of greaseproof paper and remove the lining paper. Spread the filling over the roulade and roll up. Place on an ovenproof dish, sprinkle with the remaining watercress and cheese; return to the oven for 2–3 minutes. Serve sliced.

Cook's Tip

Roll the roulade as you would a Swiss roll, using the greaseproof paper as a guide. For a good roll, tuck the end in neatly first to start the roll off.

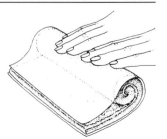

218 | Spinach Roulade

Preparation time
30 minutes, plus 30
minutes to chill

Cooking time
15–20 minutes

Oven temperature
190 C, 375 F, gas 5

Serves 4

Calories
310 per portion

You will need
50 g/2 oz concentrated butter,
  melted
350 g/12 oz spinach, cooked
3 eggs, separated
salt and pepper

For the filling
350 g/12 oz cream cheese
1 bunch spring onions, chopped
175 g/6 oz broccoli, trimmed,
  blanched and drained
4 tomatoes, peeled

Line a 23 × 30-cm/9 × 12-in Swiss roll tin with grease-proof paper and brush lightly with melted butter. Squeeze all the liquid from the spinach, chop finely or purée. Beat in the remaining butter, the egg yolks and seasoning to taste. Whisk the egg whites until just stiff and fold into the spinach. Turn into the prepared tin and cook in a moderately hot oven for 10–15 minutes.

Beat the cheese and spring onions together. Finely chop the broccoli. Halve the tomatoes, discard seeds and chop the flesh. Mix the broccoli and tomatoes into the cream cheese and season well.

Turn the cooked roulade out on to clean greaseproof paper. Carefully peel off the lining paper and trim the edges. Spread the filling evenly over three-quarters of the roulade and roll up from the unfilled end. Wrap paper tightly over the roulade and chill for 30 minutes.

Cook's Tip

Serve this splendid roulade as a dinner party starter with a simple garnish of frilled endive and radishes.

219 | Cottage Pancakes

Preparation time
10 minutes

Cooking time
30 35 minutes

Oven temperature
190 C, 375 F, gas 5

Serves 4

Calories
385 per portion

You will need
50 g/2 oz wholemeal flour
50 g/2 oz plain flour
1 egg
1 egg yolk
300 ml/½ pint water
salt and pepper
oil for frying

For the filling
25 g/1 oz butter
1 small onion, finely chopped
225 g/8 oz cottage cheese
50 g/2 oz salted peanuts, chopped
½ 1 teaspoon dried rosemary,
    crushed

Mix together the flours, egg and egg yolk, stir in about a third of the water and beat to make a smooth batter. Stir in the salt and pepper and remaining water.

Heat a little oil in a 15-cm/6-in frying pan. Pour in a little batter, so it just covers the base, and cook until the underside is golden. Turn and cook the second side. Remove and keep warm. Repeat with the remaining batter. To make the filling, heat the butter in a saucepan and fry the onion until softened, about 5 minutes. Stir in the cottage cheese, peanuts and rosemary.

Divide the filling between the pancakes and roll up. Place close together in one layer in an ovenproof dish. Cover with foil and heat through in the oven for 15–20 minutes. Serve hot.

Cook's Tip

Cottage cheese is made from skimmed milk curds which have been washed and rinsed. It is low in fat and therefore a good choice for slimmers.

220 | Provencal Pancakes

Preparation time
25 minutes

Cooking time
50 minutes

Serves 4

Calories
345 per portion

You will need
50 g/2 oz buckwheat flour
50 g/2 oz plain flour
salt and pepper
1 egg, beaten
300 ml/½ pint milk
1 tablespoon vegetable oil
oil for cooking
2 tablespoons olive oil
1 onion, chopped
2 cloves garlic, crushed
1 green or red pepper, deseeded
    and chopped
1 small aubergine, chopped
4 large tomatoes, peeled and
    chopped
1 tablespoon tomato purée
25 g/1 oz margarine, melted
2 tablespoons grated Parmesan
    cheese

Place the flours in a bowl, add salt and make a well in the centre. Add the egg, then gradually stir in half the milk and the vegetable oil. Beat until smooth; add the remaining milk. Use to make 12 small pancakes.

Heat the olive oil in a pan and cook the onion until softened. Add the garlic, pepper and aubergine and fry for 10 minutes, stirring occasionally. Add the tomatoes and tomato purée, cover and cook for 15 minutes. Season to taste. Fill the pancakes, roll up and place in an ovenproof dish. Top with the margarine and cheese; grill to brown.

Cook's Tip

Pancakes can be made in advance. Place the stack of pancakes in a plastic bag and store in the refrigerator for 2–3 days.

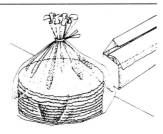

221 | Cheese Mille Feuilles

Preparation time
30 minutes

Cooking time
10 15 minutes

Oven temperature
220 230 C, 425 450 F,
gas 7 8

Serves 6

Calories
500 per portion

You will need
225 g / 8 oz frozen puff pastry,
   defrosted
cocktail gherkins to garnish

For the fillings
225 g / 8 oz blue Stilton cheese
75 g / 3 oz butter
salt and pepper
2 3 tablespoons double cream,
   lightly whipped
1 2 tablespoons milk
100 g / 4 oz Lancashire cheese,
   grated
pinch of cayenne
pinch of mustard powder
1 tablespoon chutney, chopped

Roll out pastry to about 25 × 35 cm / 10 × 14 in. Prick all over and bake in a hot oven for 10–15 minutes. Cool slightly, then cut lengthways into three even strips; crush trimmings and reserve.

Remove the rind from the Stilton. Cream the cheese with the butter and season well, adding a little cream.

Beat the milk into the Lancashire cheese, season and add the cayenne, mustard and chutney. If necessary, add a little cream to soften. Spread half the Stilton mixture over one pastry strip. Place the second strip on top, spread with the Lancashire cheese. Top with the last strip of pastry, press down gently before spreading with the remaining Stilton mixture. Mark with a knife and garnish, adding the crushed pastry as shown.

Cook's Tip

Gherkin fans make an attractive garnish. Drain the gherkins and place them on a board, then, with a sharp knife, slice them lengthways, almost to the end. Ease the slices apart to make the fans.

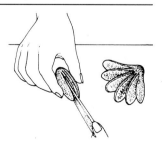

222 | Courgette Soufflé

Preparation time
20 minutes

Cooking time
1 hour

Oven temperature
180 C, 350 F, gas 4

Serves 6

Calories
145 per portion

You will need
350 g / 12 oz courgettes, diced
salt and pepper
350 g / 12 oz low-fat soft cheese
   (for example Shape cheese)
4 eggs, separated
$\frac{1}{2}$ teaspoon tarragon
pinch of cayenne

Cook the courgettes in boiling salted water until tender – about 5 minutes. Drain well, then sieve or blend in a liquidiser until smooth. Beat the soft cheese and egg yolks together. Stir in the courgettes, tarragon and cayenne. Whisk the egg whites until stiff and fold into the courgette mixture. Pour carefully into a 1.15-litre / 2-pint soufflé dish and bake, without opening the oven, for about 45–55 minutes, until well risen and golden brown on top. Serve immediately with a green salad.

Cook's Tip

It is the air incorporated in the egg whites during beating that makes a soufflé rise. Adding a pinch of salt will help to stabilise the mixture. Never beat eggs so stiffly that they look dry – if this happens they will soon collapse.

223 | Blue Cheese Soufflé

Preparation time
15 minutes

Cooking time
30 35 minutes

Oven temperature
200C, 400F, gas 6

Serves 4

Calories
310 per portion

You will need
40 g / 1½ oz butter
25 g / 1 oz plain flour
300 ml / ½ pint milk
pinch of grated nutmeg
4 egg yolks
100 g / 4 oz Danish blue cheese, crumbled
3 egg whites
salt and pepper

Melt the butter in a pan and use a little to brush the inside of a 1.4-litre/2½-pint soufflé dish. Stir the flour into the remaining butter; cook for 1 minute. Gradually stir in the milk, bring to the boil and cook for 2 minutes, stirring constantly. Add the nutmeg and allow to cool slightly. Beat in the egg yolks and cheese. Whisk the egg whites until stiff, lightly fold into the sauce and season to taste.

Turn into the prepared soufflé dish and cook in a moderately hot oven for 25–30 minutes until well risen and golden brown. Serve at once with green vegetables or a salad.

224 | Surprise Soufflé

Preparation time
20 minutes

Cooking time
1 hour

Oven temperature
190C, 375F, gas 5

Serves 4

Calories
475 per portion

You will need
4 large carrots, thickly sliced
3 large potatoes, peeled and cut into 1-cm/½-in dice
1 small turnip, cut into 1-cm/½-in dice
1 large onion, chopped
salt and pepper
8 tomatoes, peeled and deseeded
25 g / 1 oz butter
25 g / 1 oz plain flour
½ teaspoon mustard powder
300 ml / ½ pint milk
3 eggs, separated
100 g / 4 oz Cheddar cheese, grated
1 tablespoon chopped parsley to garnish (optional)

Cook the carrots, potatoes, turnip and onion in a pan of boiling salted water for 15 minutes. Drain and season to taste, then place in a 1.75-litre/3-pint ovenproof soufflé dish. Purée the tomatoes with a little seasoning and pour over the vegetables.

Melt the butter in a pan over a low heat, then add the flour and mustard powder. Cook for 2 minutes, stirring. Gradually add the milk and bring the sauce to the boil, stirring constantly. Simmer gently for 2–3 minutes. Allow it to cool slightly, then beat in the egg yolks and cheese. Whisk the egg whites until stiff and fold into the sauce. Pour the sauce over the vegetables in the soufflé dish. Bake in a moderately hot oven for about 40 minutes until risen and golden. Garnish with parsley before serving, if using.

Cook's Tip

When serving a soufflé, use a large serving spoon to reach down to the lightly cooked mixture at the bottom of the dish. Each portion should also include some of the crust.

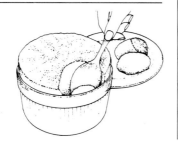

Cook's Tip

The surprise in this soufflé is the vegetable mixture at the bottom of the dish, which makes the soufflé sufficiently substantial to serve on its own.

225 | Cheese Fondue

Preparation time
15 minutes

Cooking time
10 minutes

Serves 4

Calories
435 per portion

You will need
1 clove garlic, halved
300 ml / ½ pint dry white wine
1 teaspoon lemon juice
225 g / 8 oz Danish Samsoe or
    Danbo Cheese, grated
225 g / 8 oz Danish Havarti cheese,
    grated
2 tablespoons cornflour
freshly ground black pepper
pinch of grated nutmeg
1 tablespoon Kirsch or milk

To serve
French bread
raw vegetables

Thoroughly rub the inside of a fondue pot or flameproof casserole with the garlic, then discard. Pour the wine and lemon juice into the pot and warm over a gentle heat. Add the cheese gradually and continue to heat gently, stirring until the cheese has melted. Blend the cornflour, pepper and nutmeg to a smooth paste with the Kirsch or milk and add to the melted cheese. Stir over the heat for a further 2–3 minutes. Place in the centre of the table. Serve at once with cubes of French bread and pieces of vegetable as dippers. Each guest is given a long fork with which to dip his bread and vegetables into the fondue pot. Keep the fondue warm over a spirit lamp or on a plate warmer.

Cook's Tip

To make a change from bread, accompany the fondue with a selection of vegetables to dip. Try carrots, cauliflower, celery, courgettes and different coloured peppers, all prepared and cut into bite-sized pieces.

226 | Fruit and Vegetable Kebabs

Preparation time
20 minutes, plus 1 hour
to marinate '

Cooking time
11 14 minutes

Serves 4

Calories
195 per portion

You will need
8 button onions, peeled and left
    whole
1 small green pepper, deseeded
    and cut into 8 pieces
1 small red pepper, deseeded and
    cut into 8 pieces
16 button mushrooms
2 large bananas, peeled and cut
    into 8 chunks
1 (350-g / 12-oz) can pineapple
    cubes, drained

For the marinade
6 tablespoons vegetable oil
1 tablespoon lemon juice
1 teaspoon grated orange rind
1 tablespoon finely chopped
    walnuts
salt and pepper

Blanch the onions and peppers in boiling water for 3 minutes so that they cook in the same time as the other ingredients. Drain and pat dry with absorbent kitchen paper. Thread all the ingredients on to eight kebab skewers. Lay the kebabs in a shallow dish while making the marinade. Stir the oil, lemon juice, orange rind, walnuts, salt and pepper together in a small bowl. Spoon the marinade over the kebabs and leave for about 1 hour. Grill for 8–10 minutes until evenly browned, brushing often with marinade.

Cook's Tip

In the summer, cook these colourful kebabs over a barbecue.

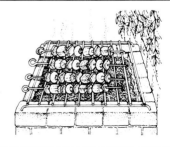

227 | Danish Blue Cheesecake

Preparation time
35 minutes, plus 3 4 hours to chill

Serves 8

Calories
375 per person

You will need
For the base
75 g/3 oz butter
175 g/6 oz wholewheat bran
  biscuits, crushed

For the topping
100 g/4 oz Danish Blue cheese
100 g/4 oz cream cheese
2 large eggs, separated
1 teaspoon French mustard
pinch of garlic salt
freshly ground black pepper
150 ml/¼ pint double cream
2 teaspoons agar-agar or 3
  teaspoons powdered gelatine
6 tablespoons water

Garnish
cucumber slices
black grapes

Melt the butter and stir in the biscuit crumbs. Press firmly into the base of a greased 20-cm/8-in loose-bottomed cake tin and chill. Soften both cheeses and beat together until creamy. Beat in the egg yolks, mustard, garlic salt, pepper and cream. Dissolve the agar-agar in the cold water in a small saucepan, then bring to the boil, stirring constantly. Beat into the cheese mixture and set aside. When on the point of setting, whisk the egg whites until stiff but not dry and gently fold in. Pour over the biscuit base and smooth the surface. Refrigerate for 3–4 hours. Garnish and serve.

Cook's Tip

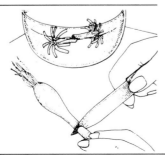

As an alternative garnish, make spring onion curls. Cut the bulb from each onion to leave about 2.5 cm/1 in of white stalk. Then make parallel cuts down the green part. When the onions are placed in iced water they will curl.

228 | Spinach and Flageolet Layer

Preparation time
25 minutes

Cooking time
1 hour 10 minutes

Oven temperature
180 C, 350 F, gas 4

Serves 4

Calories
135 per portion

You will need
450 g/1 lb fresh spinach
1 egg, beaten
1 (415-g/14½-oz) can flageolet
  beans
1 teaspoon French mustard
1 teaspoon curry powder
175 g/6 oz raspberries, puréed

Steam the spinach for 10 minutes. Keep about a quarter of the leaves aside and chop the rest very finely or liquidise in a blender or food processor. Mix in the beaten egg. Oil a 450-g/1-lb loaf tin and line with some of the reserved spinach leaves.

Drain and mash the flageolet beans. Mix with the mustard and curry powder and place in spinach-lined tin, top with the spinach mixture. Arrange remaining spinach leaves on top. Cover with foil. Place in a baking tin containing 2.5 cm/1 in of water and cook in a moderate oven for 1 hour.

Leave to cool in the tin, turn out and serve with a sauce of puréed raspberries. Accompany with hot garlic bread.

Cook's Tip

To make the sauce or coulis, simply purée fresh raspberries and press through a sieve to remove the seeds. A little lemon juice or gin may be added to sharpen the flavour.

229 | Kohlrabi with Walnuts

Preparation time
15 minutes

Cooking time
18 20 minutes

Serves 4

Calories
345 per portion

You will need
1 kg/2 lb young, tender kohlrabi
1 tablespoon vegetable oil
2 shallots, peeled and finely
    chopped
salt and pepper
grated nutmeg
120 ml/4 fl oz double cream
2 tablespoons chopped basil or
    marjoram
100 g/4 oz walnuts, coarsely
    chopped

Trim the kohlrabi, cutting off the feathery leaves and reserving for garnish. Peel the kohlrabi, cut out any tough parts, wash and halve. Cut the halves first into 1-cm/½-in slices and then into sticks.

Heat the oil in a frying pan and fry the shallots over a moderate heat until transparent, stirring continuously. Add the kolhrabi and stir until completely coated in oil.

Season with salt, pepper and nutmeg to taste. Add the cream, reduce the heat, cover and cook over low heat for 5–8 minutes until the kohlrabi is tender but still firm to the bite.

Rinse the kohlrabi leaves, pat dry and finely chop. Stir the basil into the kohlrabi mixture and transfer to a warmed serving dish. Sprinkle with the kohlrabi leaves and walnuts. Accompany with jacket-boiled new potatoes or brown rice.

230 | Walnut-filled Fennel

Preparation time
15 20 minutes

Cooking time
1½ hours

Oven temperature
180 C, 350 F, gas 4

Serves 2–4

Calories
630 315 per portion

You will need
4 large heads fennel
50 g/2 oz fresh breadcrumbs
75 g/3 oz walnuts, chopped
2 tablespoons clear honey
1 tablespoon snipped chives
1 tablespoon milk
salt and pepper
50 g/2 oz butter

For the garnish
tomato wedges
parsley sprigs

Cut out the hard core of the fennel and discard. Remove and chop up a little more fennel, ensuring there is a reasonably large cavity to fill with stuffing.

Mix the chopped fennel, breadcrumbs, walnuts, honey, chives and milk, and season well with salt and pepper. Press this stuffing into the fennel cavities and place in an ovenproof dish.

Dot the surface with butter, cover tightly with foil and bake in a moderate oven for about 1½ hours, until the fennel is tender. Garnish with tomato and parsley.

Cook's Tip

Kohlrabi looks like a large green turnip but is actually a member of the cabbage family. It is high in vitamins and low in calories.

Cook's Tip

Serve this dish as an interesting light main course. Alternatively, it can be offered as an accompaniment or an appetising starter.

231 | Baked Gnocchi

Preparation time
15 minutes

Cooking time
40 minutes

Oven temperature
200 C, 400 F, gas 6

Serves 4

Calories
520 per portion

You will need
450 ml/¾ pint milk
450 ml/¾ pint water
¼ teaspoon salt
225 g/8 oz semolina
100 g/4 oz grated Parmesan
  cheese
2 egg yolks
225 g/8 oz mushrooms, sliced
450 g/1 lb tomatoes, peeled and
  sliced
2 tablespoons chopped parsley
1 teaspoon oregano
50 g/2 oz stoned black olives,
  chopped
3 tablespoons melted butter

Bring the milk, water and salt nearly to the boil. Sprinkle in the semolina and cook, stirring, until it thickens to a purée consistency. Lower heat as much as possible and cook for 5 minutes. Remove the pan from the heat and stir in about two-thirds of the cheese and the egg yolks.

Moisten a large roasting tin and press mixture into an even-sided oblong shape. Cut neatly into squares. Place the mushrooms in a buttered ovenproof dish, cover with the tomatoes, sprinkle over the parsley, oregano and olives. Cover with the gnocchi squares, spoon over the melted butter and sprinkle with the remaining cheese. Bake for 25–30 minutes until the top is just beginning to brown.

Cook's Tip

A simple salad, such as Orange and Watercress (Recipe 123) would be an excellent accompaniment to this dish.

232 | Spinach Bake

Preparation time
20 minutes

Cooking time
35 minutes

Oven temperature
200 C, 400 F, gas 6

Serves 4

Calories
365 per portion

You will need
2 tablespoons raisins
4 tablespoons apple juice
1 kg/2 lb fresh, or 450 g/1 lb frozen
  spinach
3 litres/5 pints water
1 small onion, finely chopped
50 g/2 oz butter
salt and pepper
¼ teaspoon grated nutmeg
1 kg/2 lb potatoes, cooked, puréed
  with milk, butter and salt and
  pepper
150 ml/¼ pint soured cream
4 tablespoons fresh breadcrumbs
2 tablespoons grated Parmesan
  cheese

Soak the raisins in the apple juice. Wash the spinach several times in lukewarm water. Bring the measured water to the boil, and cook the spinach for 3 minutes. Drain in a sieve and press out the excess water. Cook the onion in the butter for 3 minutes until softened, add the spinach, raisins and apple juice, salt and pepper and nutmeg. Cook for 5 minutes over very gentle heat.

Meanwhile, pipe the creamed potato round the edge of an ovenproof dish. Turn the spinach mixture into the centre, spoon over the cream, sprinkle with the bread-crumbs and cheese and cook for 20–25 minutes until crisp and golden on top.

Cook's Tip

Soaking the raisins in apple juice plumps them up and adds flavour. Pear juice may be used instead, if preferred.

233 | Barley Casserole

Preparation time	**You will need**
5 minutes	300 g/11 oz pearl barley
	3 tablespoons olive oil
Cooking time	1 large onion, chopped
1 hour	2 cloves garlic, crushed
	1 medium carrot, chopped
Serves 4	600 ml/1 pint vegetable stock
	350 g/12 oz mushrooms
Calories	1 tablespoon lemon juice
510 per portion	2 tablespoons chopped parsley
	40 g/1½ oz ground almonds
	3 tablespoons crème fraîche
	salt and pepper
	watercress and lemon slices to
	garnish

Rinse the barley until the water runs clear; this removes the starch and stops the barley sticking. Heat 2 tablespoons of the oil in a saucepan and cook the onion and garlic for 3 minutes until softened. Add the carrot and cook for 2 minutes, stirring. Add the barley and stir to coat with the oil. Stir in the stock, bring to the boil, cover, and simmer for 45 minutes.

Meanwhile, slice the mushrooms and sprinkle with the lemon juice. Heat the remaining oil in a frying pan and cook the mushrooms for 6 minutes or until soft and the liquid has evaporated. Stir in the parsley, almonds and crème fraîche.

When the barley is cooked and the stock almost absorbed stir in the mushroom mixture and check the seasoning. Serve on a warm dish and garnish with watercress and lemon slices.

Cook's Tip

Crème fraîche is a cultured cream with a slight tang not as pronouced as that of soured cream.

234 | Stuffed Vine Leaves

Preparation time	**You will need**
20 minutes	650 ml/22 fl oz vegetable stock·
	100 g/4 oz long-grain brown rice
Cooking time	20–25 vine leaves, in brine
1 hour	1 bunch spring onions, chopped
	100 g/4 oz ground almonds
Serves 4	salt and pepper
	150 ml/¼ pint white wine
Calories	2 tablespoons cornflour
460 per portion	150 ml/¼ pint double cream

Bring 350 ml/12 fl oz of the stock to the boil in a saucepan, add the rice, cover, and cook over very low heat for 40 minutes or until tender.

Meanwhile, rinse the vine leaves in cold water. Drain. Mix the rice with half the spring onions, the ground almonds and a little salt and pepper.

Fill the vine leaves (see Cook's Tip). Place the rolls in a large, shallow pan and pour over the remaining stock, the remaining onions and the wine. Heat gently and simmer for 10 minutes. Drain off the liquid, blend the cornflour to a smooth paste with a little water, pour in some of the warm stock and return the liquid to a clean pan.

Bring the liquid to the boil. Pour over the cream and heat through. Do not boil. Transfer the rolls to a warm serving dish and spoon over a little of the liquid. Serve the remainder separately.

Cook's Tip

To fill the vine leaves, spread them on a clean work surface and place a teaspoon of the rice mixture on each. Fold in the sides and roll up carefully.

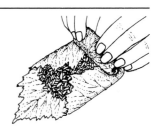

235 | Corn Fritters

Preparation time
10 minutes

Cooking time
15 minutes

Serves 4

Calories
235 per portion

You will need
40 g/1½ oz wholemeal flour
225 g/8 oz canned sweetcorn,
    drained
2 tablespoons snipped chives
2 eggs, beaten
3 tablespoons water
25 g/1 oz butter
225 g/8 oz mushrooms, sliced
225 g/8 oz tomatoes, peeled and
    chopped
1 tablespoon chopped parsley
salt and pepper
vegetable oil for cooking

Put the flour in a bowl, stir in the sweetcorn and chives, reserving a small quantity for garnish, and beat in the eggs. Add enough water to make a thick batter and transfer to a jug.

Heat the butter in a saucepan and cook the mushrooms for 3 minutes. Stir in the tomatoes, parsley and salt and pepper and set aside.

Heat a little vegetable oil in a heavy-based frying pan or griddle until hot. Pour spoonfuls of the batter on to the pan and cook quickly until golden underneath and just set on top. Turn over and quickly cook the other side. Drain on absorbent kitchen paper and keep warm while cooking the remaining batter.

Towards the end of cooking, return the mushroom mixture to the heat and warm through gently. Serve the fritters topped with the mushroom mixture and garnished with the reserved snipped chives.

Cook's Tip

Only a little oil is needed for cooking the fritters, so either brush it on with a bristle brush or use a pad of absorbent kitchen paper to rub it on, taking care not to burn your fingers!

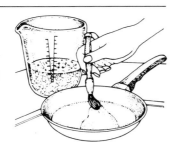

236 | Vegetable Kebabs

Preparation time
15 minutes

Cooking time
25 minutes

Serves 4

Calories
270 per portion

You will need
450 g/1 lb small new potatoes,
    scrubbed
1 medium green pepper,
    deseeded
1 large aubergine, cubed
450 g/1 lb small onions
8 bay leaves
16 button mushrooms
4 tablespoons olive oil
juice of ½ lemon
1 clove garlic, crushed
1 teaspoon tomato purée
½ teaspoon oregano
salt and pepper

Cook the potatoes for 5 minutes in boiling water. Drain thoroughly. Cut the pepper into chunks. Thread the potatoes, pepper, aubergine, onions, bay leaves and mushrooms on to 8 skewers.

Mix together the oil, lemon juice, garlic, tomato purée, oregano and salt and pepper. Brush the kebabs all over with this mixture and cook them on a barbecue for about 10 minutes each side, basting with more of the oil mixture during cooking. Alternatively cook the kebabs under a moderately hot grill for a similar time, turning once.

Cook's Tip

Serve the kebabs with a barbecue sauce. Sauté 1 onion and 1 clove garlic with 1 celery stick in a little oil. Add 175 g/ 6 oz canned chopped tomatoes, 1 tablespoon tomato purée, 1 teaspoon prepared mustard, 1 teaspoon *soy sauce and 1 teaspoon brown sugar. Simmer for 20 minutes. Serve hot.*

Desserts

The final impression of a meal is made by the dessert, so always plan it with the preceding courses in mind. Follow a light main course with a substantial treat, like Gourmet Bread and Butter Pudding, a luscious Chestnut Roulade or Orange Russe. Nectarine Brulée, on the other hand, provides the perfect, refreshing finish to a heavier main course.

237 | Iced Orange Cups

(Illustrated on title page)

Preparation time
25 minutes, plus several hours to freeze

Serves 4

Calories
225 per portion

You will need
2 oranges
50 g/2 oz caster sugar
120 ml/4 fl oz whipping cream
120 ml/4 fl oz thick Greek yogurt
50 g/2 oz raisins
2 glacé cherries, chopped
1 tablespoon brandy

Using a small sharp knife cut the oranges in half with zig-zag cuts. Scoop out the flesh with a teaspoon and press it through a sieve to extract the juice. Mix the juice with the sugar. Whip the cream until thick, then fold in the yogurt and orange juice. Pour into a shallow container and freeze until set 2.5 cm/1 inch in from the edges. Meanwhile macerate the raisins and cherries in the brandy.

Turn the mixture into a cold bowl and whisk to remove any large lumps. Stir in the raisin mixture and pour into the orange shells. Set these on a tray with absorbent kitchen paper underneath to keep them steady. Return to the freezer until firm, about 2 hours.

238 | Nectarine Brûlée

Preparation time
15 minutes

Cooking time
15 minutes

Serves 6

Calories
230 per portion

You will need
450 g/1 lb nectarines, stoned and sliced
4 tablespoons orange liqueur plus extra to flavour fruit
350 ml/12 fl oz soured cream
pinch of grated nutmeg
1 teaspoon vanilla essence
100 g/4 oz soft light brown sugar

Cover the nectarines with water in a saucepan, bring to the boil, then poach gently for 5–10 minutes or until soft. Drain and transfer to a flameproof casserole. Stir in a little of the orange liqueur to flavour.

Beat the soured cream, nutmeg, vanilla and remaining orange liqueur together until blended. Spoon the mixture over the nectarine slices then scatter the brown sugar over the top in a thick layer. Grill under a preheated hot grill for a few minutes until the sugar caramelises. Serve immediately.

Cook's Tip

Pack crumpled greaseproof paper around the oranges to make quite certain that they do not fall over in the freezer.

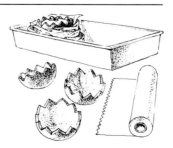

Cook's Tip

Use fresh apricots, peaches or pineapple instead of nectarines. Double cream can be used instead of soured cream. Replace the nutmeg with cinnamon and the orange liqueur with rum, if preferred.

239 | Apricot and Orange Glories

Preparation time
20 minutes, plus 2
hours to set

Serves 4

Calories
245 per portion

You will need
2 (185-g 6½-oz) cans apricot halves
    in fruit juice
1 orange jelly tablet (see Cook's
    Tip)
150 ml ¼ pint boiling water
300 ml ½ pint natural yogurt
2 tablespoons clear honey
4 fresh cherries with stalks

Drain the juice from the apricots and make up to 300 ml/
½ pint with water. Reserve four apricot halves and slice
the remainder. Dissolve the jelly tablet in the boiling
water then stir in the fruit juice. Pour into a shallow
container and chill until set.

Turn the jelly out on to a wet work surface and with a
wet knife chop it into small dice. Mix the yogurt and
honey together, then layer the jelly, yogurt and apricot
slices in four individual glass dishes. Top each with an
apricot half, hollow side up and holding a cherry as a
final touch.

240 | Fruit Baskets

Preparation time
30 minutes, plus 1½ 2
hours to stand

Cooking time
10 minutes

Oven temperature
180 C, 350 F, gas 4

Serves 4

Calories
315 per portion

You will need
100 g/4 oz plain flour
100 g/4 oz icing sugar
3 egg whites
few drops of orange essence
25 g/1 oz flaked almonds
1 ripe pear, cored and sliced
a little lemon juice

For the sauce
2 slices fresh pineapple, peeled,
    cored and chopped
120 ml/4 fl oz pineapple juice
1 2 drops yellow food colouring
120 ml/4 fl oz natural yogurt

Filling and decoration
350 g/12 oz seasonal fruit
1 tablespoon icing sugar

Sift the flour and icing sugar, then beat in the egg
whites until smooth. Stand for 1–2 hours. Stir in the
essence and almonds. Mark four 18-cm/7-in circles on
baking trays lined with non-stick baking parchment.
Spread the batter in the marked circles. Cook in a
moderate oven for 8 minutes until pale golden. Allow to
cool for about a minute, then ease off the baking trays
with a palette knife and mould (see Cook's Tip). Simmer
the pineapple, juice and colouring for 2 minutes then
blend in the liquidiser. Chill then mix in the yogurt.
Place each basket on a pool of pineapple sauce. Fill and
decorate the biscuit baskets as shown.

Cook's Tip

Vegetarian table jelly crystals
are available in 100 g/3½ oz
tubs. To use, place the
powdered crystals in a large
bowl, pour in 200 ml/⅓ pint
boiling water, stir briskly, then
add the fruit juice. Proceed as
in the recipe above.

Cook's Tip

Shaping the biscuits: cut a fine
slice off 4 oranges, so they
stand well. Grease with oil.
Carefully slide a biscuit off the
tray and lift over an orange.
Press gently and flute the
edges. Lift off when cold.

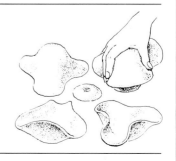

241 | Crunchy Pear Layer

Preparation time
10 15 minutes

Cooking time
35 minutes

Oven temperature
180C, 350F, gas 4

Serves 4

Calories
305 per portion

You will need
450g 1 lb cooking pears, peeled,
   cored and quartered
3 tablespoons water
1 2 teaspoons ground ginger
150g 5oz demerara sugar
50g 2oz butter
50g 2oz fresh breadcrumbs
150ml ¼ pint single cream, to
   serve

Cook the pears gently in the water with the ginger and 50g/2oz of the sugar until tender. Slice one of the poached pear quarters; reserve for decoration. Melt the butter in a frying pan and fry the breadcrumbs with the remaining sugar until crisp. Layer the pears and crunchy crumbs in a buttered ovenproof dish, finishing with a layer of crumbs.

Bake in a moderate oven for 30 minutes and serve hot or cold. Decorate with the reserved pear slices and serve with cream.

Cook's Tip

Use crushed ginger biscuits instead of the breadcrumbs, or try hazelnut biscuits for a delicious combination of flavours.

242 | Winter Fruit Compote

Preparation time
15 minutes, plus
overnight to soak

Cooking time
30 minutes

Oven temperature
190C, 375F, gas 5

Serves 4

Calories
305 per portion

You will need
225g/8oz dried apricots
100g/4oz stoned dried prunes
600ml/1 pint unsweetened
   orange juice
2 oranges
100g/4oz raisins
2 small bananas, thickly sliced
natural yogurt, to serve

Place the apricots and prunes in a bowl and pour over the orange juice. Cover and leave to soak overnight.

Using a serrated knife, peel the oranges and remove all the pith. Cut in between the membranes to separate the orange segments. Stir into the fruit mixture with the raisins and bananas and turn into an ovenproof dish. Cover and cook in a moderately hot oven for about 30 minutes. Serve warm with natural yogurt.

Cook's Tip

The fruit may be plumped in a microwave oven, if preferred. Combine the apricots, prunes, raisins and orange juice in a bowl, cover lightly and cook for 5 minutes on Full power. Cool slightly before adding the oranges and bananas.

243 | Plum Flapjack Crumble

Preparation time
15 minutes

Cooking time
30 minutes

Oven temperature
180 C, 350 F, gas 4

Serves 4

Calories
380 per portion

You will need
1 kg/2 lb plums, halved and stoned
5 tablespoons apple juice
100 g/4 oz rolled oats
50 g/2 oz soft brown sugar
1 teaspoon mixed spice
50 g/2 oz unsalted peanuts,
 roughly chopped
50 g/2 oz polyunsaturated
 margarine, melted

Place the plums in a covered pan with the apple juice and cook gently for about 10 minutes, until starting to soften. Transfer the plums with their juices to a greased 1.75-litre/3-pint ovenproof dish.

Mix together the oats, sugar, spice and peanuts in a bowl. Add the margarine and mix thoroughly. Spread evenly over the top of the plums, pressing down lightly with the back of a spoon. Bake in a moderature oven for 20 minutes, until the topping is crunchy and golden brown. Serve hot with thick Greek yogurt or vanilla ice cream, if liked.

244 | Carnival Figs

Preparation time
15 minutes plus 1 hour
to chill

Serves 4

Calories
135 per portion

You will need
8 fresh figs
1 (142-ml/5-fl oz) carton soured
 cream
4 tablespoons crème de caçao
grated chocolate or fig slices to
 decorate

Place the figs in an ovenproof bowl, pour over boiling water to cover and leave for 1 minute. Drain thoroughly and peel off the skins. Cut each fig into quarters and place in a serving bowl.

Combine the soured cream and crème de caçao and pour over the figs. Decorate with grated chocolate or fig pieces or slices. Chill for at least 1 hour before serving.

Cook's Tip

Instead of cooking fruits in sugar syrups, try using natural juices, as in this recipe. The edible leaves of herbs such as apple-scented geranium may be added to give a subtle flavour and fragrance.

Cook's Tip

Try using orange curaçao instead of crème de caçao, and decorate with grated orange rind.

245 | Orange Russe

Preparation time
30 minutes, plus several hours to set

Serves 6

Calories
350 per portion

You will need
about 21 sponge fingers
grated rind and juice of 2 oranges
1 teaspoon lemon juice
2 teaspoons agar-agar or 3 teaspoons powdered gelatine
150 g/5 oz Blue Brie cheese
100 g/4 oz curd cheese
50 g/2 oz caster sugar
2 egg whites
150 ml/¼ pint whipping cream
few strips of blanched orange rind to decorate

Base-line an 18-cm/7-in loose-bottomed cake tin. Trim the sponge fingers to 7.5 cm/3 in lengths. Stand the fingers, trimmed side down and sugar side out, around the edge of the tin (see Cook's Tip).

Heat the orange and lemon juice to just below boiling, add the agar-agar and stir until dissolved. Set aside to cool. Thinly de-rind the Blue Brie. Beat with the curd cheese, sugar and orange rind until smooth. Gradually add the cooled gelatine mixture. Leave until on the point of setting.

Whisk the egg whites until stiff but not dry, then whip the cream until it holds its shape. Fold just over half the cream into the setting cheese mixture, then add the egg whites. Pour into the biscuit-lined tin and level the surface. Refrigerate until set.

Remove from the tin to serve and decorate with the reserved cream and strips of blanched orange rind.

246 | St Clement's Cheesecake

Preparation time
30 minutes, plus 1½ hours to chill

Cooking time
5 minutes

Serves 8–10

Calories
390 315 per portion

You will need
75 g/3 oz unsalted butter
175 g/6 oz digestive or gingernut biscuits, crushed

For the filling
2 eggs, separated
50 g/2 oz caster sugar
350 g/12 oz low-fat cream cheese, lightly creamed
150 ml/¼ pint whipping cream, lightly whipped
1 (135-g/4¾-oz) packet lemon jelly (see Cook's Tip 239)
200 ml/7 fl oz boiling water

To decorate
1 large peeled orange, segmented
1 small peeled lemon, segmented
sprig of fresh mint

Lightly grease a 20-cm/8-in loose-bottomed cake tin. Melt the butter in a saucepan, mix in the crushed biscuits and press on to the base of the tin. Chill. Beat the egg yolks and sugar together until very thick and pale. Fold in the cheese and cream. Dissolve the jelly in the boiling water. Cool, then stir into the cheese mixture. Whisk the egg whites stiffly, and fold into the mixture. Pour over the biscuit base and chill until firm.

Remove the cheesecake from the tin and decorate as shown.

Cook's Tip

If the sponge fingers slither sideways in the tin, stand them upright and secure each to the tin with a tiny knob of butter.

Cook's Tip

If a loose-bottomed tin is not available, grease and line a 20-cm/8-in deep cake tin and place double thickness foil strips in a cross to lift out set cheesecake.

247 | Spiced Sultana Cheesecake

Preparation time
30 minutes

Cooking time
1 hour

Oven temperature
180 C, 350 F, gas 4

Serves 8–10

Calories
330 265 per portion

You will need
For the base
50 g 2 oz caster sugar
75 g 3 oz butter
1 egg
100 g 4 oz self-raising flour
½ teaspoon cinnamon
½ teaspoon mixed spice

For the topping
225 g 8 oz cottage cheese, sieved
225 g 8 oz low-fat soft cheese (for
   example Shape cheese)
2 eggs, separated
grated rind and juice of 2 lemons
50 g 2 oz caster sugar
2 tablespoons cornflour
150 ml ¼ pint low-fat double cream
   (for example Shape cream)
50 g 2 oz sultanas

Beat the sugar and butter together until creamy, stir in the egg, flour and spices. Mix to a soft dough and press into the base of a greased 20–25-cm/8–10-in round loose-bottomed tin. Beat the cheeses, egg yolks, lemon rind and juice, caster sugar and cornflour together. Whip the cream until it holds its shape and fold into the cheese mixture. Whisk the egg whites until stiff and add to the mixture, with the sultanas. Spoon over the base. Bake for about 1 hour, until the centre is firm to the touch. Partly cool in the tin and then remove to cool completely. Serve chilled.

Cook's Tip

Thick and creamy mandarin yogurt may be used instead of the double cream if preferred. The cheesecake will not be quite so light, but it will taste delicious.

248 | Danish Apple Pudding

Preparation time
15 20 minutes

Cooking time
25 30 minutes

Serves 4

Calories
455 per portion

You will need
575 g/1¼ lb cooking apples,
   peeled, cored and sliced
75 g/3 oz butter
sugar to taste
75 g/3 oz granulated sugar
100 g/4 oz white breadcrumbs

To decorate
150 ml/¼ pint whipping or double
   cream, whipped
redcurrant jelly (optional)

Place the apples in a saucepan with a small amount of water and cook gently, until soft. Mash with a fork, adding 25 g/1 oz of the butter and sugar to taste. Cool completely.

Melt the remaining butter in a saucepan. Add the granulated sugar and the breadcrumbs. Cook gently for 20–25 minutes, stirring frequently, until the crumbs are golden. Cool completely.

Arrange alternate layers of apple and crumb mixture in a glass serving bowl, finishing with a layer of crumbs. Decorate the apple pudding with the whipped cream, and top with teaspoons of redcurrant jelly if desired.

Cook's Tip

To prevent the breadcrumbs from becoming soggy, serve this traditional Danish cake as soon as it is assembled.

249 | Pavlova

Preparation time
30 minutes plus 8 hours to cool

Cooking time
1 hour

Oven temperature
150 C, 300 F, gas 2 then
140 C, 275 F, gas 1

Serves 6

Calories
360 per portion

You will need
For the meringue
3 egg whites
200 g/7 oz light soft brown sugar
1 teaspoon cornflour
1 teaspoon white wine vinegar
1 teaspoon vanilla essence

For the filling
150 g/5 oz Blue Brie cheese
300 ml/½ pint double or whipping cream
450 g/1 lb fresh fruit

Preheat the oven to the higher temperature. Draw a 23-cm/9-in circle on a piece of non-stick baking parchment then place this paper, pencil side down, on a baking tray. Whisk the egg whites until very stiff and dry. Gradually whisk in the sugar. Mix together the cornflour, vinegar and vanilla and whisk into the meringue mixture. Turn on to the prepared baking tray and spread inside the marked circle, making a slight wall around the edge. Place in the oven and immediately turn down the heat to the lower temperature. Bake for 1 hour then turn off the heat and leave the meringue to cool in the oven, preferably overnight.

Thinly derind the cheese, place in a bowl and beat until soft. Lightly whip the cream, add to the cheese and whisk until stiff. Prepare the fruit, reserve some for decoration and pile the remainder into the meringue case. Cover completely with the cream and decorate.

Cook's Tip

The mixture of cheese and cream in the topping adds a new dimension to this most popular of dinner party desserts. Assemble as near to the time of serving as possible for best results.

250 | Apricot Cheese Flan

Preparation time
25 minutes plus overnight to chill

Cooking time
45 minutes

Oven temperature
200 C, 400 F, gas 6 then
190 C, 375 F, gas 5

Serves 8

Calories
320 per portion

You will need
175 g/6 oz wholemeal flour
1 teaspoon ground ginger
75 g/3 oz margarine
50 g/2 oz demerara sugar
about 3 tablespoons water
1 (411-g/14½-oz) can apricot halves in natural juice
225 g/8 oz cottage cheese, sieved
225 g/8 oz low-fat cream cheese
grated rind of 1 lemon
1 tablespoon cornflour
75 g/3 oz caster sugar
1 large egg, separated
150 ml/¼ pint soured cream

Mix the flour and ginger together. Rub in the fat, stir in the sugar and add sufficient water to mix to a soft dough. Knead the pastry until smooth and use it to line a 23-cm/9-in fluted flan ring. Chill for 20 minutes then bake blind at the hotter temperature for 10 minutes. Remove paper and cook for a further 5 minutes, then leave the case to cool. Reduce the oven temperature. Drain the apricots and arrange eight halves around the edge of the flan case, finely chop the remainder and pile in the centre.

Beat the cheeses, lemon rind, cornflour, sugar and egg yolk together. Stir in the cream. Whisk the egg white until stiff and fold carefully into the mixture. Pour the filling into the flan case and bake for 30 minutes or until the centre is just set. Cool, then chill overnight.

Cook's Tip

Almonds have an affinity with apricots. Try substituting 50 g/ 2 oz ground almonds for an equivalent amount of the flour, adding a drop of almond essence to the filling and topping the cooked flan with toasted almonds.

251 | Citrus Flan

Preparation time
30 minutes, plus several hours to chill

Cooking time
30 minutes

Oven temperature
190 C, 375 F, Gas 5

Serves 6 to 8

Calories
480 360 per portion

You will need
Wholemeal pastry (see recipe 175)
75 g/3 oz caster sugar

For the filling
50 g/2 oz cake crumbs
2 tablespoons marmalade
1 large orange
1 grapefruit
50 g/2 oz cornflour
75 g/3 oz caster sugar
1 egg yolk
150 ml/¼ pint single cream
marmalade, warmed and sieved

Make the pastry, adding the sugar to the dry ingredients. Use two-thirds to line a 20-cm/8-in fluted flan ring. Bake blind for 15 minutes. Remove the paper and cook for 5 minutes more. Roll out the remaining pastry thickly and trim to two 23-cm/9-in long strips. Bake strips until brown, then use to divide flan case into four.

Mix the cake crumbs and marmalade together and spread in flan. Grate the rind of the orange and rind of half the grapefruit and keep separate. Squeeze the juice from half the orange and half the grapefruit and make up to 300 ml/½ pint with water. Slice remaining fruit. Blend the cornflour, sugar and egg yolk together in a small pan; gradually add the fruit juice and stir over a low heat until thick. Off the heat stir in the cream. Divide in half and stir orange rind into one half and the grapefruit rind into the other. Pour the custards into the sectioned flan case. Cool, then glaze with marmalade, decorate with the reserved fruit slices and chill.

Cook's Tip

Use a no-cook biscuit base instead of pastry when time is short. For extra flavour, add 50 g/2 oz finely chopped, toasted hazelnuts to the pastry.

252 | Chestnut Roulade

Preparation time
30 minutes, plus about 30 minutes to cool

Cooking time
20 minutes

Oven temperature
160 C, 325 F, gas 3

Serves 6

Calories
285 per portion

You will need
50 g/2 oz wholemeal flour
1 tablespoon cocoa powder
4 eggs, separated
150 g/5 oz caster sugar
icing sugar to sprinkle

For the filling
50 g/2 oz raisins
175 g/6 oz chestnut purée
25 g/1 oz soft brown sugar
120 ml/4 fl oz thick Greek yogurt
pinch of ground cinnamon

Sift the flour with the cocoa powder, adding back any bran left in the sieve. Whisk the egg whites until stiff, then whisk in half the sugar. Whisk the egg yolks with the remaining sugar in a large bowl until thick and pale, about 5 minutes. Carefully fold in first the flour mixture then the whisked egg whites. Turn into a greased and lined 23 × 30-cm/9 × 12-in Swiss roll tin. Shake the tin gently to level the mixture and cook in a moderate oven for 20 minutes, until firm to the touch. Turn out on to a large sheet of greaseproof paper dusted with icing sugar and discard the lining paper. Roll up from one short end, rolling the clean greaseproof paper with the roulade, and leave until cold.

Beat together the raisins, chestnut purée and soft brown sugar. Fold in the yogurt and cinnamon. Carefully unroll the roulade and spread evenly with the filling. Re-roll and dust with icing sugar.

Cook's Tip

Before rolling up the just-cooked roulade, trim off any crusty edges with a sharp knife. This will make rolling much easier.

253 | Fruity Yule Pudding

Preparation time
25 minutes

Cooking time
3 4 hours, plus 2 hours
on the day of serving

Serves 8

Calories
295 per portion

You will need
100 g / 4 oz self-raising wholemeal
  flour
100 g / 4 oz fresh wholewheat
  breadcrumbs
1 teaspoon mixed spice
1 teaspoon ground cinnamon
1 teaspoon grated nutmeg
100 g / 4 oz polyunsaturated
  margarine
75 g / 3 oz light soft brown sugar
2 eggs, beaten
1 dessert apple, peeled, cored and
  grated
1 carrot, grated
225 g / 8 oz raisins
grated rind and juice of 1 orange

Mix together the flour, breadcrumbs and spices. Beat the margarine with the sugar for about 5 minutes until soft and light, then beat in the eggs, apple, carrot, raisins, orange rind and juice. Stir in the flour mixture until evenly blended.

Press lightly into a greased 1.15-litre / 2-pint pudding basin and cover with double thickness greaseproof paper, tied down securely. Steam for 3–4 hours, topping up the water as necessary, then for a further 2 hours on the day of serving.

254 | Choux Ring

Preparation time
45 minutes

Cooking time
40 45 minutes

Oven temperature
220 C, 425 F, gas 7
then
190 C, 375 F, gas 5

Serves 8

Calories
435 per portion

You will need
300 ml / ⅟₂ pint water
100 g / 4 oz butter
150 g / 5 oz plain flour
3 4 eggs, lightly beaten
300 ml / ⅟₂ pint double cream
1 tablespoon sweet sherry
1 (225-g/8-oz) can sweetened
  chestnut purée
a little cocoa powder

Make the choux pastry, using the first four ingredients and following the instructions in the Cook's Tip below. Transfer to a piping bag fitted with a large nozzle. Dampen a large baking tray and pipe a 25-cm/10-in circle of paste on it. Pipe another circle immediately inside. Bake for 10 minutes at the higher setting, then reduce the temperature and cook for a further 35–40 minutes, until well puffed, crisp and brown. Split the choux ring in half immediately it is removed from the oven; cool.

Whip the cream and sherry together and fold into the chestnut purée. Spread the choux base with the chestnut cream and cover with the choux top. Dust with cocoa.

Cook's Tip

Dried and fresh fruit replaces much of the sugar in this light Christmas pudding; an ideal alternative for the health and weight conscious.

Cook's Tip

To make choux pastry, heat the water and butter gently until the fat melts, then bring to a rapid boil. Off the heat, immediately add all the flour. Beat vigorously, return to the heat and continue beating until the mixture forms a ball which leaves the sides of the pan clean. Cool to lukewarm, beat in enough egg to give a piping consistency, then beat until glossy.

255 | Choux Bun Star

Preparation time
25 minutes, plus 30
minutes to cool

Cooking time
20 25 minutes

Oven temperature
220 C, 425 F, gas 7

Serves 6

Calories
280 per portion

You will need
For the choux pastry
150 ml ¼ pint water
40 g 1½ oz concentrated butter
65 g 2½ oz plain flour, sifted
pinch of salt
2 eggs, beaten

For the filling
350 g 12 oz strawberry fromage
    frais

For the icing
175 g 6 oz icing sugar, sifted
about 2 tablespoons warm water
pink food colouring

Make the choux pastry, adding the salt with the flour
and following the instructions in Cook's Tip 254. Spoon
into a piping bag fitted with a large star nozzle and pipe
small stars on to a greased and dampened baking tray.
Cook in a hot oven for 15–20 minutes until well risen
and golden brown. Transfer to a wire rack and cool.

When cool, split horizontally and fill with the fromage
frais. Place the icing sugar in a bowl with just enough
water to make a thick glacé icing. Add the colouring a
few drops at a time and mix to desired colour. Arrange
the choux buns in a star shape and drizzle the icing over
the top.

Cook's Tip

**If preferred, fill the buns with
whipped cream and drizzle
melted chocolate over the top.**

256 | Corinth Pancakes

Preparation time
20 minutes

Cooking time
45 minutes

Makes 8

Calories
155 per portion

You will need
For the batter
100 g/4 oz wholemeal flour
1 egg, beaten
150 ml/¼ pint unsweetened
    orange juice
150 ml/¼ pint soda water
oil for frying
demerara sugar for sprinkling

For the filling
225 g/8 oz low-fat soft cheese
150 ml/¼ pint natural yogurt
1 tablespoon grated lemon rind
2 teaspoons lemon juice
100 g/4 oz currants
50 g/2 oz dried stoned dates,
    chopped

Place the flour in a bowl and beat in the egg. Gradually
beat in the orange juice and soda water.

Use the minimum of oil to grease a 20-cm/8-in
omelette pan. When the pan is hot, pour in enough of
the batter to cover the base with a thin film. Cook until
the pancake is brown and bubbling on the underside.
Flip or toss and cook the other side. Keep the cooked
pancake warm while making seven more pancakes.

To make the filling, beat together the cheese, yogurt,
lemon rind and lemon juice. Stir in the currants and
dates. Spread the mixture over each pancake. Fold each
one in half, then in half again, so that they are wedge-
shaped. Arrange in a flameproof dish, sprinkle with
sugar and grill to brown.

Cook's Tip

**Soda water acts as a leavener,
keeping the pancake batter
lovely and light. Add it
immediately before use or the
effect will be lost.**

257 | Carob Mousse

Preparation time
20 minutes, plus 4
hours to set

Cooking time
10 minutes

Serves 4

Calories
175 per portion

You will need
1 (100-g/4-oz) carob bar
grated rind and juice of 1 small
   orange
2 eggs, separated
1 teaspoon agar-agar or 1½
   teaspoons powdered gelatine
4 tablespoons water

For the decoration
strips of orange rind
carob curls

Place the carob in a medium heatproof bowl. Heat a medium saucepan of water until boiling, then reduce heat until simmering. Place the bowl on top and stir several times until the carob is melted. Remove from heat and stir in the orange rind and beat in the egg yolks.

Dissolve the agar-agar in the orange juice and water in a small saucepan, then bring to the boil, stirring constantly. Cool slightly and stir into the carob mixture. Whisk the egg whites to form stiff peaks and fold them into the carob mixture.

Divide between 4 individual ramekins and chill in the refrigerator until set. Decorate with the strips of orange rind and carob curls.

Cook's Tip

**Carob tastes like chocolate
and is available in health food
stores. It comes from the carob
bean and, unlike cocoa, it does
not contain caffeine.**

258 | Walnut Pie

Preparation time
25 minutes

Cooking time
55 minutes

Oven temperature
180 C, 350 F, gas 4

Serves 6

Calories
855 per portion

You will need
1 quantity shortcrust pastry (recipe
   175)

For the filling
175 g/6 oz butter, softened
225 g/8 oz muscovado sugar
3 eggs
grated rind of 2 lemons
juice of 1½ lemons
225 g/8 oz walnut halves

Make the pastry using wholemeal flour as instructed in recipe 175. Roll out on a floured surface and use to line a 20-cm/8-in flan tin. Bake blind in a moderate oven for 10 minutes (see Cook's Tip 173).

Cream together the butter and sugar. Carefully beat in the eggs, one at a time, then add the lemon rind, juice and walnuts. Mix well and turn the mixture into the flan case. Bake for 45 minutes until the filling has risen and turned golden brown. Eat warm or cold with cream.

Cook's Tip

**Pecans, which are related to
walnuts but have a milder
flavour, may be used instead.**

259 | Citrus Apple Pie

Preparation time
15 minutes, plus 30
minutes to chill pastry

Cooking time
40 45 minutes

Oven temperature
200 C, 400 F, gas 6

Serves 6

Calories
305 per portion

You will need
225 g/8 oz plain flour
100 g/4 oz unsalted butter
25 g/1 oz caster sugar
2 3 tablespoons cold water

For the filling
450 g/1 lb cooking apples, peeled,
   cored and sliced
1 orange, peeled and chopped
2 3 tablespoons water
sugar to taste
½ teaspoon ground cinnamon
   (optional)

To decorate
orange slices
apple slices brushed with lemon
   juice

Sift the flour into a bowl, then rub in the butter until the mixture resembles fine breadcrumbs. Mix in the sugar well and reserve 75 g/3 oz of this mixture. Add enough water to the remaining mixture to form a firm dough. Roll out and use to line a 20-cm/8-inch flan tin. Chill for 30 minutes.

Cook the apples and orange with the water for 5 minutes, until soft. Stir in sugar and cinnamon to taste.

Line the base of the flan with foil and dried beans and bake blind for 10 minutes. Remove the foil and beans, and bake for a further 5 minutes. Fill with the fruit and reserved flour mixture. Bake for a further 20–25 minutes, until golden. Decorate as shown and serve with cream.

Cook's Tip

**To lift pastry into a flan tin,
fold it over the rolling pin, then
lift it loosely over the tin. Press
in with fingertips.**

260 | Pear Flan

Preparation time
25 minutes, plus 30
minutes to chill

Cooking time
45 minutes

Oven temperature
190 C, 375 F, gas 5

Serves 4

Calories
350 per portion

You will need
For the pastry
100 g/4 oz plain flour
1 teaspoon ground cinnamon
50 g/2 oz butter, softened
25 g/1 oz walnuts, ground
25 g/1 oz caster sugar
1 egg yolk
2 teaspoons cold water

For the filling
2 (285-g/10-oz) cans pear quarters
   in fruit juice
1 tablespoon each currants,
   sultanas and chopped lemon
   peel
1 tablespoon cornflour
1 tablespoon lemon juice
icing sugar to sprinkle

Sift the flour and cinnamon into a bowl, rub in the butter then stir in the walnuts and sugar. Bind with the egg yolk and water. Chill for 30 minutes. Drain the pear juice into a pan and add the currants, sultanas and lemon peel. Bring to the boil and simmer for 5 minutes. Mix the cornflour and lemon juice and stir into the mixture. Cook, stirring, until thickened. Roll out the pastry to line a 19-cm/7½-in flan tin, reserving the trimmings. Prick the pastry and bake blind in a moderately hot oven for 15 minutes (see Cook's Tip 173). Fill with the pears and thickened juice; top with a pastry lattice and bake for a further 20 minutes. Dust with icing sugar when cool.

Cook's Tip

**There are three ways to make
a pastry lattice: the pastry
slats may simply be placed on
top of the filling with all the
horizontal slats underneath
and the vertical ones on top;
for a woven lattice the top
slats are threaded under and
over the bottom ones to give a
basketweave effect, and in the
twisted lattice the slats are
turned to give an even more
decorative appearance.**

261 | Orchard Tart

Preparation time
25 minutes

Cooking time
35 40 minutes

Oven temperature
200 C, 400 F, gas 6

Serves 6

Calories
355 per portion

You will need
For the pastry
100 g/4 oz plain flour
50 g/2 oz concentrated butter,
    softened
50 g/2 oz ground hazelnuts
25 g/1 oz soft brown sugar
1 egg, beaten

For the filling
4 large pears, peeled, cored and
    chopped
2-cm/$\frac{3}{4}$-in piece fresh root ginger,
    peeled and chopped
2 tablespoons clear honey
100 g/4 oz demerara sugar
3 tablespoons water
4 dessert apples, peeled, cored
    and nalved

Place the flour in a mixing bowl and add the concentrated butter; rub in until very fine. Add the hazelnuts and sugar, bind with the egg. Roll out to line a 20-cm/8-in loose-bottomed flan tin.

Place the pears in a pan with the ginger, honey, sugar and water and cook over a moderate heat for 5 minutes. Remove the pears with a slotted spoon, drain well and place in the flan case, crushing them slightly. Slice the apple halves almost through but keeping in shape and arrange rounded side up over the flan. Reduce the pan juices until thick enough to coat then spoon over the apples. Bake in a moderately hot oven for 30 minutes and serve warm with cream.

Cook's Tip

To slice the apples evenly without cutting right through place the halves, cut side down, on a work surface in front of a thin chopping board. Use a large knife held horizontally so that the board halts the descending blade.

262 | Gourmet Bread and Butter Pudding

Preparation time
15 minutes

Cooking time
30 40 minutes

Oven temperature
180 C, 350 F, gas 4

Serves 4

Calories
455 per portion

You will need
8 large slices white or granary
    bread
50 g/2 oz concentrated butter,
    melted
50 g/2 oz demerara sugar
$\frac{1}{2}$ teaspoon mixed spice
100 g/4 oz sultanas
2 eggs, beaten
1 teaspoon vanilla essence
450 ml/$\frac{3}{4}$ pint milk
1 tablespoon sherry (optional)

Remove the crusts and cut the bread into fingers or desired shapes for one large (1.15-litre/2-pint) pudding or four individual (300-ml/$\frac{1}{2}$-pint) puddings.

Brush a little melted butter inside the ovenproof dishes and cover the base with bread. Mix the sugar, spice and sultanas together and sprinkle half over the bread, drizzle with a little of the melted butter and repeat the layers, finishing with bread and melted butter. Beat the eggs, vanilla, milk and sherry together and carefully pour over. Bake in a moderate oven for 30–40 minutes until set.

Cook's Tip

The texture and flavour of this updated old favourite will be even better if the pudding is allowed to stand for 1 hour before cooking.

263 | Blackberry and Apple Crumble

Preparation time
15 minutes

Cooking time
35 45 minutes

Oven temperature
190 C, 375 F, gas 5

Serves 4

Calories
350 per portion

You will need
225 g 8 oz blackberries
450 g 1 lb cooking apples, peeled,
    cored and thinly sliced
25 g 1 oz unrefined sugar (golden
    granulated or molasses)

For the crumble
100 g 4 oz wholemeal flour
75 g 3 oz polyunsaturated
    margarine
50 g 2 oz fruit 'n fibre cereal, lightly
    crushed
15 g ½ oz unrefined sugar

Mix together the fruit and sugar and place in a 1.15-litre/ 2-pint ovenproof dish.

Put the flour into a mixing bowl and rub in the fat. Stir in the cereal and sugar. Spread this topping evenly over the fruit and bake in a moderately hot oven for 35–45 minutes, until the crumble is crisp and the fruit soft. Serve warm with custard.

Cook's Tip

All berry fruits taste good with a crumble topping. Try cranberries, loganberries, tayberries or raspberries, varying the quantity of sugar as required.

264 | Autumnal Pudding

Preparation time
20 minutes, plus 2
hours to chill and set

Cooking time
10 minutes

Serves 4

Calories
225 per portion

You will need
oil for brushing
8 thin slices wholewheat bread
150 ml/¼ pint apple juice
50 g/2 oz granulated sugar
juice of ½ lemon
2 dessert apples, peeled, cored
    and sliced
1 dessert pear, peeled, cored and
    sliced
75 g/3 oz blackberries
pinch of ground cinnamon
1½ teaspoons agar-agar or 2
    teaspoons powdered gelatine
6 tablespoons water

For the sauce
225 g/8 oz blackberries
3 tablespoons icing sugar
juice of ½ lemon
fresh fruit to decorate

Brush the insides of four individual pudding basins with oil. Cut the bread into circles and fingers to line them.

Stir the apple juice, sugar and lemon juice over low heat until dissolved. Add the apple and pear slices and poach gently for 4 minutes. Stir in the blackberries and cinnamon; cool. In a small saucepan, dissolve the agar-agar in the cold water, then bring to the boil, stirring constantly. Add to the cooled fruits. Spoon into the basins and chill. Poach the sauce ingredients gently, blend in a liquidiser and serve with the puddings, as shown.

Cook's Tip

Agar-agar, which is derived from seaweed, is the preferred setting agent for many vegetarians. If using gelatine dissolve it in a little water in a basin over a saucepan of hot water. Stir frequently.

Baking

Home-baked cakes and breads are irresistible and their commercial counterparts cannot compete for texture and flavour. Among the teatime treats in this chapter are imaginative teabreads, such as Plum Teabread and Banana and Honey Teabread, moist cakes fruity, spicy and nutty, the exotic Brazilian Ginger Bran Bread and Cheese and Pineapple Scones.

265 | Fruit Tartlets

(Illustrated on title page)

Preparation time
20 minutes, plus 30 minutes to chill pastry and 20 minutes to cool pastry cream

Cooking time
20–25 minutes

Oven temperature
190 C, 375 F, gas 5

Makes 6 medium or 12 small tartlets

Calories
630 per medium tartlet

You will need
350 g/12 oz plain flour
pinch of salt
1 egg
225 g/8 oz butter or margarine
1 tablespoon caster sugar

For the filling
50 g/2 oz caster sugar
3 egg yolks
2 tablespoons cornflour
300 ml/½ pint milk
2 to 4 drops vanilla essence

Line and grease 6 (10-cm/4-in) or 12 (5-7.5-cm/2-3-in) tartlet tins. Sift together the flour and salt into a large bowl. Make a well in the centre, drop in the egg and butter, and knead to form a soft, pliable dough. Wrap the dough and chill for 30 minutes. Roll out and use to line the tins. Prick the bases and bake blind (see Cook's Tip 173) for 10–15 minutes. Remove the beans and greaseproof paper. Bake for a further 5–10 minutes.

Mix together the sugar, egg yolks and cornflour. Heat the milk in a saucepan just to boiling point, cool slightly, then whisk into the egg mixture, return to the pan and slowly bring to the boil. Cover the surface of the mixture with dampened paper to cool. Fill the tartlets with the cold pastry cream and fruit as shown.

Cook's Tip

To prevent oxidation or drying out, warm some jam or marmalade flavoured with either lemon juice or liqueur, sieve and brush carefully over the fruit.

266 | Bakewell Tart

Preparation time
25 minutes

Cooking time
20–25 minutes

Oven temperature
180 C, 350 F, gas 4

Serves 4

Calories
900 per portion

You will need
75 g/3 oz plain flour
50 g/2 oz wholemeal flour
25 g/1 oz icing sugar
100 g/4 oz margarine
25 g/1 oz All-Bran cereal, crushed
1 egg
5 tablespoons jam

For the filling
100 g/4 oz brown sugar
100 g/4 oz margarine
2 eggs
1 teaspoon vanilla essence
2 teaspoons almond essence
100 g/4 oz fresh breadcrumbs
100 g/4 oz All-Bran cereal
50 g/2 oz flaked almonds
icing sugar for dusting

Sift the flours and icing sugar together, adding any bran in the sieve to the mixture. Cut the margarine into small pieces and rub in until the mixture resembles fine breadcrumbs. Stir in the cereal and egg and mix to a dough. Knead lightly, cover and chill.

To make the filling, cream the sugar and margarine together until light and fluffy. Gradually beat in the eggs. Stir in the essences, breadcrumbs, cereal and almonds until well mixed. Roll out the dough to line a 20-cm/8-in round, loose-bottomed cake tin. Spread the jam over the dough. Top with filling and bake for 20–25 minutes or until the pastry is crisp and the filling set. Cool for 10 minutes, remove from the tin and dust the top with icing sugar. Serve warm or cold.

Cook's Tip

For a more elaborate effect, like that shown in the photograph, reserve one-third of the pastry, roll out the base thinly, then roll out the reserved pastry, cut into strips for the lattice and arrange over the filling (see Cook's Tip 260).

Decorate the tart by spooning a little glacé icing into the holes in the lattice. Add chopped cherries and nuts.

267 | Cheese Scone Ring

Preparation time
15 minutes

Cooking time
15 20 minutes

Oven temperature
200 C, 400 F, gas 6

Makes 8 scones

Calories
180 per scone

You will need
225 g/8 oz self-raising flour
1 teaspoon baking powder
50 g/2 oz butter
50 g/2 oz Danish Blue cheese
about 150 ml/¼ pint milk

Sift the flour with the baking powder into a large bowl. Rub in the butter until the mixture resembles fine bread-crumbs. Crumble the cheese into this mixture and rub in. Using a fork, mix in enough milk to make a soft, but not sticky dough. Knead lightly.

Divide the mixture into eight equal pieces and shape each piece into a ball. Place one ball in the centre of a well buttered 20-cm/8-in cake tin and arrange the remainder around the edge so that they are just touching. Brush with milk to glaze. Bake in a moderately hot oven for approximately 15–20 minutes, or until well risen and golden brown.

268 | Passion Cake

Preparation time
30 minutes

Cooking time
1¼ hours

Oven temperature
160 C, 325 F, gas 3

Makes 1 cake

Total calories
4835

You will need
175 g/6 oz plain flour
1 teaspoon bicarbonate of soda
1 teaspoon baking powder
1 teaspoon ground cinnamon
1 teaspoon mixed spice
½ teaspoon salt
2 large oranges
175 g/6 oz light soft brown sugar
3 eggs
175 g/6 oz butter, melted
225 g/8 oz carrots, grated
100 g/4 oz walnuts, chopped

For the topping
100 g/4 oz cream cheese
50 g/2 oz unsalted butter, softened
grated rind of 1 orange
100 g/4 oz icing sugar, sifted
15 g/½ oz walnuts, chopped to decorate

Sift together the first six ingredients. Pare away the zest only of half of one of the oranges. Cut into thin strips and blanch in boiling water. Grate the remaining orange rind. Beat the sugar, eggs and grated orange rind. Beat in the melted butter. Mix in the carrots, walnuts and flour mixture. Pour into a lined and greased 18-cm/7-in square or 20-cm/8-in round cake tin. Bake in a moderate oven for about 1¼ hours, until firm to the touch. Cool in the tin for 5 minutes, then cool on a wire rack. Beat the topping ingredients together, spread over the cake and decorate as shown.

Cook's Tip

Delicious on its own, served split and buttered, or with a sweet or savoury filling. At teatime spread with blackcurrant or apricot jam, and for a lunch snack fill with sliced cucumber and slim wedges of Danish Blue cheese.

Cook's Tip

This lovely moist cake is almost irresistible. For a vanilla passion cake, substitute 1 teaspoon vanilla essence for the orange rind in the cake and omit the orange rind in the topping.

269 | Carrot and Orange Cake Alabama

Preparation time
20 minutes

Cooking time
30 35 minutes

Oven temperature
180 C, 350 F, gas 4

Makes 15 squares

Calories
250 per square

You will need
175 g/6 oz soft brown sugar
175 ml/6 fl oz groundnut oil
3 eggs, beaten
225 g/8 oz carrots, finely grated
100 g/4 oz raisins
75 g/3 oz peanuts, chopped
175 g/6 oz self-raising wholemeal
    flour
1 teaspoon bicarbonate of soda
1 teaspoon ground cinnamon
1 teaspoon finely grated orange
    rind
150 ml/¼ pint double cream,
    whipped
1–2 tablespoons chopped
    peanuts, to decorate

Mix together the sugar, oil and eggs in a large bowl. Stir in the carrots, raisins and peanuts. Mix the flour with the bicarbonate of soda, cinnamon and orange rind. Add to the bowl and mix lightly.

Turn into a greased and lined 18 × 25-cm/7 × 10-in oblong tin and bake in a moderate oven for 30–35 minutes, until firm to the touch. Cool in the tin for 5 minutes, then turn out and cool on a wire rack. Cut into squares, then top with whipped cream and peanuts to serve.

270 | Blackcurrant Nut Cake

Preparation time
15 minutes

Cooking time
40 45 minutes

Oven temperature
180 C, 350 F, gas 4

Makes 1 loaf

Total calories
2610

You will need
150 g/5 oz plain flour
2 teaspoons baking powder
½ teaspoon salt
75 g/3 oz All-Bran or Bran Buds
    cereal
100 g/4 oz butter
75 g/3 oz sugar
2 eggs
150 ml/¼ pint natural yogurt
100 g/4 oz chopped nuts
100 g/4 oz blackcurrants, fresh,
    frozen or canned

Line and grease a 1-kg/2-lb loaf tin. Sift together the flour, baking powder and salt. Stir in the cereal.

Cream the butter and sugar together until light and fluffy. Gradually beat in the eggs. Stir in the yogurt and then the flour mixture until just combined. Lightly stir in the nuts and blackcurrants (well drained, if canned). Spoon into the loaf tin; bake for 40-45 minutes. Insert a skewer in the centre of the cake; if it comes out clean the loaf is cooked. Cool for about 10 minutes before removing from the tin. Place on a wire rack to cool completely.

Cook's Tip

In America, where this cake originated, it is traditional to serve it with a cream cheese topping. Beat 175 g/6 oz cream cheese until soft and light and gradually add 450 g/ 1 lb icing sugar and 1 teaspoon vanilla essence. Beat in enough milk to give a spreading consistency, cover the cake and watch the calories climb!

Cook's Tip

This is the perfect cake for a picnic. Slice it just before setting out, reassemble the slices in the tin in which it was cooked, overwrap in foil and pack it in a picnic hamper or cooler.

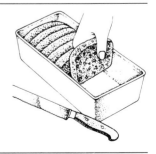

271 | Apple and Almond Layer Cake

Preparation time
20 minutes

Cooking time
1½ hours

Oven temperature
160 C, 325 F, gas 3

Makes 1 cake

Total calories
3190

You will need
150 g 5 oz soft margarine
2 large eggs, beaten
225 g 8 oz golden granulated
    sugar
1 teaspoon almond essence
225 g 8 oz self-raising flour, sifted
1½ teaspoons baking powder
350 g 12 oz cooking apples,
    peeled, cored and sliced
25 g 1 oz flaked almonds

Place the margarine, eggs, sugar, almond essence, flour and baking powder in a bowl and beat thoroughly until well combined. Alternatively use a mixer or food processor.

Spread half the cake mixture in the base of a greased 20-cm/8-in loose-bottomed cake tin. Cover with the sliced apples and put the remaining cake mixture on top of the apples in blobs. Sprinkle over the flaked almonds and bake in a moderate oven for about 1½ hours, until evenly golden and the edges shrink away from the sides of the tin. Turn out and cool on a wire rack.

Cook's Tip

**This is especially delicious
served warm with whipped
cream for dessert, though
equally good as a lovely
teatime cake.**

272 | California Christmas Cake

Preparation time
30 minutes, plus 1 hour
to macerate fruit

Cooking time
2 2¼ hours

Oven temperature
160 C, 325 F, gas 3

Makes 1 cake

Total calories
4650

You will need
350 g / 12 oz raisins
50 g / 2 oz glacé cherries, quartered
50 g / 2 oz dried apricots, chopped
3 tablespoons sherry
175 g / 6 oz margarine
175 g / 6 oz light soft brown sugar
3 eggs, beaten
50 g / 2 oz ground almonds
50 g / 2 oz almonds, chopped
few drops of almond essence
225 g / 8 oz self-raising wholemeal
    flour
1 teaspoon mixed spice
whole nuts for topping
clear honey to glaze

Soak the fruit in the sherry for 1 hour. Beat together the margarine and sugar until fluffy, beat in the eggs, then stir in the fruit mixture, ground and chopped almonds and essence. Fold in the flour and spice. Turn into a greased and double-lined 20-cm/8-in round cake tin and smooth the top. Arrange rows of nuts over the top of the cake to completely cover it. Bake in a moderate oven for 2–2¼ hours, until firm to the touch and a skewer inserted in the centre of the cake comes out clean. Cool in the tin for 30 minutes, then turn out, remove the paper and cool on a wire rack. Brush the cake with melted honey when cold and fix a ribbon around the side.

Cook's Tip

**The easiest way to quarter the
cherries and chop the apricots
is to use clean kitchen scissors,
frequently dipping the blades
in a jug of hot water.**

273 | Spiced Tea Bread

Preparation time
10 minutes plus
overnight to macerate
fruit

Cooking time
1¼ hours

Oven temperature
180C, 350F, gas 4
then
160C, 325F, gas 3

Makes 1 lb loaf

Total calories
2005

You will need
175 g/6 oz mixed dried fruit
grated rind and juice of ½ orange
1 teaspoon mixed spice
1 teaspoon ground cinnamon
freshly made tea
175 g/6 oz self-raising flour
50 g/2 oz wholemeal flour
2 teaspoons baking powder
50 g/2 oz caster sugar
1 egg, beaten
4 tablespoons oil
1 tablespoon chopped nuts

Place fruit, orange rind and spices in a basin. Make the orange juice up to 150 ml/¼ pint with tea and stir into the fruit. Leave overnight. Line and grease a 450-g/1-lb loaf tin. Mix the dry ingredients in a bowl. Beat in the egg, oil and macerated fruit mixture. Pour into the prepared tin and sprinkle the nuts on top. Bake at the hotter temperature for 45 minutes, then reduce the temperature for a further 30 minutes or until bread is firm and a skewer comes out clean. Leave for 5 minutes in the tin, then cool on a wire rack.

274 | Banana and Walnut Loaf

Preparation time
20 minutes

Cooking time
1 hour

Oven temperature
180C, 350F, gas 4

Makes 1 loaf

Total calories
2790

You will need
100 g/4 oz soft margarine
175 g/6 oz light muscovado sugar
2 ripe bananas
2 eggs
225 g/8 oz self-raising flour
1 teaspoon baking powder
50 g/2 oz walnuts, chopped
2 tablespoons milk

Cream the margarine with the sugar until soft and light. Mash the bananas and mix in well. Break the eggs into the mixture and beat well. Gently fold in the sifted flour and baking powder, then stir in the walnuts and milk. Turn into a lined and greased 1-kg/2-lb loaf tin and bake in a moderate oven for 1 hour, until well risen and golden brown. Turn out and cool on a wire rack. Serve sliced, spread with butter if liked.

Cook's Tip

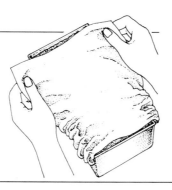

If a cake or loaf such as this one begins to brown too much before it is fully cooked, cover loosely with a piece of foil.

Cook's Tip

A great favourite with children, this, and so easy to make that even a relatively young child could attempt it with suitable supervision.

275 | Brazilian Ginger Bran Bread

Preparation time
20 minutes plus 2 hours to macerate fruit

Cooking time
1¼ hours

Oven temperature
180C, 350F, gas 4

Makes 18 slices

Calories
145 per slice

You will need
100 g/4 oz sultanas
100 g/4 oz raisins
100 g/4 oz currants
100 g/4 oz glacé cherries, washed, dried and halved
175 g/6 oz dark brown sugar
200 ml/7 fl oz strong black coffee
1 large egg
100 g/4 oz cottage cheese, sieved
50 g/2 oz bran
200 g/7 oz plain flour
2 teaspoons ground ginger
½ teaspoon bicarbonate of soda

Soak the fruits and sugar in the coffee for 2 hours. Baseline and grease a deep 20-cm/8-in square cake tin. Beat the egg and cheese into the fruit mixture. Stir in the remaining ingredients, mixing thoroughly. Pour into the prepared tin and bake for 1¼ hours until well-risen and firm. Cool in the tin for 5 minutes and then on a wire rack. Serve sliced, spread with butter.

276 | Plum Teabread

Preparation time
30 minutes

Cooking time
1¼ hours

Oven temperature
190C, 375F, gas 5

Makes 12 slices

Calories
180 per slice

You will need
225 g/8 oz cottage cheese
175 g/6 oz light soft brown sugar
2 large eggs
50 g/2 oz walnuts, chopped
175 g/6 oz plums, stoned
225 g/8 oz self-raising flour

Line and thoroughly grease a 900-g/2-lb loaf tin. Sieve the cottage cheese and beat in the sugar. Add the eggs and walnuts. Reserve two plums; chop the rest. Stir the chopped plums and flour into the mixture and spoon into the prepared tin. Bake for 30 minutes. Press four plum halves as decoration along the centre of the loaf and bake for a further 45 minutes, covering with foil if it over-browns, until cooked through. Cool on a wire rack and serve sliced, spread with butter.

Cook's Tip

Instead of spreading the slices of bread with butter, try using a light cream cheese. The flavours are wonderfully complementary.

Cook's Tip

For a more elaborate decoration on the top of this loaf, use almonds to transform each inverted plum half to a sunburst.

277 | Banana and Honey Teabread

Preparation time
20 minutes

Cooking time
1¼–1½ hours

Oven temperature
180 C, 350 F, gas 4

Makes 1 large loaf

Total calories
2830

You will need
200 g/7 oz self-raising flour
¼ teaspoon bicarbonate of soda
pinch of salt
75 g/3 oz butter
50 g/2 oz soft brown sugar
175 g/6 oz sultanas
100 g/4 oz walnuts, chopped
2 medium bananas, peeled
2 tablespoons clear honey
2 eggs

Line and grease a 900-g/2-lb loaf tin. Sift together the flour, soda and salt into a large bowl. Rub in the butter until the mixture resembles fine breadcrumbs. Stir in the sugar, sultanas and walnuts.

Mash the bananas in a bowl. Add the honey and eggs and whisk together. Add to the dry ingredients and mix well.

Pour into the prepared loaf tin and level the surface with the back of a metal spoon. Bake in a moderate oven for 1¼-1½ hours, or until a warmed skewer inserted into the centre comes out clean.

Allow to cool in the tin for 5 minutes. Then turn on to a wire rack, remove lining paper and cool completely. Serve sliced and buttered.

278 | Apricot Bars

Preparation time
20 minutes

Cooking time
25–30 minutes

Oven temperature
180 C, 350 F, gas 4

Makes 18

Calories
125 per bar

You will need
175 g/6 oz butter, softened
175 g/6 oz soft brown sugar
225 g/8 oz plain flour, sifted
½ teaspoon bicarbonate of soda
100 g/4 oz rolled oats
½ teaspoon salt
15 g/½ oz butter, melted
1 (285-g/10-oz) can apricot halves, drained
grated rind of 1 lemon
caster sugar to decorate

Beat the softened butter with the sugar. Mix in the flour, bicarbonate of soda, oats and salt. Brush a 20 × 30-cm/8 × 12-in tin with the melted butter and spread over half the crumb mixture. Chop the apricots and mix with the lemon rind. Spread on to the crumb base and cover with the remaining mixture. Cook in a moderate oven for 25–30 minutes, cut into bars and leave to cool in the tin. Sprinkle over a little caster sugar.

Cook's Tip

It is important to preheat the oven for at least 15 minutes before baking a cake. If the temperature is too low, the texture of the cake is liable to be coarse.

Cook's Tip

To soften the butter, cut it into large cubes and place it in a bowl with cold (room temperature) water to cover. Allow to stand for a few minutes, then pour off water. Alternatively heat in a microwave for 1–2 minutes.

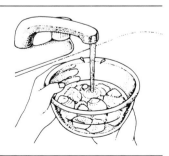

279 | Blue Cheese Loaf

Preparation time
20 minutes

Cooking time
1 hour

Oven temperature
190 C, 375 F, gas 5

Makes 1 loaf

Total calories
1865

You will need
100 g 4 oz self-raising wholemeal
    flour
100 g 4 oz self-raising flour
½ teaspoon baking powder
1 teaspoon mustard powder
½ teaspoon salt
50 g 2 oz butter
100 g 4 oz Danish Blue cheese
2 celery sticks, finely chopped
50 g 2 oz walnuts, chopped
1 large egg
120 ml 4 fl oz milk
sesame seeds or poppy seeds
    (optional)

Sift the flours, baking powder, mustard and salt into a mixing bowl, adding back any bran left in the sieve. Rub in the butter until the mixture resembles fine breadcrumbs. Crumble the cheese and rub in. Mix in the celery and walnuts. Beat the egg and milk together, add to the dry ingredients and mix well to make a fairly stiff consistency.

Spoon the mixture into a lined and greased 450-g/1-lb loaf tin. Level the top and sprinkle with sesame or poppy seeds, if liked. Bake in a moderately hot oven for 1 hour, or until well browned. When cooked, a skewer inserted into the centre of the loaf will come out clean. Cool the loaf in the tin for 5 minutes, then turn out on to a wire rack, remove the lining paper and cool.

Serve warm or cold, sliced and spread with butter.

280 | Caraway Rolls

Preparation time
25 30 minutes, plus
time to rise and prove

Cooking time
20 minutes

Oven temperature
230 C, 450 F, gas 8

Makes 8

Calories
170 per roll

You will need
25 g / 1 oz fresh yeast or 15 g/½ oz
    dried yeast (see Cook's Tip)
1 teaspoon sugar
250 ml / 8 fl oz lukewarm water
15 g /½ oz butter or margarine
275 g / 10 oz strong white bread
    flour
50 g/2 oz bran flakes, crushed
1 teaspoon caraway seeds
½ teaspoon salt

Blend the fresh yeast and sugar with a little of the water to form a smooth paste. Add the remaining water. Leave until frothy. Rub the butter or margarine into the flour and stir in the bran flakes, caraway seeds and salt. Add the yeast mixture and mix well to form a soft dough. Knead for about 10 minutes. Place the dough in a bowl and cover loosely with a large oiled plastic bag or cling film. Leave in a warm place until doubled in size. Turn the dough on to a floured surface and knead for a further 4 minutes. Shape into eight rolls, place on a greased baking tray and leave in a warm place until doubled in size. Brush with a little milk and bake in a hot oven for about 20 minutes.

Cook's Tip

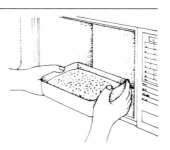

To cook in your microwave, turn the loaf mixture into a 900-ml / 1½-pint rectangular dish. Microwave on full power for 12 minutes then stand for 10 minutes before cooling on a wire rack.

Cook's Tip

If using dried yeast, you will need 15 g /½ oz. Sprinkle the dried yeast over the water, stir in the sugar and leave until frothy, about 10 minutes.

281 | Savoury Cheese Flowerpot Bread

Preparation time
30 minutes plus about 3 hours for rising

Cooking time
45 minutes

Oven temperature
200 C, 400 F, gas 6

Makes 1 (675-g/ 1½-lb) flowerpot loaf

Total calories
1680

You will need
350 g/12 oz strong wholemeal flour
¼ teaspoon salt
15 g/½ oz butter
1 sachet easy-blend dried yeast
25 g/1 oz walnuts, chopped
100 g/4 oz low-fat hard cheese, finely grated (for example Shape cheese)
75 g/3 oz celery, chopped
150 ml/¼ pint warm water
beaten egg to glaze
1 tablespoon kibbled wheat

Mix the flour and salt together. Rub in the butter and stir in the yeast. Thoroughly mix in the walnuts, cheese and celery. Add the water to make a dough and knead for 10 minutes. Leave to rise in a large bowl, covered with a lightly oiled plastic bag, in a warm place, until double in size – about 2 hours.

Knock back, knead and shape to fit a well greased unused flowerpot measuring about 15 cm/6 in in depth and width. Cover with plastic again and leave to rise for about 1 hour. Glaze and sprinkle with kibbled wheat. Bake for 45 minutes until golden. The bottom of the bread should sound hollow when tapped. Cool on a wire rack and serve sliced, lightly spread with butter.

Cook's Tip

Season the flowerpot before use by brushing the inside very thoroughly with oil. Place the empty pot in a moderately hot oven (200 C, 400 F, gas 6) for 15 minutes. Allow to cool completely before use.

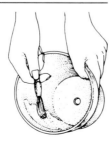

282 | Peanut Cookies

Preparation time
10 minutes

Cooking time
12 minutes

Oven temperature
180 C, 350 F, gas 4

Makes 12

Calories
95 per cookie

You will need
50 g/2 oz butter, softened
50 g/2 oz soft brown sugar
50 g/2 oz salted peanuts, roughly chopped
½ teaspoon mixed spice
75 g/3 oz self-raising flour
1 tablespoon orange juice

Cream the butter and sugar together until light and fluffy, then stir in the peanuts, spice, flour and juice to form a soft, not sticky, dough. Break the mixture into 12 equal-sized pieces and roll each into a ball. Place well apart on greased baking trays, flattening them slightly with a fork. Bake for 10–12 minutes or until firming. Leave on trays until firm enough to transfer to a wire rack to cool completely.

Cook's Tip

Mixed spice usually includes cinnamon, cloves and nutmeg, but Jamaica pepper or coriander may be added.

283 | Cheese and Pineapple Scones

Preparation time
20 minutes

Cooking time
15 minutes

Oven temperature
200 C, 400 F, gas 6

Makes 12 scones

Calories
145 per scone

You will need
275 g/10 oz wholemeal flour
4 teaspoons baking powder
pinch of salt
65 g/2½ oz butter
50 g/2 oz low-fat hard cheese, finely grated (for example Shape cheese)
1 (227-g/8-oz) can crushed pineapple, drained
3 tablespoons milk
1 large egg, beaten
milk to glaze

Mix the flour, baking powder and salt together. Rub in the butter until the mixture resembles fine breadcrumbs. Stir in the cheese and pineapple. Bind to a dough with the milk and egg.

Roll out 1 cm/½ in thick and cut out twelve 6-cm/2½-in rounds. Place on a greased baking tray. Brush with milk and bake for about 15 minutes, until risen and golden. Cool on a wire rack. Serve split, spread with butter and pineapple jam.

284 | Nut Flapjacks

Preparation time
5 minutes

Cooking time
40 minutes

Oven temperature
160 C, 325 F, gas 3

Makes 12

Calories
215 per flapjack

You will need
100 g/4 oz vegetable margarine
4 tablespoons golden syrup
75 g/3 oz soft brown sugar
225 g/8 oz rolled oats
75 g/3 oz walnuts, chopped
grated rind of 1 orange
¼ teaspoon salt

For the decoration
fromage frais or quark (optional)
orange slices (optional)

Grease a 19-cm/7½-in square, shallow tin.

Put the margarine and syrup in a pan and melt over low heat. Remove from the heat and stir in the sugar, oats, walnuts, orange rind and salt until well mixed. Turn the mixture into the tin and bake for 40 minutes or until just starting to bubble at the edges. Cool for 5 minutes to firm up slightly. Cut into squares and leave until stiff enough to lift out on to a wire rack to cool completely.

Decorate as shown, if liked.

Cook's Tip

Baking powder loses its potency if stored for a long time. If dubious about that tin at the back of the cupboard, sprinkle 1 teaspoon of the baking powder into a little hot water. It should fizz enthusiastically.

Cook's Tip

Coconut makes a very good addition to these flapjacks. Reduce the amount of oats by 75 g/3 oz and substitute desiccated coconut.

Not Quite Vegetarian

The recipes in this chapter have been carefully selected to give choice to those who follow a vegetarian diet most of the time, but who make occasional excursions into fish-eating in order to benefit from the highly nutritious food content of fish.

285 | Smokie Wheat Salad

Illustrated on back jacket

Preparation time
15–20 minutes, plus overnight soaking and 1 hour to chill fish

Cooking time
5 minutes

Serves 4—6

Calories
400–265 per portion

You will need
175 g/6 oz cracked wheat
450 g/1 lb smoked haddock fillet, skinned and cubed
300 ml/½ pint boiling water
3 celery sticks, chopped
3 spring onions, chopped
2 tomatoes, peeled and sliced
fresh mint to garnish

For the dressing
4½ tablespoons olive oil
1½ tablespoons wine vinegar
1 tablespoon finely chopped mint

Place the cracked wheat in a large bowl, cover with cold water and leave to soak overnight.

Put the haddock in a pan, cover with measured water and poach for 5 minutes. Drain and chill.

Fold the cooked fish, celery, onions and tomatoes into the drained cracked wheat. Whisk the oil, vinegar and chopped mint and pour over the fish mixture. Toss well and garnish with mint leaves.

286 | Caesar Salad

Preparation time
10 minutes

Cooking time
15 minutes

Oven temperature
150 C, 300 F, gas 2

Serves 4

Calories
235 per portion

You will need
5 anchovies in oil
1 clove garlic, crushed
8 thin slices French bread
1 cos lettuce
25 g/1 oz Parmesan cheese, grated

For the dressing
1 egg
2 tablespoons white wine vinegar
3 tablespoons olive oil
a few drops of Tabasco sauce
salt and pepper

Mash together the anchovies, garlic and a little of the anchovy oil. Spread the mixture over the bread slices and place, anchovy side up, on a baking tray. Bake for 15 minutes until crisp. Cut each slice in half. Tear the lettuce into large pieces. Place in a serving dish with the bread. Sprinkle the cheese on top.

For the dressing, place the egg in simmering water for 50 seconds, remove, cool slightly, then crack into a small bowl, spooning out the set white. Add the vinegar, oil, Tabasco and salt and pepper to the egg and whisk with a fork until thick.

Pour the dressing over the bread and lettuce in the bowl, and toss to coat the leaves.

Cook's Tip

A quick way of 'chopping' spring onions: wash and trim them, then hold them over a bowl and snip them up from green end towards the root.

Cook's Tip

Add the dressing as close as possible to serving time to prevent the salad from becoming limp and the crisp bread from becoming soggy.

287 | Salade Nicoise

Preparation time
20 minutes

Cooking time
5 minutes

Serves 4

Calories
270 per portion

You will need
275 g/10 oz frozen whole green
  beans
1 (200-g/7-oz) can tuna
1 small hearty lettuce
50 g/2 oz black olives
2 hard-boiled eggs, quartered
4 tomatoes, quartered
¼ cucumber, sliced
½ red pepper, deseeded and sliced

For the dressing
4 tablespoons oil
1 tablespoon wine vinegar
1 teaspoon sugar
½ teaspoon prepared mustard
1 clove garlic, crushed
salt and pepper

Cook the beans in boiling salted water for 5 minutes, drain and allow to cool. Drain the tuna fish and flake. Separate the lettuce into leaves and place in a salad bowl. Top with the remaining salad ingredients, including the beans and tuna. Combine the ingredients for the dressing in a screw-topped jar and shake well to mix. Pour over the salad and toss carefully together. Serve with crusty French bread.

288 | Fruit and Tuna Salad

Preparation time
15 minutes

Serves 4

Calories
185 per portion

You will need
1 (200-g/7-oz) can tuna
2 dessert apples, cored and diced
1 orange, segmented
1 banana, sliced
shredded white cabbage to serve
  (optional)

For the dressing
150 ml/¼ pint soured cream
1 tablespoon milk
1 tablespoon lemon juice
1 teaspoon caster sugar
½ teaspoon salt
1 tablespoon prepared mustard
freshly ground black pepper

Drain and flake the tuna. Place in a bowl with the prepared fruit. Mix together the ingredients for the dressing and toss into the salad. Serve on a bed of shredded white cabbage, if you like.

Cook's Tip

To keep eggshells intact while boiling, start in cold water. Bring the water to the boil, turn off heat, cover and leave for 15 minutes. Plunge the hard-boiled eggs into cold water to stop green rings forming on yolks.

Cook's Tip

A curried apple and tuna salad is a tasty variation. Peel and grate the apples and mix them with the tuna, omitting the oranges and banana. Substitute 1 teaspoon curry powder for the prepared mustard in the dressing and add just enough to moisten the mixture. Mound on a bed of shredded cabbage or lettuce.

289 | Cheese 'n' Tuna Pizza

Preparation time
15 minutes

Cooking time
20 minutes

Oven temperature
220 C, 425 F, gas 7

Serves 4

Calories
520 per portion

You will need
175 g/6 oz potatoes, cooked and
    sieved
175 g/6 oz self-raising flour
1 teaspoon baking powder
½ teaspoon salt
1 tablespoon pizza seasoning or
    mixed herbs
2 tablespoons oil
2 tablespoons water

For the topping
1 (295-g/10½-oz) can condensed
    mushroom soup
200 g/7 oz can tuna, flaked
2 tablespoons chopped spring
    onion or onion
50 g/2 oz rolled oats
100 g/4 oz Cheddar cheese, grated

Place the potatoes in a large bowl. Sift the flour, baking powder and salt on to them. Stir in the seasoning or herbs, the oil and enough water to make a soft dough. Knead gently until smooth. Roll out and place in a large pizza pan or on a baking tray about 23 × 33 cm/9 × 13 in.

To make the topping, mix together the soup and tuna. Spread over the dough base; sprinkle over onion, oats and cheese. Bake for 20 minutes or until cooked and golden. Serve hot. If serving cold, transfer to a wire rack to cool completely.

290 | Mediterranean Pasta

Preparation time
10 minutes

Cooking time
20 25 minutes

Serves 4

Calories
545 per portion

You will need
350 g/12 oz pasta shells
1 onion, sliced
1 2 cloves garlic, crushed
50 g/2 oz butter, melted
350 g/12 oz courgettes, trimmed
    and sliced at an angle
1 (198-g/7-oz) can tuna in oil,
    drained
salt and pepper
½ 1 teaspoon dried basil
225 g/8 oz tomatoes, peeled and
    cut into wedges
25-50 g/1 2 oz green or black
    olives (optional)

Put the pasta shells into a large saucepan of salted boiling water and simmer gently for 10–15 minutes, until just tender. Drain and set aside.

Gently fry the onion and garlic in butter for 5 minutes until soft. Add the courgettes and continue cooking for 3–4 minutes. Then add the tuna, seasoning and basil and heat through. Carefully stir in the tomatoes, without breaking them.

Turn the pasta into a warm serving dish and pour over the tuna mixture. Scatter with olives and serve at once.

Cook's Tip

This nutritious pizza owes much to the pantry. All the ingredients are common store-cupboard items and because the dough does not need to prove, the pizza does not take long to make.

Cook's Tip

This is a quick and tasty lunch or supper dish. Serve with a green salad and vinaigrette dressing.

291 | Fish Bake

Preparation time
35 minutes

Cooking time
35 45 minutes

Oven temperature
190 C, 375 F, gas 5

Serves 4

Calories
300 per portion

You will need
450 g/1 lb white fish fillet, skinned
3 tablespoons oil
1 onion, sliced
1 green pepper, deseeded and
    diced
2 celery sticks, chopped
salt and pepper
1 tablespoon cider vinegar
1 (397-g/14-oz) can chopped
    tomatoes
100 g/4 oz fresh breadcrumbs
grated rind of 1 lemon
50 g/2 oz cheese, grated
2 tablespoons chopped parsley
lemon twist to garnish

Cut the fish fillets into chunks and place in an ovenproof dish. Heat the oil in a small pan, add the onion, pepper and celery and cook until soft but not browned. Spoon the mixture over the fish, season to taste and pour on the vinegar and tomatoes.

Mix all the topping ingredients, seasoning to taste. Spoon this topping over the tomatoes, then bake in a moderately hot oven for about 30 minutes, until golden brown. Serve piping hot, with brown rice or baked potatoes and a crisp salad.

Cook's Tip

Add some chopped peanuts or walnuts to the topping and stir in some chopped fresh herbs if you like. Suitable fish are haddock, plaice, cod, coley or whiting.

292 | Haddock and Spinach Roulade

Preparation time
30 minutes

Cooking time
25 minutes

Oven temperature
200 C, 400 F, gas 6

Serves 4

Calories
480 per portion

You will need
350 g/12 oz smoked haddock
150 ml/¼ pint milk
25 g/1 oz butter
25 g/1 oz plain flour
175 g/6 oz soft cheese with black
    pepper
2 hard-boiled eggs, chopped
450 g/1 lb frozen chopped spinach,
    defrosted
4 eggs, separated
salt
½ teaspoon grated nutmeg
75 g/3 oz brie, rind removed
25 g/1 oz dried breadcrumbs

Line and grease a 33 × 23 cm/13 × 9-in Swiss roll tin. To make the filling, poach the haddock in the milk for 10 minutes. Drain and reserve 200 ml/7 fl oz of the cooking liquid, or make it up to this amount with extra milk. Flake fish. Whisk the butter, flour and cooking liquid over low heat until boiling. Stir in half the soft cheese, fish and eggs.

For the roulade, cream the remaining soft cheese with the spinach, egg yolks, salt and nutmeg. Cut the Brie into small pieces and stir in. Whisk the egg whites until stiff and fold in, adding the breadcrumbs, a spoonful at a time. Pour into the tin; bake for 8–10 minutes.

Reheat the filling. Turn the roulade out on to greaseproof paper, spread the filling over quickly and, with the aid of the paper, roll up the roulade. Serve at once.

Cook's Tip

After adding the roulade mixture to the tin, tilt it quickly so that the mixture flows into all the corners.

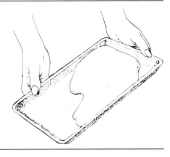

293 | *Whiting and Fennel Soufflés*

Preparation time
40 minutes

Cooking time
20 25 minutes

Oven temperature
220 C, 425 F, gas 7

Serves 6

Calories
285 per soufflé

You will need
225 g/8 oz whiting fillets
150 ml/¼ pint milk
½ onion, chopped
1 small carrot, chopped
1 bay leaf
1 head fennel, with a few leaves
50 g/2 oz butter
75 g/3 oz plain flour
150 ml/¼ pint single cream
2 eggs, separated
salt and pepper
pinch of cayenne
100 g/4 oz low-fat hard cheese,
    grated (for example Shape
    cheese)

Poach the fish in the milk with the onion, carrot and bay leaf for 10 minutes. Cool. Trim the fennel, cut into four and simmer in water for about 8 minutes, until soft. Keeping the cooking water, drain and chop the fennel. Drain the fish (reserving the milk for the sauce) and flake. Discard the flavouring vegetables. Make a thick sauce: melt the butter in a pan, stir in the flour then gradually add the milk, cream and 150 ml/¼ pint of the fennel water, stirring continuously. Beat in the yolks, and stir in the fish and fennel. Season well and add the cayenne. Whisk the egg whites until stiff and fold into the fish mixture. Divide the mixture between six individual soufflé dishes (each holding about 150 ml/¼ pint) and sprinkle with cheese. Bake for 20–25 minutes.

Cook's Tip

Fish is an excellent food, low in carbohydrate and high in protein. All fish are a good source of B vitamins and minerals such as iodine and calcium.

294 | *Prawn Risotto*

Preparation time
15 minutes

Cooking time
38 43 minutes

Serves 4

Calories
375 per portion

You will need
1 onion, chopped
2 tablespoons oil
1 clove garlic, crushed
1 red pepper, deseeded and diced
225 g/8 oz long-grain brown rice
750 ml/1¼ pints water
salt and pepper
100 g/4 oz frozen cut French
    beans
225 g/8 oz peeled cooked prawns
4 tablespoons grated Parmesan
    cheese

Cook the onion in the oil with the garlic until soft but not browned. Add the pepper and rice and cook for 3 minutes, stirring frequently. Pour in the water and add seasoning to taste. Bring to the boil, cover and simmer gently for 30 minutes. Add the beans and prawns, without stirring in, re-cover and continue to cook for 5–10 minutes. When most of the liquid has been absorbed and the beans are just cooked, stir in the Parmesan cheese and serve at once.

Cook's Tip

On the fishmonger's slab, look for prawns with firm unbroken heads and tails that are intact and undamaged. They should have a mild fresh sea smell with no trace of ammonia.

295 | Russian Fish Plait

Preparation time
30 35 minutes, plus
30 minutes to cool fish

Cooking time
35 40 minutes

Oven temperature
220 C, 425 F, gas 7

Serves 4

Calories
390 per portion

You will need
1 (227-g/8-oz) packet frozen puff
   pastry, defrosted
beaten egg to glaze

For the filling
20 g/¾ oz margarine
20 g/¾ oz plain flour
150 ml/¼ pint milk
1 tablespoon chopped parsley
freshly ground black pepper
2 hard-boiled eggs, chopped
100 g/4 oz smoked haddock,
   cooked and flaked
75 g/3 oz button mushrooms,
   sliced

For the garnish
lemon and cucumber slices
parsley sprigs

Whisk the margarine, flour, milk, parsley and a pinch of
pepper in a medium saucepan over a moderate heat
until the sauce thickens, then cook gently for 1 minute.
Add the chopped eggs and flaked haddock. Cool.

   Roll out the pastry to a 30-cm/12-in square. Lift on to
a damp baking tray. Place the filling in a 10-cm/4-in
wide panel down the centre and scatter over the mushrooms. Brush the pastry edges with beaten egg and cut
from the filling to the edge in 1-cm/½-in wide strips
down both sides. Fold the strips over the filling to
resemble a plait. Glaze and bake in a hot oven for 30–35
minutes. Serve hot or cold, garnished with lemon and
cucumber twists and sprigs of parsley.

Cook's Tip

*You can easily omit the small
amount of fish in this recipe
and increase the quantity of
egg or mushrooms. This is
delicious served hot or it
travels well, packed up cold,
for an unusual picnic dish.*

296 | Neptune Flans

Preparation time
20 minutes

Cooking time
40 45 minutes

Oven temperature
200 C, 400 F, gas 6

Makes 4

Calories
655 per flan

You will need
1 (396-g/14-oz) packet frozen
   shortcrust pastry, defrosted

For the filling
1 (198-g/7-oz) packet frozen
   buttered smoked haddock
1 (198-g/7-oz) packet frozen
   haddock or cod steaks
salt and pepper
1 tablespoon chopped parsley
2 eggs, beaten
300 ml/½ pint milk
2 tablespoons double cream

For the garnish
2 tomato slices, halved
4 lemon slices, halved
parsley sprigs

Roll out the pastry on a lightly floured surface and use to
line four individual fluted flan rings, placed on a baking
tray. Poach the fish in simmering water for about 15
minutes, until cooked. Drain and flake well, then season
and stir in the parsley. Divide the fish evenly between
the flan cases. Beat the eggs and milk together and stir
in the cream. Pour into the flans and cook in a moderately
hot oven for 25–30 minutes, until set and golden brown.
Garnish and serve with a crisp green salad.

Cook's Tip

*For a special occasion,
substitute 100 g/4 oz smoked
salmon for the smoked
haddock, adding it to the
poached haddock or cod in the
flan cases. Garnish each flan
with red lumpfish caviar.*

297 | Salmon Quiche

Preparation time
25 minutes

Cooking time
50–55 minutes

Oven temperature
200 C, 400 F, gas 6
then
180 C, 350 F, gas 4

Serves 4

Calories
725 per portion

You will need
1 quantity shortcrust pastry (recipe 175)

For the filling
150 g/5 oz Cheddar cheese, grated
2 spring onions, chopped
2 tablespoons chopped red pepper
1 (213-g/7.5-oz) can red or pink salmon
3 eggs
300 ml/½ pint milk
salt and pepper

Make the pastry as instructed in recipe 175. Roll out on a lightly floured surface and use to line a 23-cm/9-in flan tin or flan ring placed on a baking tray. Bake blind in a moderately hot oven for 10 minutes (see Cook's Tip 173).

Sprinkle the flan case with 100 g/4 oz cheese, the onions and red pepper. Drain and flake the salmon and spread over. Beat the eggs with the milk, season and pour over the filling. Sprinkle with the remaining cheese and bake in a moderate oven for 40–45 minutes.

298 | Pissaladière

Preparation time
30 minutes, plus about 2¼ hours to rise dough

Cooking time
30 minutes

Oven temperature
200 C, 400 F, gas 6

Serves 4

Calories
465 per portion

You will need
250 g/8 oz plain flour
½ teaspoon salt
7 g/¼ oz fresh yeast
4–5 tablespoons warm water
1 egg, beaten
1 tablespoon vegetable oil

For the topping
4 tablespoons olive oil
450 g/1 lb onions, sliced
4 large tomatoes, peeled and sliced
2 cloves garlic, crushed
salt and pepper
1 (50-g/1¾-oz) can anchovy fillets, drained and halved
12–14 black olives, halved and stoned

Sift the flour and salt into a bowl. Cream the yeast with some of the water and leave for about 15 minutes. Add to the flour with the egg, oil and remaining water; mix to a soft dough. Knead for 8–10 minutes until smooth and elastic. Leave to rise, in a covered bowl in a warm place, for about 2 hours. Turn on to a lightly floured surface, knead for a few minutes, and shape into a 28 cm/11 in round. Place on a greased baking tray and pinch up the edges.

Heat the olive oil, add the onions and cook until soft. Add the tomatoes, garlic and seasoning and cook for 5 minutes. Spoon all over the dough. Top as shown and leave in a warm place for 10 minutes. Bake in a moderately hot oven for 15–20 minutes.

Cook's Tip

Pick over the drained canned salmon before flaking to remove any bones or pieces of skin.

Cook's Tip

Serve the pissaladière with one of the salads featured in this book.

299 | Haddock Lasagne

Preparation time
25–30 minutes

Cooking time
about 1 hour

Oven temperature
190 C, 375 F, gas 5

Serves 4

Calories
705 per portion

You will need
450 g/1 lb haddock
300 ml/½ pint water
about 300 ml/½ pint milk
25 g/1 oz butter
1 onion, chopped
1 tablespoon plain flour
75 g/3 oz Danish blue cheese,
   crumbled
1 (198-g/7-oz) can sweetcorn with
   red peppers
salt and pepper
175 g/6 oz no-need-to-precook
   lasagne
150 ml/¼ pint double cream
150 ml/¼ pint natural yogurt
1 large egg, beaten
1 teaspoon dried tarragon
1 small packet plain potato crisps
tomato slices to garnish

Poach the haddock in the water for about 10 minutes. Drain; make up the stock to 600 ml/1 pint with milk. Remove skin and bones and flake the fish. Melt the butter in a large saucepan and cook the onion for 5 minutes. Stir in the flour, whisk in the milk stock and bring to the boil. Remove from the heat, add the cheese, fish, drained sweetcorn and seasoning. Layer the fish sauce and dry lasagne sheets in a buttered 1.75-litre/3-pint shallow ovenproof dish, cover with foil and bake in a moderately hot oven for 25 minutes. Mix the cream, yogurt, beaten egg and tarragon. Pour over the lasagne, to cover completely, and sprinkle with the crisps. Bake uncovered for a further 15–20 minutes. Garnish.

Cook's Tip

This fish version of a popular dish makes a welcome change from the more usual meat sauce. It is important to use the no-need-to-precook lasagne as the sauce in the recipe is very liquid to allow the pasta to cook properly.

300 | Health Bun

Preparation time
10 minutes

Serves 2

Calories
360 per portion

You will need
2 granary or wholemeal buns
25 g/1 oz low-fat spread
1 (200-g/7-oz) can tuna in brine
2 tablespoons cottage cheese
1 celery stick, finely chopped
3 walnut halves, chopped
1 tablespoon mayonnaise
½ teaspoon grated horseradish
2 celery sticks to garnish

Split the bread buns in half and spread with the butter or low-fat spread. Drain the tuna and flake into a bowl with the cottage cheese, celery, walnuts, mayonnaise and horseradish. Divide the mixture between the rolls and garnish each with a crisp stick of celery.

Cook's Tip

The filling for these buns makes a delicious dip, served with celery sticks.

301 | Pilaff with Plaice

Preparation time
5 minutes

Cooking time
45 minutes

Serves 4

Calories
450 per portion

You will need
25 g/1 oz butter
1 small onion, finely chopped
225 g/8 oz long-grain brown rice
pinch of turmeric
900 ml/1½ pints vegetable stock
   (see Cook's Tip 11)
100 g/4 oz mushrooms
1 courgette, sliced
1 small red pepper, deseeded and
   diced
450 g/1 lb plaice fillets, skinned
   and cut into strips
½ teaspoon ground cinnamon
salt and pepper
50 g/2 oz sunflower seeds

Melt the butter in a large saucepan. Cook the onion for 3 minutes until softened. Stir in the rice, turmeric and half the stock. Simmer for 30 minutes. Stir in the mushrooms, courgette and pepper, and a little more stock, and cook for a further 5 minutes. Stir in the fish strips, cinnamon, salt and pepper and a little more stock and cook for a further 5 minutes or until the fish is cooked and the stock absorbed. Turn into a warm serving dish, scatter over the sunflower seeds and serve immediately.

302 | Oriental Fish

Preparation time
20 minutes

Cooking time
20–25 minutes

Serves 4

Calories
355 per portion

You will need
750 g/1½ lb cod fillet, skinned and
   cubed
1 tablespoon cornflour
1 tablespoon dry sherry
2 tablespoons soy sauce
bunch of spring onions
2 celery sticks
225 g/8 oz carrots
1 leek, washed
5 tablespoons vegetable oil
1 clove garlic, crushed
225 g/8 oz canned bamboo
   shoots, sliced
150 ml/¼ pint vegetable stock
salt and pepper
spring onion curls to garnish
   (optional)

Place the fish cubes in a bowl, then mix in the cornflour, sherry and soy sauce. Cut the spring onions and celery into 5-cm/2-in strips. Cut carrots and leek into fine strips.

Heat 1 tablespoon of the oil and cook the garlic for 1 minute. Add vegetables and stir-fry for 3 minutes. Add the stock and seasoning; cover, and cook for a further 5 minutes. Turn into a serving dish and keep hot. Heat 2 tablespoons of the remaining oil and fry the fish cubes, in batches, for 3–4 minutes turning them frequently. Place cooked fish on top of vegetables and serve at once, garnished with spring onion curls, if liked.

Cook's Tip

**Sunflower seeds pack even
more protein than nuts and are
an excellent addition to fish
dishes, salads, crumble
mixture, breads and cookies.**

Cook's Tip

**Use a firm-fleshed fish for this
dish, such as cod, huss,
haddock or halibut. Even with
firm fish the cubes tend to fall
apart to some extent during
cooking.**

303 | Plaice Gougere

Preparation time
10 minutes

Cooking time
1 hour

Oven temperature
200 C, 400 F, gas 6

Serves 4

Calories
760 per portion

You will need
1 medium onion, sliced
150 g/5 oz butter
175 g/6 oz plain flour
300 ml/½ pint milk
350 g/12 oz plaice fillets, skinned
  and cut into strips
100 g/4 oz canned sweetcorn
100 g/4 oz mushrooms, sliced
3 tablespoons cider
2 tablespoons natural yogurt
salt and pepper
300 ml/½ pint water
4 eggs, beaten
75 g/3 oz Cheddar cheese, grated
1 tablespoon dry breadcrumbs
chopped parsley

Cook the onion in 25 g/1 oz of the butter for 8 minutes until golden. Stir in 25 g/1 oz of the flour and cook for 1 minute. Remove the pan from the heat and gradually stir in the milk. Bring to the boil, stirring, and cook for 1 minute. Stir in the fish, sweetcorn, mushrooms, cider, yogurt and salt and pepper.

Melt the remaining butter in a saucepan with the water. Bring to the boil, take off the heat and immediately beat in the remaining flour until just smooth. Beat in the eggs a little at a time, then stir in the cheese. Spoon the paste round the edge of a greased 1.15-litre/2-pint ovenproof dish. Spoon the fish sauce into the middle, sprinkle with the breadcrumbs and bake for 40–45 minutes or until crisp and golden. Scatter parsley on top and serve immediately.

Cook's Tip

A gougère makes a marvellous lunch dish, virtually complete in itself (though you can add a salad from this book if you like). Don't be put off by the choux pastry. It is very easy to make.

304 | Goujon Salad

Preparation time
20 minutes

Cooking time
12–15 minutes

Serves 4

Calories
520 per portion

You will need
1 iceberg lettuce, shredded
1 bunch spring onions, chopped
1 red pepper, deseeded and cut
  into strips
¼ cucumber, halved lengthways
  and sliced
2 tablespoons sunflower oil
1 tablespoon lemon juice
150 ml/¼ pint soured cream
2 tablespoons snipped chives
8 small sole fillets, skinned
1 large egg
1 tablespoon water
salt and pepper
about 150 g/5 oz dry white or
  wholewheat breadcrumbs for
  coating
oil for deep frying

Mix the lettuce, onions, pepper and cucumber together. Beat together the oil and lemon juice. In a separate bowl mix together the soured cream and chives. Cut the fish fillets diagonally into strips about 1 cm/ ½ in wide. Beat the egg with the water and season generously with salt and pepper. Coat the fish in the egg mixture, drain, then toss in the breadcrumbs to coat.

Heat the oil to 180 C, 350 F, add the goujons a few at a time and cook until crisp and golden. Drain on absorbent kitchen paper. Keep hot while cooking the remaining goujons. Pour the oil and vinegar dressing over the salad and toss well. Place the goujons on a warmed plate and serve with the salad. Serve the soured cream sauce separately.

Cook's Tip

Red peppers (which are simply ripe green peppers) are a good source of vitamins A and C. Look for plump, firm pods with bright colour. To deseed, slice off the top, then cut round the pith to remove the core and seeds cleanly.

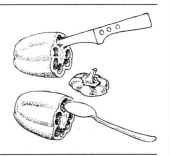

Index

Almond:
  Almond potatoes 68
  Spinach with flaked almonds 100
Apple:
  Apple and almond layer cake 271
  Citrus apple pie 259
  Creamy Waldorf salad 113
  Danish apple cake 248
Apricot:
  Apricot bars 278
  Apricot cheese flan 250
  Apricot and orange glories 239
Artichoke hearts, garnished 31
Aubergine:
  Aubergine fans Georgia 89
  Aubergine galette 201
  Aubergine layer 88
  Aubergine and onion gratin 92
  Aubergines bonne femme 91
  Aubergines au gratin 190
  Macaroni and aubergine layer 90
  Stuffed aubergines 82
Autumnal pudding 264
Avocado and cheese mousse 30

Bakewell tart 266
Banana and honey teabread 277
Banana and walnut loaf 274
Barley casserole 233
Bean:
  Bean cobbler 54
  Bean curry 50
  Bean and pasta curry 53
  Bean and pasta soup 2
  Bean pâté 62
  Bean and rice casserole 47
  Broad bean salad 120
  Butter beans in sesame 49
  Caerphilly bean salad 105
  Chilli bean tacos 51
  Colourful bean salad 58
  Dressed bean and onion salad 118
  Egyptian salad 56
  Kidney bean coleslaw 57
  Kidney bean and Stilton salad 59
  Mushroom and bean salad 119
  Provençal beans 46
  Rice and bean salad 60
  Rice and beans 166
  Spinach and flageolet layer 228
  Sweet and sour butter beans 48
  West African bean salad 55
Beansprout and cheese salad, crunchy 111
Blackberry and apple crumble 263
Blackcurrant nut cake 270
Blue cheese see Cheese
Bread and butter pudding 262
Breakfast special 214
Broccoli flan 171
Broccoli ring 98
Brussels sprouts and carrot salad 124

Cabbage salad, crunchy 117
Caesar salad 286
Cannelloni, Corsican 163
Caraway rolls 280
Carob mousse 257
Carrot:
  Carrot aigrettes 169
  Carrot and apple salad 126
  Carrot and cumin quiche 176
  Carrot and mushroom loaf 79
  Carrot and orange cake Alabama 269
  Carrot soup 7
Cashew:
  Potato and cashew curry 65
Cauliflower omelettes 198

Celery with mushrooms 77
Celery salad Flavia 127
Cheese:
  Blue cheese dip 36
  Blue cheese loaf 279
  Blue cheese and mandarin salad 110
  Blue cheese parcels 184
  Blue cheese soufflé 223
  Caerphilly bean salad 105
  Cheese and apple pie 188
  Cheese balls 27
  Cheese courgettes 84
  Cheese croustades 24
  Cheese fondue 225
  Cheese mille feuilles 221
  Cheese and onion flans 185
  Cheese and pineapple scones 283
  Cheese scone ring 267
  Cheese and semolina bake 189
  Cheese 'n' tuna pizza 289
  Cheesy banana muffins 203
  Cheshire salad 108
  Crunchy beansprout and cheese salad 111
  Crunchy Brie 28
  Danish blue cheesecake 227
  Derby and lentil loaf 37
  Light cheese and pineapple salad 109
  Mushroom and Leicester salad 106
  Savoury cheese flowerpot bread 281
  Smoked cheese and nut salad 34
  Spinach cheese salad 107
  Stilton-stuffed mushrooms 74
  Two-cheese salad 112
Cheesecakes 246–7
Chestnut roulade 252
Chestnut soup 5
Chick pea:
  Felafel in pitta pockets 61
  Leek and chick pea chowder 1
  Spanish chick peas 63
Chicory:
  Chicory in mustard sauce 99
  Chicory and sesame salad 125
  Creamed chicory and mushrooms 75
Chilli bean tacos 51
Chinese-style stir-fry 101
Choux bun star 255
Choux ring 254
Christmas cake, Californian 272
Cidered hot pot 95
Citrus flan 251
Cod:
  Oriental fish 302
Corn fritters 235
Cottage pancakes 219
Courgette:
  Cheese courgettes 84
  Courgette and cauliflower macaroni 160
  Courgette gratin 193
  Courgette soufflé 222

Egg:
  Cauliflower omelettes 198
  Egg tatties 72
  Frittata 200
  Potato and courgette omelette 197
  Provençal eggs 195
  Soufflés 222–4, 293
Egyptian salad 56

Family pie 180
Felafel in pitta pockets 61
Feta parcels 182
Fig:
  Carnival figs 244
Fish bake 291
Fondue 225
Frittata 200
Fruit. See also Apple etc.
  Fruit baskets 240
  Fruit coleslaw 116
  Fruit tartlets 265
  Fruit and tuna salad 288
  Fruit and vegetable kebabs 226
Fruity yule pudding 253
Nutty fruit salad 210
Orchard fruit 261
Winter fruit compote 242

Ginger bran bread, Brazilian 275
Glamorgan sausages 29
Gnocchi, baked 231
Goujon salad 304
Grapefruit and avocado salad 14
Grapefruit and chicory salad 131
Grapefruit sorbet 15
Greek salad 33
Green salad with peanut dressing 133
Gumbo, vegetarian 143

Haddock lasagne 299
Haddock and spinach roulade 292
Hazelnut:
  Brown rice and hazelnut salad 135
  Hazelnut toasts 216
Health bun 300
Hummous 212

Kohlrabi with walnuts 229

Lasagne 157–8, 299
Leek:
  Leek and chick pea chowder 1
  Leek flans 175
  Leek pie 178
  Leek, potato and coriander bake 194
  Leek and potato soup 10
  Leeks au gratin 94
  Tofu with leeks 208
Lentil:
  Creamed lentils 64
  Derby and lentil loaf 37
  Lentil croquettes 42
  Lentil moussaka 38
  Lentil patties 43
  Lentil and peanut layer 40
  Lentil and vegetable bake 39
  Spiced lentil dhal 44
  Walnut and lentil loaf 41

Macaroni:
  Courgette and cauliflower macaroni 160
  Macaroni and aubergine layer 90
  Macaroni special 148
  Macaroni tomatoes 162
  Red pepper macaroni cheese 191
Marrow:
  Marrow lasagne 157
  Stuffed marrow rings 83
Melon and grapefruit cocktail 13
Muesli, spiced 215
Mulligatawny soup 3
Mung bean and fresh herb risotto 138
Mushroom:
  Celery with mushrooms 77
  Country mushroom soup 12
  Cream of mushroom soup 11
  Greek mushroom salad 19
  Mushroom and avocado starter 23
  Mushroom and bean salad 119
  Mushroom and celeriac salad 122
  Mushroom and cucumber side salad 121
  Mushroom flan 172
  Mushroom fondue 76
  Mushroom gougère 170
  Mushroom and Leicester salad 106
  Mushroom pasta with pine nuts 145
  Mushroom pâté 26
  Mushroom puffs 187
  Mushroom puffs with spicy sauce 25
  Mushroom slaw 114
  Mushroom vols-au-vent 181
  Mushrooms indienne 21
  Mushrooms Montebello 73
  Stilton-stuffed mushrooms 74

Nectarine brûlée 238
Noodles, Szechuan 165
Nuts. See also Almond etc.
  Crumbly nut roast 192

Nut flapjacks 284
Nutty fruit salad 210
Nutty ribbon pasta 153
Okra:
  Okra salad 135
  Sunflower okra with mushrooms 93
Onion soup, creamy 9
Orange:
  Iced orange cups 237
  Orange and beetroot salad 132
  Orange russe 245
  Orange and watercress salad 123
Orchard tart 261

Pancakes:
  Continental-style pancakes 78
  Corinth pancakes 256
  Cottage pancakes 219
  Provençal pancakes 220
  Stuffed pancakes 199
Parsnip:
  Parsnip casserole 96
  Parsnip croquettes 103
Party dip, speedy 35
Passion cake 268
Pasta:
  Creamy curried pasta 168
  Gratin of pasta 156
  Mediterranean pasta 290
  Mushroom pasta with pine nuts 145
  Nutty ribbon pasta 153
  Pasta with aubergine 149
  Pasta with bolina cheese sauce 155
  Pasta pesto 144
  Pasta al pomodoro 154
  Pasta with ratatouille sauce 152
  Pasta slaw 115
  Wholemeal pasta salad 137
Pasties, quick 183
Pavlova 249
Pea:
  Crispy pea croquettes 45
  Green pea and potato curry 52
  Pea soup 4
Peanut cookies 282
Peanut dip with crudités 22
Pear:
  Crunchy pear layer 241
  Pear flan 260
  Pears with mustard cream mayonnaise 16
  Savoury pear mousse 17
Pepper:
  Red pepper macaroni cheese 191
  Turkish pepper salad 129
Pissaladière 298
Pizzas 196, 289
Plaice:
  Pilaff with plaice 301
  Plaice gougère 303
Plum flapjack crumble 243
Plum teabread 276
Potato:
  Almond potatoes 68
  Creamed swede duchesse 66
  Egg tatties 72
  Mediterranean potatoes 67
  Potato cake with cheese topping 71
  Potato and cashew curry 65
  Potato and courgette omelette 197
  Potatoes Madras 70
  Spiced potatoes 80
  Stir-fried potatoes 69
Prawn risotto 294
Provençal pancakes 220
Pumpkin pie 179

Radish salad 130
Rainbow quiche 174
Ravioli 161
Rice:
  Brown rice and hazelnut salad 146
  Brown rice salad 147
  Mung bean and fresh herb risotto 138
  Pilaff with plaice 301
  Prawn risotto 294
  Rice and bean salad 60

Rice and beans 166
Rice and mushroom bake 140
Rice salad Gado Gado 141
Risotto with spinach and herbs 139
Spiced rice and courgette salad 142
Vegetable risotto 137

St Clement's cheesecake 246
Salade niçoise 287
Salmon quiche 297
Savoury bake 87
Soufflés 222–4, 293
Spaghetti with walnut sauce 150
Smoked haddock:
  Neptune flans 296
  Russian fish plait 295
  Smokie wheat salad 285
Sole:
  Goujon salad 304
Spiced sultana cheesecake 247
Spiced tea bread 273
Spinach:
  Spinach bake 232
  Spinach, cauliflower and courgette bhaji 97
  Spinach cheese salad 107
  Spinach and flageolet layer 228
  Spinach with flaked almonds 100
  Spinach lasagne 159
  Spinach noodles 151
  Spinach and potato patties 202
  Spinach roulade 218
Stilton-stuffed mushrooms 75
Sunflower okra with mushrooms 93
Sunflower snacks 209
Surprise soufflé 224
Swede:
  Creamed swede duchesse 66
Sweet and sour butter beans 48
Szechuan noodles 165

Tabbouleh 136
Tofu:
  To make a salad dressing with tofu 205
  Chinese-style tofu 207
  Crunchy tofu 205
  Tofu and avocado spread 213
  Tofu cakes 204
  Tofu with leeks 208
Tomato:
  Macaroni tomatoes 162
  Savoury stuffed tomatoes 20
  Tomato and carrot soup 8
  Tomato coupé 18
  Tomato ring salad 134
  Tomato roulade 217
  Tomato sauce 81
  Tomato triangles 186
Tropical salad 164

Vegetable burgers 85
Vegetable curry 104
Vegetable kebabs 236
Vegetable lasagne 158
Vegetable parcels 86
Vegetable pâté 32
Vegetable pie 177
Vegetable risotto 167
Vegetable terrine 81
Vegetarian nuggets, crispy 102
Vine leaves, stuffed 234

Waffles, savoury 206
Waldorf salad, creamy 113
Walnut:
  Banana and walnut loaf 274
  Kohlrabi with walnuts 229
  Walnut dip 211
  Walnut-filled fennel 230
  Walnut and lentil loaf 41
  Walnut pie 258
Watercress and Brie quiche 173
Whiting and fennel soufflés 293
Winter radish salad 128
Winter warmer 6

Yule pudding, fruity 253